GETTING BACK ON MISSION

Reforming Our Church Together

CATHOLICS FOR RENEWAL

garratt
PUBLISHING

garratt
PUBLISHING

Published in Australia by
Garratt Publishing
32 Glenvale Crescent
Mulgrave,VIC 3170
www.garrattpublishing.com.au

Cover Design by Guy Holt Design
Typesetting by Mike Kuszla
Cover image: He Qi's painting After Resurrection depicts Jesus' disciples – women
and men – empowered by their new faith in the Risen Christ, setting out on
God's mission to bring the light of the Gospel to the world. It also suggests today's
disciples searching for a way to make the Church a true sign of the Kingdom in the
21st century
Photographs © p. iii AAP Photos, *Pope Francis blesses a man as he washes inmates' feet at
a Maundy Thursday service at Rebibbia prison in Rome* (2015), p. 40 iStock, p. 82 iStock,
p. 108 iStock, p. 148 *Photo by Lalesh Aldarwish from pexels,* p. 228 *photo published with
permission from the Photo Collection of the Melbourne Diocesan Historical Commission
(MDHC),* p. 270 *pexels photo 433333*

Paperback ISBN 9781925009651
eBook ISBN 9781925009156

A catalogue record for this
book is available from the
NATIONAL
LIBRARY   National Library of Australia
OF AUSTRALIA

Cataloguing in Publication information for this title is available from the National
Library of Australia.
www.nla.gov.au

The authors and publisher gratefully acknowledge the permission granted to
reproduce the copyright material in this book. Every effort has been made to trace
copyright holders and to obtain their permission for the use of copyright material.

The publisher apologises for any errors or omissions in the above list and would be
grateful if notified of any corrections that should be incorporated in future reprints
or editions of this book.

**All proceeds from sales of *Getting Back on Mission* received by Catholics for
Renewal will be directed towards the mission of Catholics for Renewal.**

Is this the Catholic Church we want?

Cardinal Raymond Burke and acolytes (c. 2014)

Or is this the Church we want?

Pope Francis blesses a man as he washes inmates' feet at a Maundy Thursday service at Rebibbia prison in Rome (2015)

Endorsements

I wish Getting Back on Mission *well and hope this book helps navigate our Church's sacred pastors to the wisdom and action needed to get us out of this mess.*

> – Mary McAleese, former President of Ireland.

Getting Back on Mission *provides us with a blueprint for the reformation of the Catholic Church so necessary for it to be faithful to the mission of Jesus. The bishops and religious leaders are called to listen to the laity and to implement standards of governance where accountability, inclusiveness and transparency become the norm and not optional extras. Only then will it have any chance of reclaiming its credibility among the faithful.*

> – Rosemarie Joyce CSB, former President,
> Catholic Religious Australia, Marriage Tribunal Judge.

Getting Back on Mission *is an extraordinary work – a labour of love by Catholic women and men whose abundant faith in God's Spirit, steadfast commitment to the Gospel, and uncompromising dedication to intellectual and theological rigor can be found on every page of the document. This work reflects the exemplary manner in which a relatively small group of Catholics throughout Australia have pioneered a new way to exercise lay leadership, committing their gifts, talents, and expertise to the remaking of an institution torn apart by corruption and clericalism. This document is a model and manual for any Catholic who seeks to exercise lay leadership more effectively in their own region.*

> – Deborah Rose-Milavec and Russ Petrus,
> Co-Directors, FutureChurch, USA.

Those Christians hoping that their faith will appeal to their children have every reason to share passionate insights on Church reform so that the vessel might be more fit for purpose. Faith seeking understanding thrives when there is an openness to all that is best in a world which espouses primacy of conscience, democratic participation and transparent governance. Synodality, subsidiarity, and collegiality are the key. In Getting Back on Mission, **Catholics for Renewal** *have provided a realistic, hopeful and authentically Catholic roadmap for the forthcoming Australian Plenary Council.*

> – Frank Brennan SJ AO, CEO of Catholic Social Services Australia.

Reading Getting Back on Mission *by* **Catholics for Renewal** *– from the perspective of Ireland, where I live, and where our Church is facing similar challenges – I am enormously impressed by the clarity of its analysis of the problems we are faced with, and the list of recommendations, though challenging, are as necessary here as in Australia.*

– Tony Flannery CSsR, co-founder of the Association of
Catholic Priests Ireland, author of *A Question of Conscience,*
Londubh Books (2013).

Catholics for Renewal *speaks for the wider church reform movement in correctly identifying the crisis facing the church and is right to point to the serious limitations of current church governance in Australia. Good governance has three essentials: accountability, transparency and inclusion. This new book is a most comprehensive compendium of necessary reforms for consideration not only by the Plenary Council 2020/21, but immediately by every church leader as a matter of urgency.*

– Emeritus Professor John Warhurst AO, Chair of Concerned Catholics
Canberra Goulburn, and Member of Australian Bishops' Church
Governance Review Panel.

In one document, **Catholics for Renewal** *has captured all the major issues confronting the Catholic Church in Australia. Although prepared primarily for the Plenary, the origins of this book are to be found in the hearts and minds of so many Catholics (mainly the laity) who over many years have refused to walk away from the Church, despite many understandable reasons for doing so. After years of rejection by the hierarchy, the Plenary (hopefully) provides an opportunity for their voices to be heard. It is a balanced and fair document, carefully and lovingly prepared by hearts and minds fully open to the ongoing revelations of our God. It speaks of and to God's Australian people today."*

– Michael Gill, Former President of the Law Council of Australia,
Convenor for Voice of Catholic Australian Laity (VOCAL).

This absolute mine of information calls on Australian Catholics to leave behind a clericalist, self-engrossed church and embrace a renewed vision that includes full lay participation with a faith inspired by Jesus and the gospel message, while at the same time embracing the very modern virtues of equality and accountability.

— Paul Collins, Broadcaster, church historian,
writer and commentator on Catholicism.

The Australian Catholic Plenary Council is of a piece with the participatory mode of governance Pope Francis wants generalised throughout the Church today. Getting Back on Mission *can only do good in supporting that process with which Catholics in Australia have little experience in the Church. But as citizens of a democratic, pluralist society, we have the skills and experience to make a vital contribution to the Church in these times that require reform urgently, breaking out of the time warp in which much official teaching exists. I commend* Getting Back on Mission *to your consideration.*

— Michael Kelly SJ, Chief Executive Officer, UCAN Services.

Some have blamed the appalling sexual abuse of children within the Catholic Church on the Second Vatican Council, the sexual revolution and the decline of Eucharistic devotion. Commissions of inquiry in the United States, Ireland, the Netherlands and Australia have found more worldly explanations in the Church's structures and canon law. Getting Back on Mission *by* **Catholics for Renewal** *provides a program for reform of these earthly causes along the lines recommended by the Australian Royal Commission into the Institutional Responses to Child Sexual Abuse. The Church will ignore it at its peril.*

— Kieran Tapsell, author of *Potiphar's Wife: The Vatican's Secret and Child Sexual Abuse* ATF (2014).

The forthcoming Plenary Council 2020/21 provides a unique opportunity for Australian Catholics to reflect on their own faith journey, their relationship to Church, and the situation of the Church in relation to civil and canonical norms. The Church's governance needs careful review as recommended by the Royal Commission. **Catholics for Renewal** *are to be commended for actively engaging in the process of reflection, analysis and engagement.*

— Susan Pascoe AM, former and founding Commissioner
of the Australian Charities and Not-for-Profit Commission,
former Director of Catholic Education Victoria,
Member of Australian Bishops' Church Governance Review Panel,
Chair of Community Directors Council.

Divide and conquer has been a favored strategy of Rome since the time of Julius Caesar and it is still used today by the Church. When a problem or issue emerges in one country or another, Rome simply dismisses it by saying it's only an American problem or it's only an issue in Europe but doesn't reflect the whole Church. Getting Back on Mission *by* **Catholics for Renewal** *accurately reflects similar statements coming from Europe, the United States, Latin America and now Australia. These statements can no longer be dismissed as simply regional. Australia's very isolation has intensified its experience and has in effect made it the canary in the coal mine. As such* Getting Back on Mission *must be regarded as particularly cautionary for the future of the Church.*

> – Gerry Bechard, Parish Priest, Ss. Simon & Jude, Westland, Michigan, USA; founder 'Elephants in the Living Room' blog on Catholic institutional blindness to clerical child sexual abuse.

Want to know what the Plenary Council 2020/21 should be dealing with? Then read **Catholics for Renewal**'s Getting Back on Mission. *All the key issues, big and small, are listed with practical steps on how to deal with them – and with an eye to history, theology and Canon Law. The Plenary Council is a council of bishops, but the Church is overwhelmingly lay. The bishops should be pleased that so many are so keen for the Church's success as to produce this sophisticated document.*

> – Eric Hodgens, a Senior Priest of the Melbourne Archdiocese, a 'retired Pastor Emeritus' who 'writes a bit'.

For those interested in the Plenary Council 2020/21, here is a most comprehensive exploration of the issues that confront the Catholic Church in Australia today. Getting Back on Mission *by* **Catholics for Renewal** *represents the reflections, thoughts and methodical research of many Catholics who contributed to the various stages of bringing to birth this important book. It covers issues of governance, lay participation, liturgical reform, inclusion of women, people of diverse sexualities, gender and marital status, clericalism, training and professional development of clergy and church leaders and much more. All Australian Catholics interested in the Church's future will find this book informative, challenging and essential to understanding the issues that should be addressed at the Plenary Council 2020/21.*

> – Peter Maher, Editor of *The Swag* National Council of Priests Quarterly Magazine, former Parish Priest of St Joseph's Newtown in Sydney.

Getting Back on Mission *is a well researched document that is grounded in the larger Tradition of the Church and the contemporary reality of Australia. This insightful writing is exciting, creative, courageous and visionary in its scope and depth. As such, it deserves a thorough and thoughtful reading.*
– Rev. Jim Clarke Ph.D., Senior Lecturer in Spirituality, Loyola Marymount University, Los Angeles, USA.

I see the Plenary Council of the Australian Catholic Church as crucial to the future of our Church. The world needs the Church more now than perhaps at any time in its history. In order to meet this need, the institutional Church must get its house in order with the grace of God and the good will of the people of God. In "Getting back on mission", **Catholics for Renewal** *has provided invaluable guidance for the Church.*
– Kevin Mogg, former Episcopal Vicar for Social Services for the Archdiocese of Melbourne (27 years), founder of Catholic Social Services Victoria, former Rector of Corpus Christi Seminary for Victoria and Tasmania

It took the world-wide catastrophe of sexual abuse of minors by Catholic clerics and the discovery of the systemic cover-up and enabling by Catholic Bishops to force the People of God to finally realize that toxic clericalism still reigns supreme. Getting Back on Mission by **Catholics For Renewal**, *Australia, is far more than an evidentiary document for the Australian Plenary Council to be held in 2020/21. It is a clear, concise, detailed, factual and prophetic examination of the distortions, failures and subversion perpetrated by the clerical culture. This historic work, inspired by the disastrous debacle of sexual abuse in the Church that was exposed by the Royal Commission, is far more than another cry for reform that falls on the deaf ears of the hierarchy. It is a glaring exposition of reality. It is a prophetic description of what has been, what is and what will be if the clerical establishment continues to run from this reality.* Getting Back on Mission *is both terrifying because it tells the truth and hopeful because it comes from believing, courageous and determined members of the People of God who are making the future happen.*
– Thomas Doyle, Doctor of Canon Law, former Dominican priest, internationally acknowledged expert in the canonical and pastoral dimensions of clerical child sexual abuse, expert witness before the Australian Royal Commission into Institutional Responses to Child Sexual Abuse, received Priest of Integrity Award from The Voice of the Faithful in 2002.

ABOUT
CATHOLICS FOR RENEWAL
AND THIS BOOK

About the book

The core of this book is the formal submission of *Catholics for Renewal* to the Australian Plenary Council to be held over two sessions in 2020 and 2021. It is presented as a resource for the people of God in discussing their expectations of the Council.

The submission was researched and written in response to an invitation from the bishops of Australia to all Christ's faithful in Australia to:

> engage in an open and inclusive experience of listening, dialogue and discernment about the future of the Catholic Church in Australia ... to get together with friends, family or colleagues ... to spend time thinking and talking about your experiences of faith, life and the Church ... and to respond to the question: *What do you think God is asking of us in Australia at this time?*

The bishops also stated that it was important for the Plenary Council to hear responses from as many people as possible. Consequently, *Catholics for Renewal* recognised "a graced opportunity to renew the Church in Australia".

The submission was lodged on 6 March 2019 and immediately shared on the website: www.catholicsforrenewal.org.au. Subsequently, Garratt Publishing offered to make the document available as a book that could be of wider interest to all those seeking renewal of the Church. It was agreed that some new material and refinements should be included to support this purpose. Supplementary information, a foreword from Robert Fitzgerald AM, and discussion questions for each part have been included. The discussion questions are intended to support our bishops' desire that the faithful "spend time thinking and talking about your experiences of faith, life and the Church".

Since 6 March, important data on the current state of the Church in Australia has been published by the National Centre for Pastoral Research concerning Mass attendance and the 2016 Commonwealth Census. To ensure that the book is as up-to-date as possible some of this new data has been added to the original text and tables and appropriately noted. Additional text and a new recommendation (2.10) regarding the Church's teaching on homosexuality have been included.

Also included are references to several recent developments which are relevant to the content of the book and ensure that it is as current as possible. We note the welcome decision of the Australian Catholic Bishops Conference and Catholic Religious Australia, on 1 May 2019, to proceed with a national review of the governance and management structures of Catholic dioceses and parishes, as recommended by the Royal Commission into Institutional Responses to Child Sexual Abuse (and in the manner proposed in our Recommendation 3.2).

In keeping with a commitment to engagement of the people of God with the leaders of our Church, we have included as a supplement contact details for the Apostolic Nuncio, diocesan bishops, eparchs, ordinaries, auxiliary bishops, and Australian Catholic Bishops Conference. We hope that Supplement 1 will serve as a useful reference document for readers who are prepared to share their views with their diocesan bishop in particular, and thus contribute to a better articulation of the sense of faith of the faithful (*sensus fidei fidelium*).

About the author

The author of this book is *Catholics for Renewal*, a group of committed Catholic women and men who call for a renewed Catholic Church that follows Jesus Christ more closely. The group established itself in 2011 and officially incorporated in the State of Victoria.

The first action of the group, in 2011, was to draft an *Open Letter to Pope Benedict XVI and the Bishops of Australia* stating that the institutional Church had alienated many Catholics and had become disconnected from, and irrelevant to the lives of many Catholic children. The letter called for an open, transparent, accountable, compassionate and outward-facing Church, totally committed to justice, peace, ecumenism, dialogue with other faiths, and advocacy for the rights of the oppressed and disadvantaged while tending practically to their needs. It also called for an end to the Church's patriarchal attitude to women and asked every bishop to convene a diocesan synod to discuss how each local church might be a more authentic witness in the 21st century. Over 8000 Australian Catholics endorsed and signed the letter.

In 2012 the group called on the Australian Catholic Bishops Conference to convene a Plenary Council in 2015.

Catholics for Renewal made written submissions to both the Victorian Parliamentary Inquiry into the Handling of Child Abuse by Religious and Other Organisations (2012-2013) and the Royal Commission into Institutional Responses to Child Sexual Abuse (2012-2017). It presented evidence at the public hearings of both inquiries, expressing particular concern that Church leaders had protected paedophiles, and worse, had thus exposed further children to sexual abuse. The focus of the submissions and evidence was reform of church governance and the introduction of mandatory criminal reporting of child sexual abusers.

In February 2017, the group drafted another *Open Letter to the Bishops of Australia* calling on them to "Please Listen and Act Now" on seven key areas exposed by the Royal Commission: clericalism, accountability, equality of women, diocesan synods, priestly formation, redress for abuse victims/survivors, and Vatican inaction on child sexual abuse, dysfunctional governance, and the selection of bishops. Some 4000 Australian Catholics endorsed and signed this letter.

The 2019 Submission to the Plenary Council is the group's most recent endeavour for the renewal of the Catholic Church in Australia. The book includes as appendices the earlier Open Letters whose signatories expressed support for many of the book's proposals.

Acknowledgments

Catholics for Renewal wishes to thank Garratt Publishing for the generous and collaborative approach it has brought to this endeavour.

Catholics for Renewal particularly acknowledges the work of the Australian Catholic Coalition for Church Reform comprising 13 separate renewal groups seeking urgent reform of the institutional Church. A statement from the Coalition calling for Church reform is contained in Supplement 4, a further indication of the extensive commitment by Australian Catholics to the need for Church reform.

We are grateful to Anne Doyle for her voluntary professional proof-reading of the submission text. Her eyes found things that those familiar with it could not see.

Special thanks go to the expert commentators who each wrote an introduction to a Part of the book: Clare Condon SGS, Marilyn Hatton, Elizabeth Proust, Bruce Duncan CSsR, and Peter Wilkinson.

Contents

Supplements   303

Index   327

Foreword

When I was asked to write this foreword by *Catholics for Renewal*, I was not asked to endorse the specific proposals, but rather to join with those who have generously worked, prayed, reflected and discerned a way forward for a revitalised and renewed Church. Like so many thousands around Australia, they have entered into the journey of the Australian Plenary Council 2020/21 with a genuine hope that a transformed Church can emerge. A new conversation has arisen within the Church and I hope a new dawn for the Church, both in this country and beyond, will slowly unfold as a consequence.

My personal hopes and aspirations for our church are deeply and profoundly grounded in what I heard, saw and experienced in the recent Royal Commission into Institutional Responses to Child Sexual Abuse. And so it is important to reflect on the truth revealed by those who came forward and the learnings from the evidence, research and deep analyses. More importantly, it should help inform how we must respond.

Child sexual abuse by Catholic clergy, religious and lay people may be explained by a combination of psychosexual and other related factors on the part of the individual perpetrator, and a range of institutional factors, including theological, governance and cultural factors. The same theological, governance and cultural factors that contributed to the occurrence of abuse also contributed to the inadequate responses of Catholic institutions to that abuse. And they lie at the heart of the loss of integrity and legitimacy more generally, both within and outside the Church.

Many contributing factors collectively gave rise to personal and institutional failures including unhealthy clericalism, mandatory celibacy and inadequate selection, training and formation of religious and clergy. The absence of professional development and ongoing pastoral supervision exacerbated such weaknesses. The absence of females and their participation in leadership roles is also very likely to have affected the responses to abuse once known.

Poor governance, inadequate leadership, and an unhealthy culture that preferences secrecy and the Church's own interests contributed to the collective failure of the Catholic Church. Conflicts of interest were not dealt with adequately, and incentives were not aligned with the stated values of the Church. The interests of children, and then later adult survivors, were not paramount or even adequately addressed until at least the mid 1990s.

Our response to what has been revealed rests as much in the Gospel as it does in the learnings of the Royal Commission. For in the Gospel it was the voice of the oppressed and marginalised that Christ used to declare a new order. It was through his engagement with the poor that Christ proclaimed the truth and the light. He admonished those who sought to maintain the status quo and those who fought to maintain the privileges of power and influence.

There is enormous pain in many parts of the Church. For clergy and religious, the revelation that some of their colleagues abused children is almost overwhelming. For lay people, the fact that trusted priests, religious and lay leaders, often friends and mentors, offended against children has been devastating. For many parents, the failure of their fellow parishioners to believe them and their children is deeply wounding. For survivors, the Church's cold indifference still hurts.

Yet, the Church risks further losing the trust and confidence of the people of God and the broader community, unless the lessons are learnt and governance is improved and renewal occurs. More specifically, the current governance arrangements are increasingly losing legitimacy with the Church's own community of faithful.

Reform of Church governance arrangements, even within current canon law, is vital if the Church is to be a relevant, responsive, sacred and transformative body in spreading the Word of God to the faithful and beyond.

Current Church governance, and some of the canons that underpin it, are based (intentionally or unintentionally) on a fear of the non-ordained, especially women, a fear of outside influence (even where that is good), an arrogant assertion of the position of the Church in the world, and maintaining the unique privilege of an ordained class. It too often dismisses open, transparent and accountable approaches in favour of secrecy, complexity and legalistic approaches. It shuns genuine participation. And there are strong forces within the Church that seek the *status quo*.

Good church governance must be based in hope not fear. It must arise out of humility not arrogance. It must, at its core, embrace the participation of all the faithful in order to regain legitimacy.

For me, good governance is essential to a renewed Church but is not an end in itself. It is an enabler for the fulfilment of the purpose and mission of our Church. It is intrinsically relational in nature, creating relationships between people, and between people and processes, to achieve a desired end within an institutional and societal context of norms and values.

Church governance should be based on a stewardship model that recognises that the organisation is governed for the benefit of promoting the word of God, for the benefit of the community of the faithful equally (without fear or favour) in the best interests of the people and community it serves, and recognises the interests of the broader community within which it is located.

The outcome of good governance is to drive good cultures, support good leadership and build trust in the institution. It allows the institution's purpose to be fulfilled responsibly with regard to both Church and societal norms. It will allow good practice to be infused with all that is important in our faith-filled mission.

But most importantly, it must promote integrity, legitimacy, and the just exercise of authority. Too much of current church governance concentrates on authority, too little on integrity and legitimacy.

We have the capacity to reshape our institutions and the Church at large:
• To create a Church that is genuinely safe for children and vulnerable adults and which acts in their best interests.

- To create a Church that is genuinely responsive to the voices of those who have come forward to tell their stories, express their pain and seek healing and hope in a better Church.
- To create a Church whose governance and leadership is competent, engaged and open to evidence, learning and improvement.
- To create an ongoing conversation with the people of God, and to genuinely invite them into the governance and leadership of the Church.
- To create a Church more truthful, transparent and accountable to the faithful and the community at large.
- To create a Church in which the community's trust can be restored.
- To create a Church authentically based on the Gospels and the revelations of Jesus Christ – one that seeks to heal not to hurt, to include not to exclude, to nurture not control.
- To create a Church that loves, that acts justly, and that walks humbly in the presence of God.

Along with so many others, the voice of *Catholics for Renewal* is a clarion call for renewal. I hope and pray that the Plenary Council 2020/21 will be an opportunity for the Church in Australia to explore the evidence, engage in open dialogue, and discern a new course for the Church. I remain encouraged by the transformative words of Pope Francis and live in hope that good words will be followed by good action. The time for resolute action is upon us. The time to govern out of hope not fear is now.

Robert Fitzgerald AM
(in a personal capacity only)
Former Commissioner, Royal Commission into Institutional
Responses to Child Sexual Abuse

Preface

Vatican II stated that "the Church, inspired by no earthly ambition, seeks but a solitary goal: to carry forward the work of Christ himself under the lead of the befriending Spirit".[1]

The work of Jesus Christ was the proclamation and inauguration of the Kingdom of God on earth. That was the mission which God gave Jesus and which Jesus passed on to the Church. *Catholics for Renewal* believes that for too long the Church in Australia has been 'off mission' and must urgently get back to carrying forward the work of Christ. We believe that God's mission and the Kingdom of God must be the priority focus of the Plenary Council 2020/21. The Kingdom of God is one of Love, Justice, Compassion, Peace, Truth, Freedom, and Equality. The Church in Australia must be the sign of that Kingdom.

The Church in Australia currently finds itself in a real and huge existential crisis. The signs are everywhere: massive disaffiliation by baptised Catholics, falling Mass attendance and use of the sacraments, few vocations to the priesthood and religious life, bishops isolated from their people, many parishes merged and without priests, flagging confidence in the hierarchical leadership, and the massive fallout from disgraceful conduct of clergy revealed by the Royal Commission into Institutional Responses to Child Sexual Abuse. Recent events concerning two senior cardinals have added to the crisis.

> … Catholics for Renewal believes that for too long the Church in Australia has been 'off mission' and must urgently get back to carrying forward the work of Christ … God's mission and the Kingdom of God must be the priority focus of the Plenary Council 2020/21 …

The crisis was building for decades, but no single moment marked the point when the Church went 'off mission', and those who identified the crisis early on were easily dismissed as exaggerating or 'crying wolf'. The depth of the crisis only came into full view with the revelation of the widespread criminal sexual abuse of children by priests and religious, and the systematic and secretive cover-ups of these crimes by bishops wanting to protect the abusers, contain the financial costs, and avert reputational damage. By then, the essential qualities of the Kingdom had been abandoned.

The extent of the tragedy, how it happened, and what remedial actions are needed were the subject of two major government inquiries: the Victoria Parliamentary Inquiry into the Handling of Child Abuse by Religious and Other Organisations (2012-13) and the Royal Commission into Institutional Responses to Child Sexual Abuse (2012-17).

Catholics for Renewal made contributions to both inquiries, and our conviction was that a fundamental reason for the failure of the Church to be a credible sign of the Kingdom was, and is, its dysfunctional governance. Vatican II envisaged the Church's governance to be collegial, synodal, co-responsible, and in accord with the principle of subsidiarity – recognising the "whole people's supernatural discernment"[2]. In Australia, little notice was taken of any part of that call. Bishops continued to operate as independent monarchs, avoided synods, refused to establish the needed structures for effective co-responsibility, and routinely requested Rome to make decisions that should have been taken locally.

... until the equality of women is recognised and accepted, the culture of clericalism and secrecy uprooted, and bishops made accountable to their people, the Church in Australia will never be the sign of the Kingdom ...

We believe that the dysfunctional governance of the Church in Australia – and elsewhere – will persist until the key elements of good governance are in place: accountability, transparency, and inclusion. We also believe that until the equality of women is recognised and accepted, the culture of clericalism and secrecy uprooted, and bishops made accountable to their people, the Church in Australia will never be the sign of the Kingdom.

Good church governance demands synodality: a genuine listening to the *sensus fidei* of Christ's faithful. There are proper canonical structures for this - particular councils, diocesan synods, diocesan and parish pastoral councils – and until they are established in every diocese across the nation, without exception, the dysfunctional governance and lack of synodality will continue.

Much of the dysfunction also stems from a pervasive and pernicious culture and mindset known as 'clericalism'. It flourishes within the clergy, but is reinforced by a laity conditioned to defer to the clergy and to accept subservience. Clericalism was inculcated over a long period in the formation program for priests and religious, and became deeply ingrained; this has to be eradicated now.

Vatican II identified many fundamental rights and duties of Catholics, but most of the laity are unaware of their rights. To take up their proper role and responsibilities in the Church in Australia, the People of God need to know their rights and duties and to understand them. We believe a 'charter' of rights and responsibilities is due and should be developed and promulgated urgently.

... whenever we gather, Christ is among us, and the Spirit stirs ...

Most Catholics in Australia are now aware of significant failings amongst their bishops, and regular Mass attenders will know of the many deficiencies in parish ministry. We believe that these failings are holding back God's mission and are obstacles to the building of the Kingdom of God. We have sought to identify them and to recommend change.

While we are appalled by the crisis which has befallen the Church in Australia, and challenged by its enormity, we are not without hope that our Church can be renewed. For whenever we gather, Christ is among us, and the Spirit stirs.

Catholics for Renewal believes that the Plenary Council 2020/21 is a graced opportunity to renew the Church in Australia. We gladly accept our responsibility to contribute to that opportunity.

Recommendations

Following is a complete list of the recommendations by *Catholics for Renewal*, extracted from the parts of the book where the relevant matters are discussed.

Part 2: People of God

Recommendation 2.1:

> that the Plenary Council 2020/21 develop a Charter of Rights and Duties for Christ's Faithful in Australia, based on those set out in the 1983 *Code of Canon Law*, particularly Canons 210–223, augmented by those contained in the Synod of Bishops document *Justice in the World*, and updated using the fresh insights contained in Pope Francis's Apostolic Exhortations *Evangelii Gaudium* (2013) and *Episcopalis communio* (2018), his Encyclical Letter *Laudato Si'* (2015), the *Directory for the Pastoral Ministry of Bishops* (*Apostolorum successors*, 2004)[3], and the most recent documents of the International Theological Commission (2014, 2018)[4].

Recommendation 2.2:

> that the Charter incorporates the right of Australian Catholics to have made available to them by their diocesan bishops all the canonical structures recommended by Vatican II, and other necessary avenues for effective pastoral dialogue, so that they can express their needs and desires with freedom and confidence.[5]

Recommendation 2.3:

that the Charter incorporates the right of Christ's faithful to expect their diocesan bishops, as a matter of course, and in order to fulfil their missionary obligation, as stressed by Pope Francis, to:

i) "listen to everyone and not simply to those who would tell them what [they] would like to hear";

ii) "be bold and creative in rethinking the goals, structures, style, and methods of evangelization in their respective communities";

iii) ensure that proposals of goals will not prove illusory by including "an adequate communal search for the means of achieving them"; and

iv) "not walk alone, but rely on [all the faithful] as brothers and sisters under [their] leadership, in a wise and realistic pastoral discernment".[6]

Recommendation 2.4:

that the Charter incorporates the right of all persons (and groups) who have suffered abuse or injustice at the hands of an ordained cleric, professed religious or church-employed person, to receive just redress.

Recommendation 2.5:

that the Charter incorporates the right of all the faithful to know:

i) the quality of pastoral ministry they are entitled to receive from their pastors;

ii) the standards of ethical conduct their pastors will uphold and follow;

iii) what mechanisms will be put in place to guarantee accountability and transparency; and

iv) what actions will be taken to ensure gender balance throughout the Church.

Recommendation 2.6:

> that the Charter incorporates the right of every Australian bishop, priest, religious or layperson accused of doctrinal error and/or failure of leadership, to be afforded due process and a fair trial in accord with the standards of Australian civil justice.

Recommendation 2.7:

> that the Charter incorporates the right of Christ's faithful in Australia to be invited to express their opinion when new bishops are to be selected and to be moved, and that a new process be drawn up to ensure this is enabled.[7]

Recommendation 2.8:

> that the Charter incorporates the right of Christ's faithful in parishes to be recognised as living communities of faith, and be consulted whenever there is a proposal to divide, merge, amalgamate, cluster, or close a parish.

Recommendation 2.9:

> that the Charter be officially promulgated, published in print and digital format, be widely disseminated on all official Catholic Church websites, and be displayed in print at the entrance of every church, and every Catholic educational, health and welfare institution throughout the nation.

Recommendation 2.10:

> that the Plenary Council request the Holy See to review urgently the provisions of the Catechism regarding homosexual people in light of modern understanding of God-given human sexuality.

Part 3: Church Governance

Our recommendations on Church Governance comprise three groups:
A – those requiring immediate implementation pre-Council
B – those requiring determination by the Plenary Council

C – those outside the direct competence of the Plenary Council requiring referral by the Council to the Holy See.

A   Recommendations requiring immediate implementation pre-Council;

Recommendation 3.1:

> that each diocesan bishop, prior to the first session of the Council, convene a diocesan synod or assembly or other means of engagement and dialogue to ascertain the *sensus fidei* of the faithful in his care; and that these synods/assemblies be accepted as an integral part of preparing the Plenary Council agenda. At this diocesan synod/assembly, the diocesan bishop should seek guidance on how to select the non-religious lay faithful who will represent the diocese at the Plenary Council 2020/21.[8]

Recommendation 3.2:

> that the ACBC immediately expedite implementation of the Royal Commission's recommendation that the ACBC conduct a national review of the governance and management structures of dioceses and parishes (**Recommendation 16.7**) with results to be made public during the lead up to the Plenary Council. This review should valuably inform considerations of the Plenary Council and ensure a more thorough appreciation of these critical governance issues.

B   Recommendations requiring determination by the Plenary Council:

Recommendation 3.3:

> that the Plenary Council legislate that each diocesan bishop must establish a diocesan pastoral council, and that its membership is to be gender balanced and reflect the diversity of the faithful in the diocese. Vatican II intended that diocesan pastoral councils support and guide bishops in their pastoral ministry.

The International Theological Commission has stated that "the diocesan pastoral council proposes itself as the permanent structure most favourable to the implementation of synodality in the particular church".[9] The selection process for members of this council should not only follow the canonical guidelines (C. 512) but be based on merit and independence, comprising members of the faithful committed to "carry forward the work of Christ himself under the lead of the befriending Spirit".[10]

Recommendation 3.4:

that the Plenary Council legislate that each parish priest must establish a parish pastoral council, and that its membership is to include men and women, and to attempt to represent the diversity of the faithful in the parish.

Recommendation 3.5:

that the Plenary Council legislate that at least once every five years, each diocesan bishop must convene a diocesan synod, recognising that a diocesan synod is the "instrument 'par excellence' for assisting the bishop to order his diocese", represents "the summit of diocesan participation structures", and "occupies a place of primary importance".[11] Moreover, when its membership reflects the diversity of vocations, ministries, charisms, skills, social backgrounds and geographical origins of the faithful within the diocese, it is an 'event of grace'. At least half those called to be synod members should be non-religious lay men and women balanced in their numbers [cf. Instruction on Diocesan Synods, 1997].

Recommendation 3.6:

that the Plenary Council legislate that each diocesan bishop convene a diocesan assembly between diocesan synods as an alternative less restrictive means of engaging the faithful. The International Theological Commission states that a diocesan assembly expresses and promotes communion and co-responsibility and contributes to the planning of integrated pastoral care and its evaluation. As such, a diocesan assembly is important to the synodal journey of a particular church and can serve as the ordinary preparation for a diocesan synod and also a plenary council.[12]

Recommendation 3.7:

that the Plenary Council legislate that a plenary council must be convened by the Australian Episcopal Conference at least once every fifteen years, and that at least one third of those to be called are non-religious laypersons with gender equality.

Recommendation 3.8:

that the Plenary Council legislate that each diocesan bishop be required to prepare in a synodal manner, with the clergy and laity of their diocese, a diocesan pastoral plan, to cover a forward period of no less than 5 years. The legislation should require regular reviews and updating before it expires. The pastoral plan must be circulated widely and online as a public document.

Recommendation 3.9:

that the Plenary Council legislate that each diocesan bishop be required to prepare and publish an annual report on the state of his diocese, and that it include information on:

i) the implementation of the diocesan pastoral plan;
ii) membership of the diocesan pastoral council and presbyteral council;
iii) Catholic Education (primary, secondary, tertiary);
iv) Mass attendance and reception of the sacraments;
v) Rite of Christian Initiation of Adults (RCIA);
vi) health, aged care and welfare activities;
vii) the financial situation (Profit & Loss Statements, Balance Sheets) of the diocese;
viii) state of the clergy and seminarians;
ix) employees of the diocese;
x) the bishop's personal appraisal of the pastoral and other challenges/risks currently being faced;

xi) decisions made or proposals being considered to address them; and

xii) significant achievements and developments.

Recommendation 3.10:

that the Plenary Council legislate that each parish priest, in consultation with his parish pastoral and financial councils, is to prepare and publish an annual report on the pastoral and financial state of the parish.

Recommendation 3.11:

that the Plenary Council legislate that bishops and presbyters are to be held accountable for their pastoral, administrative and financial decisions.

Recommendation 3.12:

that the Plenary Council develop a more suitable, inclusive and open process for the selection of bishops in Australia, having regard to Recommendations 4.9 – 4.13 below. Explicit in the qualities required of the candidate should be their qualifications and skills to lead and to govern. The process for selection should be transparent and public, with due regard for necessary confidentiality.[13]

Recommendation 3.13:

that the Plenary Council develop a professional formation program for bishops and parish pastors to ensure that they have the necessary skills for:

i) leadership based on Christian values;

ii) listening to the *sensus fidei fidelium*;

iii) commitment to gender equality; and

iv) an understanding of Australian standards of best practice for good governance.

Recommendation 3.14:

that the Plenary Council commit to gender balance in the

leadership of the Church, starting with women with appropriate skills and qualifications being appointed to senior executive positions in all dioceses.

C Recommendations outside the direct competence of the Plenary Council requiring referral by the Council to the Holy See

Recommendation 3.15:

that the 1983 *Code of Canon Law* be amended to:

i) repeal Canon 129;

ii) require the Quinquennial Report, prepared by each diocesan bishop on the state of the diocese entrusted to him (C. 399), to include information necessary to establish compliance with best-practice standards of accountability, transparency and inclusion;

iii) allow an unredacted copy of each Quinquennial Report to be kept in the secret archives of the diocese, with access to legitimate researchers after say 20 years;

iv) ensure that any bishop accused of a failure in his governance of the diocese entrusted to him, be accorded a fair trial with due process; namely, with notification of the charges made against him, with access to the names of his accusers and the details of their accusations, with access to legal counsel, and with the opportunity to question his accusers under oath in an official court of law;

v) ensure that the pontifical secret does not prevent reporting to the civil authorities of child sexual abusers at large, regardless of whether there are mandatory criminal reporting laws in the State concerned; and

vi) require Church authorities to report knowledge of child sexual abusers at large regardless of whether there are mandatory criminal reporting laws in the State concerned (with exemptions for jurisdictions where human rights are at risk).

Recommendation 3.16:

that the Holy See commit to gender balance in the leadership of the Church at all levels.

Recommendation 3.17:

that the Holy See recognise the equality of women by appointing suitable and competent women as the prefect and secretary of a number of dicasteries of the Holy See (say half of all dicasteries).

Recommendation 3.18:

that the Holy See be asked to take note of the *sensus fidei fidelium* in Australia with regard to the ordination of women to the priesthood and to the diaconate; and that it review the Church's position regarding women and the sacrament of Holy Orders, commencing with the Order of the Diaconate.

Recommendation 3.19:

that the Holy See be asked to ensure a regular turnover of clerical staff in its various dicasteries; that those appointed be lay and clerical persons selected from across the world; and that they be persons who have 'the smell of the sheep'[14] and are fully committed to accountability to Christ's mission, who actively seek to be informed by the *sensus fidei fidelium*, and who have a lively culture of pastoral awareness and sensitivity.[15]

Recommendation 3.20:

that the Holy See be asked to remove the requirement of compulsory celibacy for diocesan priests,[16] noting that:

i)   married priests currently minister in Australia;

ii)   the compulsory nature of the celibacy discipline denies the faithful of ministers they need; and

iii)   it blights the ministry of some priests who do not have the gift of celibacy.

Recommendation 3.21:

> that the Holy See consider changes to the period of appointment
> and tenure of bishops in Australia[17] which would include:
>
> i)   the introduction of initial appointments by the Bishop of
> Rome for a 5-year period for all diocesan and titular bishops;
>
> ii)   the introduction of re-appointments for 5-year periods,
> subject to the individual bishop satisfying a review and
> assessment of his pastoral ministry and governance by the
> priests and faithful of his diocese;
>
> iii) a transparent and accountable review and assessment process
> which respects the confidentially of the participants and the
> reputation of the bishop;
>
> iv) the review and assessment process to be initiated and
> conducted by the Apostolic Nuncio;
>
> v)   the compiled report on the assessment to be sent to the
> Holy See by the Apostolic Nuncio; and
>
> vi) the individual bishop subject to review to be given a copy of
> the report sent to the Holy See.

Part 4: Pastoral Leadership and Parish Ministry

Recommendation 4.1:

> that the Plenary Council review the role of the ministers of
> the sacraments to ensure that the priorities of their ministry
> reflect a sound understanding of the relationship between Word,
> sacrament and ministry.

Recommendation 4.2:

> that the Plenary Council thoroughly examine the empirical
> evidence of the decline in the reception of the sacraments to:
>
> i)   identify the failures in the life of the community to which it
> attests; and
>
> ii)   address the causes of and remedies to those failures.

Recommendation 4.3:

> that the Plenary Council re-examine the Pastoral Strategies recommended by the Pastoral Projects Office in 2007 and legislate for appropriate action at diocesan and parish level.

Recommendation 4.4:

> that all adult catechumens, before being baptised, be given a copy of the proposed Charter of Rights and Duties for Christ's Faithful in Australia and have it explained to them.

Recommendation 4.5:

> that bishops who confer the sacrament of Confirmation be more mindful of the gifts of the Spirit received in the sacrament, particularly wisdom, knowledge and understanding, and understand that they have a duty to respect those gifts in the confirmed and to listen to what Christ's faithful have to say.

Recommendation 4.6:

> that the Plenary Council legislate to restore the use of the Third Rite of Reconciliation in the Church in Australia to at least twice each year, during Lent and Advent, and that this Rite be properly explained to Christ's faithful.

Recommendation 4.7:

> that, as there is a critical need to ensure that child sexual abusers are not left unidentified and at large in the community, the Plenary Council should carefully examine the seal of confession as it currently operates in the First Rite,[18] with a view to:
>
> i) maintaining its essential purpose while conforming to civil laws requiring reporting knowledge of child sexual abusers at large obtained in a sacramental confession; and
>
> ii) mandating that absolution be deferred, conditional on the abuser penitent self-reporting the crime(s) committed to the civil authorities of the jurisdiction where the crime(s) was committed and providing proof of the self-reporting.

Recommendation 4.8:

that the sexual abuse of a child or minor[19] be declared a 'reserved sin' with absolution reserved to a diocesan bishop; and that absolution be deferred, conditional on the abuser penitent self-reporting the crime(s) committed to the civil authorities of the jurisdiction where the crime(s) were committed and providing proof of the self-reporting.[20]

Recommendation 4.9:

that the Plenary Council legislate to ensure that all priests, permanent deacons, religious and lay members of Christ's faithful in a diocese are given the opportunity to have a co-responsible and participatory role in the selection of their own bishop(s).[21]

Recommendation 4.10:

that the Plenary Council legislate to ensure that the Apostolic Nuncio, as part of his responsibility, must seek out and welcome any nominations, recommendations or expressions of concern from Christ's faithful in particular dioceses in regard to the selection or appointment of a new bishop for that diocese.

Recommendation 4.11:

that the Plenary Council legislate to make it obligatory for the Apostolic Nuncio to advise Christ's faithful in a particular diocese when the selection process for a bishop of their diocese is to begin and end, and to invite their participation.

Recommendation 4.12:

that all metropolitan archbishops and diocesan bishops are to encourage and facilitate the participation of Christ's faithful in every selection process where the appointment of a new auxiliary bishop in needed.

Recommendation 4.13:

that bishops be persons of prayer, humility, faith and courage, live close to the people committed to their care, and be true pastors, leaders, and agents of renewal for the sake of the Kingdom of God.[22]

Recommendation 4.14:

that all bishops develop and adopt a mindset of pastoral ministry which LISTENS carefully and constantly to the *sensus fidei* of Christ's faithful in their diocese, learn to govern with synodality, co-responsibility, accountability, transparency, inclusion, and subsidiarity, and embrace women as equals.

Recommendation 4.15:

that all bishops engage:
i)   a professional supervisor to 'look over' or 'oversee' how they personally approach and conduct their ministry; and
ii) a regular spiritual director.

Recommendation 4.16:

that the program of priestly formation present the priesthood as a gift of service to the community of Christ's faithful, not as something that elevates the priest above the lay faithful or separates the priest from them.

Recommendation 4.17:

that the program of priestly formation must instil a mindset that:
i)   welcomes collaborative and co-responsible lay and ordained ministries;
ii)   respects the inherent value of lay ministries; and
iii) does not view ordained persons as superior in dignity to laypersons.

Recommendation 4.18:

that priests and bishops retain close ties with their own family members, and with colleagues and parishioners who will support them outside their professional and ministerial roles; and tell them what they need to hear, not what they want to hear.

Recommendation 4.19:

that priests and bishops allow some trusted persons into their personal lives as close friends – including but not limited to brother priests – who know them well, who will be honest with them and keep them grounded, and who will always be there for them.

Recommendation 4.20:

that the review of the *National Program of Priestly Formation,* as recommended by the Royal Commission, be immediate, independent, and comprehensive, with particular focus on the systemic factors related to:

i)   initial selection and ongoing assessment of candidates for the priesthood;

ii) adequate personal and psychosexual development and integration; and

iii) initial and on-going professional education and formation for pastoral ministry.

Recommendation 4.21:

that candidates seeking admission to the program of formation for the priesthood should:

i)   be at least 24 years of age;

ii) have gained a university degree or trade qualification;

iii) have worked for three years in their chosen field or trade;

iv) have demonstrated financial independence; and

v)   have demonstrated a capacity for independent living.

Recommendation 4.22:

that a National Protocol for the Assessment of Candidates for the Priesthood be immediately developed and adopted. It should include:

i) having access to a highly skilled, multi-disciplinary team of professional persons, external to seminary staff, with extensive expertise in clinical psychiatry and psychology and a comprehensive understanding of the sub-cultures of religious life and diocesan priesthood;

ii) using this team for the initial and on-going assessment of candidates for the priesthood (and religious life);

iii) establishing a training and mentoring program for selected clinicians to become members of this team; and

iv) a clear statement of the pre-requisites for candidates for formation for the priesthood.

Recommendation 4.23:

that during their formation for the diocesan priesthood, seminarians remain living, for the most part, in the general community, and preferably in non-institutional settings with a model to be developed.

Recommendation 4.24:

that all staff involved in the formation of candidates for the priesthood must have an adequate and accurate self-knowledge, a high level of professional training and substantial pastoral experience.

Recommendation 4.25:

that the personal, professional and pastoral formation of priests be holistic, ongoing and reviewable, covering their relational, psychological, emotional, and spiritual development. They must be trained to understand that they will be accountable to pre-determined standards of ethical behaviour set out in an official code of conduct.

Recommendation 4.26:

that priests and bishops always approach and conduct their ministry with humility and in the spirit of service, according to Gospel values and for the building up of the Kingdom of God.

Recommendation 4.27:

that those candidates who voluntarily embrace celibacy for the sake of the Kingdom of God, be fully informed of the loss of generativity it involves, guided in how to embrace and grieve for this loss, and how to live celibacy creatively and lovingly.

Recommendation 4.28:

that the Plenary Council take particular note of the outcomes of the Pan-Amazonian Synod, especially as it relates to the ordination of *viri probati*.[23]

Recommendation 4.29:

that the Plenary Council reflect seriously on the grave shortage of priests in certain dioceses and the impediments hindering faithful from frequent access to the Eucharist and the other sacraments, and legislate to permit the ordinaries of such dioceses, in consultation and collaboration with the Australian Catholic Bishops Conference, to put forward to the Holy See concrete proposals for the ordination to the priesthood of suitable and mature married men of deep faith and proven virtue, who are natural leaders and have the support and respect of their communities.[24]

Recommendation 4.30:

that, if after a period of trial, the ministry of married priests proves successful and acceptable to the clergy and other faithful in the dioceses where it exists, a later plenary council should review the situation and, if opportune, recommend that the presence and ministry of married priests be accepted as a normal and permanent part of priestly ministry throughout Australia.

Recommendation 4.31:

that discussion and study of women's ordination to the priesthood not be shut down, but allowed to continue, as it is an issue which calls for new efforts of analysis and synthesis within the context of a more dynamic and evolutionary concept of reality.[25]

Recommendation 4.32:

that the Plenary Council, although it cannot legislate on this issue, respectfully listens to the *sensus fidei* of Christ's faithful in Australia on the matter of the ordination of women, and reports in full what it hears to the Holy See.

Recommendation 4.33:

that the Plenary Council or the ACBC legislate or make provision, with the approval of the Holy See, for the ordination of suitable and mature single, married, and widowed women to the permanent diaconate and appointment for this ministry.

Recommendation 4.34:

that each diocesan bishop, after consulting his council of priests and diocesan pastoral council, should convene a diocesan synod to hear the *sensus fidei* of the faithful of the diocese on women deacons in ministry, and make his decision in the Spirit based on the needs of the diocese and what he has heard.

Recommendation 4.35:

that the Plenary Council or the ACBC develop suitable criteria for the selection and screening of suitable female candidates for the diaconate, and a suitable program with active mentorship for their initial and ongoing formation.

Recommendation 4.36:

that the Plenary Council or the ACBC develop and implement a suitable program for the preparation and education of the faithful of the dioceses where women deacons are introduced, so that their ministry will be welcomed and appreciated.

Recommendation 4.37:

that the approved ministries of women deacons include:
i) the solemn conferral of Baptism;
ii) keeping and dispensing the Eucharist;

iii) assisting at and blessing marriage in the name of the Church;
iv) bringing Viaticum to the sick and dying;
v) reading and explaining the Sacred Scriptures to the faithful;
vi) instructing and exhorting the faithful;
vii) presiding at the worship and prayer of the faithful;
viii) administering the sacramentals[26]; and
ix) officiating at funeral and burial services.[27]

Recommendation 4.38:

that the ACBC support lay Catholic civil celebrants and encourage them to include prayers and blessings in the marriage services of Catholics if and when the Catholic spouse(s) request(s) them.

Recommendation 4.39:

that more ministers be available to young people when they are preparing for marriage, and to accompany them at their time of great happiness as they set out on their marriage journey.

Recommendation 4.40:

that the Plenary Council legislate to allow diocesan bishops to give lay Catholic male and female civil marriage celebrants the authority to witness marriages in the name of the Church.[28]

Recommendation 4.41:

that the Plenary Council legislate to allow people to be married in parks and gardens, in the bush, on beaches, or wherever they feel the presence of God is more powerfully present; and that it simplify the system for granting permission (e.g. delegating authority to Parish Priests and Administrators).[29]

Recommendation 4.42:

that the Plenary Council make an unequivocal national commitment to widespread liturgical education in the spirit and principles of *Sacrosanctum Concilium*[30].

Recommendation 4.43:

that the Plenary Council make a similar commitment to immediately establish a professional training program for liturgists in the spirit of Vatican II throughout Australia, with the aim of having them develop, promote and implement meaningful liturgical reform in all dioceses.

Recommendation 4.44:

that the Plenary Council reawaken in parishes and dioceses throughout Australia a passion for the Rite of Christian Initiation of Adults (RCIA) which is true to the Vatican II spirit.

Recommendation 4.45:

that the Plenary Council seek to ensure that parish communities have meaningful liturgies, supported by quality resources, especially for baptism, liturgical presiding, and homiletics.

Recommendation 4.46:

that the Plenary Council strongly encourage the creation and renewal of sacred spaces in the spirit of Vatican II.

Recommendation 4.47:

that all formation programs for candidates for the priesthood and diaconate include professional training in Vatican II liturgical teaching and the best of contemporary liturgical insights.

Recommendation 4.48:

that all diocesan bishops and superiors of religious institutes provide adequate and ongoing training in Vatican II liturgical celebration and homiletics for all their priests and deacons – especially those sourced from overseas – who are engaged in parish ministry and experience difficult in communicating. The training must include pastoral eloquence, speech therapy, accent modification, voice production, and homiletics.

Recommendation 4.49:

that diocesan bishops and superiors of religious institutes take steps to identify those of their priests and deacons who are experiencing difficulty in providing the faithful with balanced and dignified liturgical celebrations and easily understood and scripture-related homilies.

Recommendation 4.50:

that on an annual basis, a professionally prepared qualitative and quantitative survey be conducted anonymously in every parish and church throughout the nation, with an adequate sample of respondents, to assess the pastoral effectiveness of priests and deacons. Those surveyed are to be shown the results and offered the opportunity for further professional development.

Recommendation 4.51:

that there be an urgent retraining of all clerics – including overseas-trained priests – whose liturgical understanding and practices, especially in homiletics, are not in tune with Vatican II, or suited to the needs of the local worshipping community. This is necessary for the sake of the clerics themselves, but above all in justice to the people of God.

Recommendation 4.52:

that the Plenary Council legislate for the conducting of a regular and thorough review of liturgical music to ensure that it is suited to our times and Australian culture.

Recommendation 4.53:

that the Plenary Council legislate for the urgent and ongoing review of liturgical texts, including a reconsideration of previous texts which were prepared using a synodal process.

Recommendation 4.54:

> that the Plenary Council carefully examine how the spirituality, sacred rituals, dance, music and customs of Australia's First Peoples might be more effectively incorporated into Australian liturgical celebrations and worship.

Recommendation 4.55:

> that the Plenary Council:
> i)   make public the current policies and migration agreement(s) with the Commonwealth Government in relation to the recruitment of priests and seminarians from churches outside Australia;
> ii) review the current situation of overseas-born priests working in parish ministry in the territorial dioceses;
> iii) recommend a full-scale research project looking at its origins, extent, arrangements, the welfare of the priests, the quality and effectiveness of their ministry, present and future needs, and policy settings and implications; and
> iv) recommend that a major part of the research project include extensive consultation with the overseas priests themselves, with those parish communities who have experience of the ministry of these priests, with their Australian-born brother priests, with Australian bishops, and with the bishops and superiors of the religious congregations in their own countries who have sent them to Australia.

Recommendation 4.56:

> that the Plenary Council formally recognise and support the ministry of pastoral associates and their leadership role in parish communities: and that their employment conditions include just remuneration, a reasonable workload and work-life balance, the opportunity for advancement in responsibility and remuneration, support for professional development, supervision and spiritual direction, security of employment, and encouragement to belong to professional associations.

Recommendation 4.57:

that all dioceses put in place dedicated support services for pastoral associates and lay ecclesial ministers, including a special ministry to them - similar to the Ministry to Priests office - with full-time staff, an adequate budget, and space.

Recommendation 4.58:

that seminary formation prioritise education and training in collaborative team ministry, especially with women, that all ministers – lay and clerical – in all dioceses receive the same education and training; and that special education and training, with women, be given to priests from overseas churches, to assist them in understanding collaborative team ministry, particularly at the early stage of their ministry in Australia.

Recommendation 4.59:

that all parishes in all dioceses, regardless of size or wealth, be given the opportunity to employ pastoral associates or other qualified lay leaders; and that these persons be given the resources and support to gain the necessary skills to minister effectively to their parish communities.

Recommendation 4.60:

that the Plenary Council re-evaluate the recent practice of amalgamating, merging, and clustering parishes, and consider the establishment of smaller parishes with qualified religious and lay leaders, supported by structures which bolster co-responsible pastoral ministry and good governance between the lay faithful and the ordained clergy.

Recommendation 4.61:

that all diocesan bishops make more frequent parish pastoral visitations, and during these, give the highest priority to listening to all Christ's faithful in the community in a setting that allows meaningful dialogue.[31]

Recommendation 4.62:

> that all diocesan bishops recognise and support the various leadership roles within parishes, commission their ministry, and provide appropriate structures.

Recommendation 4.63:

> that all diocesan bishops instruct all the parishes in their diocese to develop, in a synodal and co-responsible manner, a parish pastoral plan which articulates the parish vision, mission and goals, in harmony with the diocesan pastoral plan. The plan should be reviewed and updated on a periodic (e.g. 5-yearly) basis.

Recommendation 4.64:

> that the Plenary Council legislate for the establishment of a consultative process for parishes when a new parish priest is to be appointed; and that it should respect parish traditions and the giftedness of the incoming pastor.

Recommendation 4.65:

> that diocesan bishops actively promote and support co-responsible and consensus decision-making in diocesan and parish pastoral councils, and discourage autocratic decision-making.

Recommendation 4.66:

> that parish communities more actively identify and reach out to those parishioners who have drifted away from active participation in parish life, visit them, and assure them of a welcome should they return.

Recommendation 4.67:

> that the Plenary Council consider the possibility of the Archdiocese of Melbourne being broken up into two or more smaller dioceses to afford Christ's faithful in the archdiocese a greater sense of ecclesial community and to enjoy a closer pastoral relationship with their diocesan bishop.

Part 5: Plenary Council: Process and Procedures

Recommendation 5.1:

> that the ACBC immediately seek from the Holy See an exemption from certain aspects of C. 443 to ensure that at least one third of all those to be called to the Council are non-religious lay men and women and gender balanced; and that every particular church will have a basic representation at the Plenary Council of 1 priest (elected by his peers), and minimal 1 male and 1 female non-religious layperson, to be selected in a manner determined at a diocesan synod or assembly convened prior to the Plenary Council.

Recommendation 5.2:

> that the ACBC allocate to the 22 particular churches with more than 50,000 faithful a scaled-up gender-balanced non-religious lay representation, increasing to a maximum of 10 representatives for dioceses with more than 500,000 faithful, to ensure that the Plenary Council hears adequately from the full diversity of voices within the particular churches.[32]

Recommendation 5.3:

> that among the non-religious lay faithful to be selected/elected to represent the particular churches, special consideration be given to members of the indigenous, ethnic, LGBTIQ, and youth communities.

Recommendation 5.4:

> that the ACBC limit to 5 the number of retired titular bishops living in Australia who may be called to the Plenary Council; and that it invite all these bishops, as a group, to vote for those of their number whom they wish to be called. The 5 with the greatest number of votes are to be called.

Recommendation 5.5:

> that among those called to attend the Plenary Council, there be up to 5 permanent deacons.

Recommendation 5.6:

> that the ACBC invite to the Plenary Council as guests a suitable number of experts, auditors, observers and special guests who may include:

i)   selected Catholic clerics, religious and laypersons with particular expertise;

ii)   selected representatives of Catholic Episcopal conferences from the Asia-Pacific region;

iii) selected ministers and members of other Christian churches; and

iv)   selected leaders of non-Christian faith communities.

All these guests should be invited to speak at the general assemblies and in the working groups, but they cannot vote.

Recommendation 5.7:

> that the ACBC makes a decision as soon as possible on who and how many are to be called to the Council, and who and how many are to be invited as guests to attend the Council, and how they are to be selected or appointed.

Recommendation 5.8:

> that each diocesan bishop, prior to the first session of the Council, convene a diocesan synod or assembly to ascertain the *sensus fidei* of the faithful in his care, and that this be an integral part of preparing the Plenary Council agenda. At this diocesan synod/ assembly, the diocesan bishop should seek guidance on how to select the lay faithful who will best represent the diocese at the Plenary Council 2020/21.

Recommendation 5.9:

> that prior to the first session of the Council, the ACBC draw up and make public the agenda for the Council, which should

contain a *Lineamenta* or 'preparatory document' including the questions to be addressed, a 'schemata' of the draft legislation or propositions to be presented at the Plenary Council, and well-researched background papers on the questions.

Recommendation 5.10:

that the 'rules of procedure' for voting at the Council be drawn up well in advance of the first session, be put out for comment and feedback, and generally follow the guidelines set out in *Episcopalis communio* and the procedures used at the two recent ordinary assemblies of the Synod of Bishops.

Recommendation 5.11:

that, after the 2020 (first) session of the Plenary Council, the President of the Council should commission a detailed report on the session, make it public, and invite comment and feedback from Christ's faithful. If necessary, the President might seek further clarification of the *sensus fidei fidelium* on certain issues.

Recommendation 5.12:

that, after the working committees have discussed the detailed draft legislation on specific issues with advice from experts (*periti*), the drafts be voted on by those with a consultative vote; and if they have majority support, they are to go forward to the general assembly of the 2021 (second) session of the Council.

Recommendation 5.13:

that all draft laws and propositions which have received majority support from the working committees should be voted on in the general assembly, paragraph by paragraph, by all those with a consultative vote. If the draft paragraph or proposition receives the support of two-thirds or more of those with a consultative vote, it should immediately go forward to the bishops for their deliberative vote. Draft paragraphs which gain the support of less than two-thirds but of more than half, may be redrafted and put to another vote. Draft paragraphs which gain the support of half or less of those with a consultative vote should be set aside permanently.

Recommendation 5.14:

that all draft legislation which receives support from two-thirds or more of those with a consultative vote must go forward to the bishops for their deliberative vote; and that the bishops, unless they perceive some grave doctrinal or other reason to be an obstacle, should vote in favour of the draft legislation. The tally of the consultative and deliberative votes should be made public.

Recommendation 5.15:

that if a draft law or proposition fails to gain the support of a two-thirds majority vote of the bishops, the reasons why it failed, in their prudential judgment, must be made public and recorded in the minutes of the Council to be sent to the Holy See.

Recommendation 5.16:

that the text of the Council's legislation be written in a tone that is welcoming and pastoral; in a style that is clear, open and inviting, not moralizing, judgmental or controlling; that it be framed in the context of the Council's understanding of contemporary Australian society and the place of the Church in that society; and that it set out clearly its vision of how the Church might better progress God's mission in Australia.

Recommendation 5.17:

that the liturgical celebrations at the Council incorporate in a symbolic and meaningful manner, wherever possible, the language, rituals, spirituality and culture of Australia's First Peoples.

Notes

1   Vatican II, *Gaudium et Spes*, n. 3.
2   Vatican II, *Lumen Gentium*, n. 123, Congregation for Bishops (2004), retrieved from http://www.vatican.va/roman_curia/congregations/cbishops/documents/rc_con_cbishops_doc_20040222_apostolorum-successores_en.html
4   International Theological Commission, *Sensus fidei in the life of the Church* (2014); *Synodality in the life and mission of the Church* (2018).
5   Pope Francis, *Evangelii Gaudium*, n. 31; *Episcopalis communio*.
6   *Ibid.* n. 33.
7   Cf. Also, our Recommendations 3.12 and 4.9-4.13.
8   Cf. our Recommendation 5.8.
9   International Theological Commission (2018). *Synodality and the Mission of the Church*, n. 81. Retrieved from http://www.vatican.va/roman_curia/congregations/cfaith/cti_documents/rc_cti_20180302_sinodalita_en.html
10 Vatican II, *Gaudium et Spes*, n. 3.
11 *Successores Apostolorum*, n. 67; n. 166.
12 International Theological Commission, *Synodality and the Mission of the Church*, Rome, 2018, n. 82.
13 Cf. Also, our Recommendations 2.7 and 4.9-4.13.
14 Glatz, C. (2013). *Pope Francis: Priests should be "Shepherds living with the smell of the sheep"*, The Catholic Telegraph. Retrieved from https://www.thecatholictelegraph.com/pope-francis-priests-should-be-shepherds-living-with-the-smell-of-the-sheep/13439
15 *Ibid.*
16 Note: Australia's National Council of Priests recently called for optional celibacy and married priests, and planned to take the issues to the Vatican – see Joanne McCarthy, *We live in joyful hope: Plan to allow married Catholic priests,* Sydney Morning Herald, 16 September 2018. Retrieved from https://www.smh.com.au/national/we-live-in-joyful-hope-plan-to-allow-married-catholic-priests-20180916-p5042e.html
17 Cf. Recommendation 3.12 for a more inclusive and open process for the selection of bishops in Australia, and the importance of qualifications and skills to lead and to govern.
18 See also Recommendations 3.12 and 3.13.
19 CIC, Canon 97 defines a minor as a person aged under 18 years, while a minor under at the age of 8 years is presumed to have the use of reason. In Australia, a minor is a person under the age of 18 years.
20 Cf. Pope Francis, Christmas Eve address to Curia, 2018. C. 982 could provide a template for conditional absolution. See also Kieran Tapsell's submission to the 21-24 February 2019 Summit of Presidents of Episcopal conferences in Rome to discuss child sexual abuse.
21 Cf. Recommendations 2.7 and 3.12.
22 Matt 19:12.
23 Retrieved from https://cruxnow.com/news-analysis/2019/03/08/as-debate-on-married-priests-reignites-ordaining-viri-probati-faces-hurdles/
24 Cf. Vatican II, *Lumen Gentium*, n. 29 as a potential model for the restoration of a married priesthood in the Latin Church.
25 Vatican II, *Gaudium et Spes*, n. 5.

26 *Catechism of the Catholic Church*, n. 1667: Sacramentals are sacred signs which bear a resemblance to the sacraments. They signify effects, particularly of a spiritual nature, which are obtained through the intercession of the Church. By them men (sic) are disposed to receive the chief effect of the sacraments, and various occasions in life are rendered holy.

27 Vatican II, *Lumen Gentium*, n. 29.

28 Cf. Canon 1112 §1. Where there are no priests and deacons, the diocesan Bishop can delegate lay persons to assist at marriages, if the Episcopal Conference has given its prior approval and the permission of the Holy See has been obtained; §2: a suitable lay person is to be selected, capable of giving instruction to those who are getting married and fit to conduct the marriage liturgy properly.

29 Current law should permit this: Canon 1118 §1: a marriage between Catholics, or between a catholic party and a baptised non-Catholic, is to be celebrated in the parish church. By permission of the local Ordinary or of the parish priest, it may be celebrated in another church or oratory; §2: the local Ordinary can allow a marriage to be celebrated in another suitable place; §3: a marriage between a Catholic party and an unbaptised party may be celebrated in a church or in another suitable place.

30 Vatican II, *Constitution on the Sacred Liturgy*.

31 It is insufficient for the bishop to meet only the parish pastoral council or address only the faithful attending the parish Mass.

32 At 31 December 2017 there were 13 particular churches with a Catholic population of less than 50,000, 9 with 51,000-100,000, 6 with 100,000-200,000, 4 with 200,000-500,000 and 3 with more than 500,000. Cf. *Official Catholic Directory*, 2018-2019, *op. cit*. Cf. Table 5.5 for possible formulae for allocation of numbers.

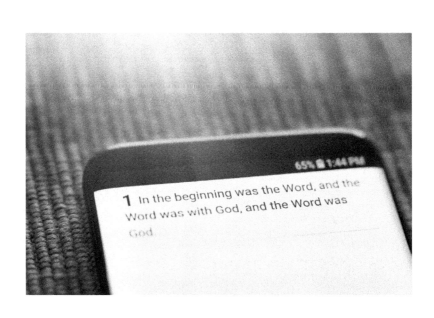

PART 1

GOD'S MISSION, THE KINGDOM OF GOD AND THE SIGNS OF THE TIMES

The Second Vatican Council of the Catholic Church urgently called all Catholics into dialogue with the changing world. It summoned us to listen, discern and respond to the signs of the times. Such a societal change of epoch proportion has demanded responsibility from every one of us. In Australia, some 50 years on, we are challenged to act now, so that the mission of God can live afresh. The church community, through rigorous analysis, needs to keep identifying and responding to the scientific, societal, cultural and spiritual realities evolving in our time. We are to bring discerning, faith-filled and prayerful hearts and minds to this reality. The mission of God calls for no less.

- Clare Condon SGS, former Congregational Leader of the Sisters of the Good Samaritan, former President Catholic Religious Australia, and former Co-Chair of the National Committee for Professional Standards

1.1 Introduction

When the Plenary Council 2020/21 was launched at Pentecost 2018 all Christ's faithful in Australia were invited to listen to the Spirit and to one another, to dialogue with friends, family and colleagues, to think and talk about their experiences of faith, life and the Church, and to respond to the question: *What do you think God is asking of us in Australia at this time?*

This submission of *Catholics for Renewal*, a group of committed Catholics with strong support throughout Australia, who want their Church renewed and more closely conformed to Jesus Christ and his mission, is our attempt to answer that question.

In responding, we begin with God's plan and the mission he gave to Jesus, who passed it on to the Apostles and the Church befriended by the Spirit. We examine the Kingdom of God, which Jesus proclaimed and inaugurated, and which the Father wants made present and built up in Australia and the world (Part 1).

...we address a range of specific issues, including church structures, clericalism, the selection, screening and formation of candidates for the priesthood, the place of women in the Church, their admission to sacred orders, and the selection of bishops...

We then state our understanding of the 'us' – the People of God – and the signs of this time in which we live (Part 2).[1]

In considering 'what' God is asking of us, we place much focus on good governance in the Church (Part 3), and pastoral leadership and parish ministry (Part 4). Within these major areas we address a range of specific issues, including church structures, clericalism, the selection, screening and formation of candidates for the priesthood, the place of women in the Church, their admission to sacred orders, and the selection of bishops.

Finally, we address several matters of concern related to the Plenary Council, particularly the process of determining who and how many will attend the Council, and the procedures for voting at the Council (Part 5).

The title of our submission is 'Getting back on mission'. It expresses our conviction that, over the past several decades, the Church in Australia has gone 'off mission'. We see the task ahead as getting the Church back 'on mission'.

The findings and recommendations of the Victorian Parliamentary Inquiry into the Handling of Child Abuse by Religious and Other Organisations (2012-2013) and the Royal Commission into Institutional Responses to Child Sexual Abuse (2012-2017) feature significantly in this submission, for both did a huge service to the Catholic Church in Australia. They exposed many of its failures and shortcomings and proposed significant remedial action. They also highlighted the flaws and deficiencies of its leaders, the bishops, who clearly were not listening to their own people's sense of faith (*sensus fidei fidelium*) or giving them a share in the governance of their church.

These public inquiries found that the Catholic Church in Australia had gone 'off mission' and had fallen into a huge and worsening crisis. For almost three decades, the Catholic Church in Australia has been drifting, out of touch with its own people and the wider society, and without effective and credible leadership. Ironically and sadly, most diocesan bishops saw no need to LISTEN to the people committed to their care. That has to change, and now.

Our Church must get back 'on mission', and the Plenary Council should be a good start. But it is not an enterprise belonging to the hierarchy alone. The renewal of the Church in Australia requires all Christ's faithful to be engaged – in prayer, study, discernment, and dialogue. Everyone has to work together co-responsibly, in communion with the Spirit of faith, hope and love. That way we can find our way back to God's mission, with leadership that is truly accountable, transparent and inclusive.

1.2 God's plan and mission

In God's plan of salvation, the Father sent his Son on a mission to become 'one with us', to suffer and die for us, and to rise again to give us hope. To ensure that God's mission would continue, Jesus established a Church, born by the sending of the Spirit.

God's mission has a Church, the People of God, who have "a solitary goal: to carry forward the work of Christ himself under the lead of the befriending Spirit – to give witness to the truth, to rescue and not to sit in judgment, to serve and not to be served".[2]

Rather than the Church having a mission, it is God's mission which has a church. The People of God are partners with God in recreating the world, and they do it through the witness of their personal lives, and the witness and service of their local faith communities, including family, parish, and school.

1.3 The Kingdom of God

God's first act of mission was creation, and its dynamic evolutionary process, sustained by God in every instant, reached its fullest expression in Jesus, who revealed God's plan through the image of the Kingdom of God. Jesus' whole message can be summed up in two words: 'Abba/Father' and 'Kingdom'. The Kingdom of God was Jesus' vision and inspiration. He spoke of it continually,[3] never defining it, but describing it in parables: it is like a banquet, a treasure in a field, the good seed among the darnel, a mustard seed, yeast, a merchant looking for pearls, a dragnet. He taught us to pray for its growing presence in the world: "May your Kingdom come and your will be done on earth as it is in heaven."[4]

St Paul said the Kingdom is "not food or drink, but righteousness and peace and joy in the Spirit".[5] It is where the dynamic evolutionary process is brought to perfection because God's will is done and all creation is brought to wholeness and completion. The partnership between God and humankind in the process will then have achieved the total triumph of God's rule, so that the world will be free from the powers that enslave humanity, a world where there is justice and peace, unity and happiness, fullness and plenty, joy and an end to suffering.[6]

...The Church is not identical to the Kingdom, but is meant to be the 'sign', 'sacrament' and 'servant' of the Kingdom of God and it cannot be separated from it. Its task is to 'proclaim the Kingdom' and work for its completion: a just and reconciled world...

The Kingdom is bigger than the Church, which Jesus calls to carry on the mission he received from his Father. The Church is not identical to the Kingdom, but is meant to be the 'sign', 'sacrament' and 'servant' of the Kingdom of God and it cannot be separated from it.[7] Its task is to 'proclaim the Kingdom' and work for its completion: a just and reconciled world. It has to uncover the Kingdom in the world, and encourage and build on the work of the Spirit in the world.

...If there was ever a time when the Church in Australia needed a VISION to unite the People of God, to give them hope, and inspire them, it is now...

In general terms, the Kingdom of God is built by proclamation and witness. Proclamation takes place in activities such as liturgical celebrations, inculturation in various settings, and interreligious dialogue. Witness is given by working to promote justice, peace, reconciliation and safeguarding the integrity of creation. Both proclamation and witness are sustained by prayer and contemplation.

The partnership with God in the dynamic evolutionary process to bring about the Kingdom constantly calls for a radical conversion, a cultural and spiritual transformation, a *metanoia*.[8] It demands deep spirituality and a constant struggle with hope. St Paul writes:

> For the creation waits with eager longing for the revealing of the children of God; for the creation was subjected to futility, not of its own will but by the will of the one who subjected it, in hope that the creation itself will be set free from its bondage to decay and will obtain the freedom of the glory of the children of God. We know that the whole creation has been groaning in labour pains until now; and not only the creation, but we ourselves, who have the first fruits of the Spirit, groan inwardly while we wait for adoption, the redemption of our bodies. For in hope we were saved. Now hope that is seen is not hope. For who hopes for what is seen? But if we hope for what we do not see, we wait for it with patience.[9]

If there was ever a time when the Church in Australia needed a VISION to unite the People of God, to give them hope, and inspire them, it is now. The symbol of the Kingdom of God, translated into the cultural terms of our day, can give the Church in Australia the clearest possible vision for meaning, direction, sense of mission and sense of community. Currently, there is no clear vision, and the day-to-day life of the Church is not a clear sign of the Kingdom; in fact, in many ways, it is a counter-sign, and Australians see it as that.

The Kingdom was Jesus' curriculum[10], for it is built by educating intelligent, caring and responsible persons, and forming confident, creative, open, and concerned individuals who will be active Kingdom-centred citizens working for its coming. Jesus said: "Strive first for the Kingdom of God and his righteousness."[11]

We are all pilgrims searching for justice, freedom, peace, life and happiness, invited to be involved in the wider community and to "take on the smell of the sheep, to put aside our own eagerness in order to see and listen to others, to have a face-to-face encounter with others and their physical presence which challenges us, to spiritually draw near to others and the new forms of poverty and vulnerability, and to befriend the poor and be evangelised by them".[12] As pilgrim people, we are called to "share the joys and hopes, the griefs and anxieties of the other people of our age, especially those who are poor or afflicted",[13] to be available to others, engaging their questions and believing they have something worthwhile to say. But others will only express themselves when they believe they are appreciated.

Even with a vision, there is no clearly defined 'road map'. We must, therefore, continuously seek out the Kingdom, scrutinising the 'signs of the times' in our own church, in our society and our culture, and interpret them in the light of the Gospel. This requires humbly recognising and celebrating the Kingdom realities which others have already made present, including non-Christians, atheists and agnostics.[14]

The Kingdom calls for a 'contemplative presence' to discern and respond, to be gracious, to trust, and to collaborate. The Church does not save the world; God does that. It only cooperates with God in the building up of the Kingdom. Its task is to respond to God, to be relevant, and involved.

Kingdom values impact on how power is used in the Church and in civil society, for they shed light on the ministries, charisms, and gifts given by the Spirit, and they build bridges between the different ministries. To embrace Kingdom values is to embrace the call to mission, humbly and authentically present the face of Christ to the world, and become a credible sign of the Kingdom, already present and to come.

Jesus inaugurates the order of things that constitutes the final horizon of the Kingdom of God: it will result in a "new heaven and a new earth".[15] The Kingdom is where God's will is being done and the dynamic evolutionary process is thus brought to wholeness and completion. It is a world free from all the powers that enslave humanity, where there is justice and peace, unity and happiness, fullness and plenty, joy, and an end to human suffering.[16]

1.4 Reading the signs of the times

To carry forward the mission of Christ under the lead of the Spirit, "the Church has always had the duty of scrutinising the 'signs of the times' and of interpreting them in the light of the Gospel. We have to recognise and understand the world in which we live, its expectations, its longings, and its often dramatic characteristics".[17] The Church must always adjust its strategies and organisation to ensure that it can, having regard to the changing times, continue to "carry forward the work of Christ himself under the lead of the befriending Spirit".[18] Some signs that must be scrutinised concern the world, others Australia specifically. Here we highlight a number that we consider particularly important.

... To carry forward the mission of Christ under the lead of the Spirit, "the Church has always had the duty of scrutinising the 'signs of the times' and of interpreting them in the light of the Gospel...

We have included much statistical data to illustrate some signs, but they are not in themselves the signs. The signs of the times express a moral norm to be discerned, and here, in the statistics we cite, we have tried to identify those events which express moral norms.

1.5 People on the planet and on the move

In 1800 less than 1 billion people were living on planet Earth.[19] Today (2017) there are 7.6 billion, and soon there will be more: 8.6 billion in 2030, 9.8 billion in 2050, and possibly 11.2 billion in 2100.

While each year an extra 84 million live on the planet, the rate of increase has decreased by more than half since 1962. Some countries are already experiencing negative growth,[20] and by 2100 worldwide growth is predicted to end.

People are also on the move. In 2017, there were 258 million international migrants worldwide,[21] including 80 million migrants living in Asia, 78 million in Europe, 58 million in North America, 25 million in Africa, 10 million in South and Central America, and 8 million in Oceania. Two-thirds live in just 21 countries, including 50 million in the USA, Saudi Arabia, Germany and Russia alone, 9 million in the UK and Northern Ireland, and 7.2 million in Australia.

... In 2017 there were 68.5 million people worldwide who were refugees or who had been forcibly displaced ...

In 2017 there were 68.5 million people worldwide who were refugees or who had been forcibly displaced.[22] In recent times the main drivers of this tragedy have included civil war, foreign invasion, terrorism, religious and political persecution, famine, ethnic cleansing, denial of human and civil rights, and environmental disasters. Other factors are the quest for civil and religious freedom, physical safety, employment and economic opportunities, and better prospects for children.

Since 1945, Australia has resettled over 800,000 refugees and displaced persons and consistently ranks high among the world's resettlement countries.[23] However, Australia now has one of the most restrictive immigration detention systems in the world: mandatory, indefinite, off-shore, and closed to legal challenge. At 30 June 2014, the average Australian immigration detention period was 11 months and 20 days, despite it being known that prolonged detention has devastating and long-lasting impacts on mental health, especially of children.[24] In 2015-16 Australia accepted 17,555 refugees including a special allocation for persons displaced by the conflicts in Syria and Iraq.[25]

1.6 People in Australia

In 1800, Australia's European population (excluding its indigenous peoples) was 5217 persons.[26] In February 2019, Australia's total population, including its indigenous peoples, reached 25.26 million.[27] Annual population growth rate peaked at 2.2% in 2008, but has since dropped to 1.6%. Australians constitute just 0.33% of all the people on planet Earth.

Australia has been a destination for international migrants since 1800. In 1947 one in ten of its 7.6 million people was born overseas, and in 2019, more than one in four (29%) of its 25.26 million people. Now, for the first time since the 1890s, one in every two Australians (52%) was either born overseas or has at least one parent born overseas.[28] Since 2008 around 170,000 permanent places have been allocated annually to new immigrants and refugees: two thirds to skilled people and the balance to mostly family members and refugees. Since 2008 international migrants have contributed to 62% of Australia's population growth.[29]

For 200 years Australia's immigrants came predominantly from the UK and Europe; now, more than half come from Asia. In 2016-17, 38,264 arrived from India, 29,604 from China, and 12,180 from the Philippines.[30] Australia also hosts over 2 million 'temporary migrants' – on short-term and long-term (12 months or more) stays. They include skilled workers, overseas students, working holiday makers, and New Zealand citizens under special arrangements.

1.7 People and religion

People have always held religious beliefs. In 2010 the vast majority of the Earth's people adhered in some way to four main religious faiths: Christianity (2.4 billion/31.5%), Islam (1.8 billion/23.2%), Hinduism (1.1 billion/15.0%), Buddhism (500 million/7.1%), and Folk (400 million/5.9%) and other religions (1.0%). Some 1.2 billion (16%) of all people had no or no-stated religious beliefs. The Catholic population worldwide at December 2016 was 1.3 billion, constituting 17.7% of the world's people.

In Australia, the 2016 Census confirmed a fast-changing and decreasing religious affiliation. Whereas in 1901, Christians made up 96% of the total (non-indigenous) population of 4.5 million, and in 1966 still constituted 88% of the total (excluding indigenous) population of 11.9 million, in 2016, just 52% of Australia's 23.4 million (including indigenous) people self-identified as Christian. While the number of non–Christians increased substantially (+ 1.85 million) over the previous 50 years, Australians who said they had no religion or did not state a religious affiliation increased by 5.75 million (Figure 1.1).

FIGURE 1.1: RELIGIOUS IDENTITY OF AUSTRALIAN POPULATION, 1966 AND 2016

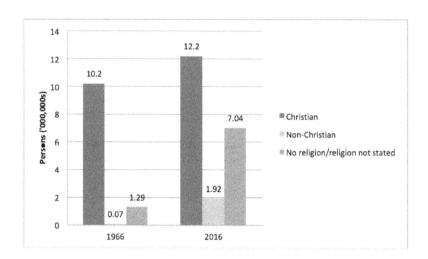

Source: ABS, 1966 and 2016 Commonwealth Census. Notes: 1. The 1966 Census contained no specific date on the Muslim population. In the 1971 Census, Muslims numbered 22,311. 2. No religious includes secular and other spiritual beliefs. 3. In the Census, since the question on religious identity is 'optional, the total of respondents (21.2 million) does not equal the total population of 23.4 million.

Muslims (604,000/2.6%) are now the largest non-Christian faith group in Australia (Figure 1.2) followed by Buddhists (564,000/2.4%), Hindus (440,000/1.9%), Sikhs (126,000/0.5%) and Jews (91,000/0.4%). But the fastest growing group is those who state they have 'no religion', which has doubled since 2001. In the 2006 Census, 3.7 million persons (18.7%) self-identified as having 'no religion', but in 2011 that number increased to 4.8 million (22.3%), and in 2016 to 7.0 million (30.1%).

Recent research on the views of Australian teenagers about religion and diversity[31] found that most have a largely positive view of religion and religious diversity, though many are concerned about the impact of religion on life in Australia and are well aware of the tensions between religious rights and other human rights. Among the 1200 13 to 18-year-olds surveyed the research found six main spirituality types: 'this worldly' (23%), 'indifferent' (15%), 'spiritual but not religious' (18%), 'seekers' (8%), 'nominally religious' (20%), and 'religiously committed' (17%). Over half (52%) did not identify with any religion, yet 37% believed in God. Of the 46% who identified with a religion, 38% were Christian, 3% Muslim, 2% Buddhist, and 1% Hindu. 'Other' and 'not sure' were 2% each.

FIGURE 1.2: RELIGIOUS AFFILIATIONS OF AUSTRALIAN POPULATION, 2016

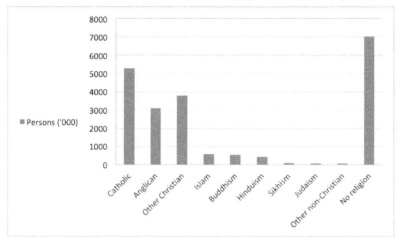

Source: ABS, Cat. 2071.0: Census of Population and Housing, 2016. Religion in Australia.

The teens surveyed also: i) affirm and are open to religious diversity and think that different faiths should have religious freedom; ii) think having people of many different faiths makes Australia a better place to live (91%); iii) think students should be allowed to wear religious clothes or jewellery to school (90%); iv) think that all religious groups should be free to practise their religion the way they want to (88%); v) believe that religion causes more problems in society than it solves (44%); and vi) think that people with very strong religious beliefs are often too intolerant of others (50%).[32]

1.8 Catholics in Australia

The Australian Catholic population in 2016 was 5,291,834, or 22.6% of the total population of 23.4 million. Since 2011, Catholics have, for the first time, decreased in both number (from 5.44 million in 2011) and percentage of the population (from 25.3% in 2011 to 22.6%) (Figure 1.3). A more significant decrease was averted due of the large intake of Catholic immigrants.

FIGURE 1.3: TOTAL AUSTRALIAN AND CATHOLIC POPULATION, 1835-2017

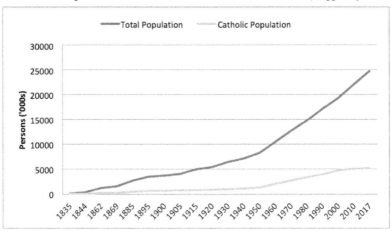

Source: Colonial and Commonweath Censuses, various years; ABS. Cat. No. 3105.0.65.001, *Australian Historical Population Statistics*. Official Catholic directories, various titles and various years.

Recently published data from the 2016 Commonwealth Census[33] also show that the Catholic population is getting older: the median age is 40 years (33 years in 1996), with just 19.8% aged

14 years and under (23% in 1996), and 16.6% aged 65 years and over (10.9% in 1996). There are also fewer males (90.6 to 100 females) in the Catholic population (94.6 in 1996); but 20.6% of all Catholics in 2016 had university degrees compared to 9.7% in 1996.

Catholics, especially younger ones, are increasingly disaffiliating from the Church, and 'ex-Catholics' now possibly number around 1 million. There has also been a major decrease in Catholic church-going. In 2011 just 662,000 (12.2% of total) Catholics regularly attended Mass, with 14 dioceses having attendance rates of less than 10%[34] in stark contrast to the rates of attendance in 1947 (63%) and 1960 (53%)[35]. Young people aged 15-24 years, who make up 13.4% of all Catholics, have the lowest attendance rate (6.9%), while female Catholics have a higher attendance rate (60.7%) than their portion (52.9%) of all Catholics. This is also the case for Catholics born in non-English speaking countries (33.6% attendance rate compared to their portion [17.9%] of all Catholics).[36]

> ...Catholics, especially younger ones, are increasingly disaffiliating from the Church, and 'ex-Catholics' now possibly number around 1 million. There has also been a major decrease in Catholic church-going...

The results of the 2016 Mass attendance count, released in April 2019, confirm that average regular weekly Mass attendance has continued to fall since 2011, with just 623,356 Catholics regularly attending Mass each week. This is a decrease of 39,000 Catholics (-5.9%) attending Mass on a regular weekly basis and a 0.4% decrease in the rate of attendance over the 5-year period. Seventeen dioceses now have an attendance rate of less than 10%.[37]

The main source countries of Catholic immigrants are also changing rapidly. Before 1828, the majority of Catholics were English-born. After 1828, the Irish-born were the majority, peaking at 228,000 (40%) in 1891. By 1961, the Australian-born were the clear majority (77.5%), while those born in the UK and Ireland had dropped to just 3.3%, and European Catholics had become a significant presence: Italians (8.0%), Dutch (1.6%), Poles (1.5%),

Maltese (1.4%), Germans (1.4%), and Yugoslavs (1.2%). In 1961, Asian Catholics were few (16,721/0.6%), as were Africans (11,577/0.4%).[38]

That situation has now changed significantly (Table 1.1). Since 2011 Australian-born Catholics have decreased in both number and percentage, as have those born in Europe, particularly those born in Italy and the Netherlands. But Catholic immigrants from Asia, the Middle East and Central and South America have increased significantly in both number and percentage. The greatest numbers are now coming from the Philippines, Vietnam, India, Iraq, Brazil, Colombia and Chile. Philippines-born Catholics in 2016 (174,621/3.3%) now outnumber all other migrant groups, except for those born in the UK and Ireland (186,020/4.5%). Within a decade Catholic Filipinos are likely to become the largest overseas-born group.

1.9 Women in Australia and the Church

At June 2016 women made up 50.3% of the total Australian population. Within the Catholic population they made up 52.47% and outnumbered men by 261,595.

A clear sign of the times in Australia is the determined struggle to ensure that women are regarded and treated as equal to men. Traditional male-dominated professions, such as medicine, have a poor culture towards women and there is little evidence of family-friendly work practices or concern for the toll such a culture takes physically and emotionally on young women.

> ...A clear sign of the times in Australia is the determined struggle to ensure that women are regarded and treated as equal to men...

The Australian Institute of Company Directors (AICD) has acknowledged that it is no longer acceptable to have company boardrooms dominated by men, and set a target of 30% representation of women on ASX 200 Boards by 2018 (now 29.7%).[39]

Gendered violence in Australia is a critical concern and the data paint a disturbing picture:

- On average, one woman a week is murdered by her current or former partner.[40]
- 1 in 4 women have experienced emotional abuse by a current or former partner since the age of 15.[41]
- 1 in 5 women have experienced sexual violence since the age of 15.[42]
- 85% of Australian women have been sexually harassed.[43]

- Almost 40% of abused women continued to experience violence from their partner while temporarily separated.[44]
- 1 in 6 women have experienced stalking since the age of 15.[45]

There has been some positive movement in education, with areas historically closed to women – science, technology, engineering, mathematics and medicine (STEMM) – being slowly prised open. In recent years over half of all Science and PhD graduates have been women. However, less than one in five senior researchers at Australian universities and research institutes is a woman, and STEMM faculties struggle to attract women. Secondary schools now actively encourage young women to pursue STEMM careers, but this workforce has the greatest attrition rates for women aged 35–45 years.[46]

... In the Catholic Church generally, there has been a tradition of offending women through a form of male domination known as clericalism ...

In the Catholic Church generally, there has been a tradition of offending women through a form of male domination known as clericalism. It is actually the 'virus of misogyny' for which there is a freely available serum for immunisation – it is called 'equality'. In the Church in Australia, women are still treated as inferior, and many Catholic women have had painful and damaging experiences of exclusion and judgment by bishops. Nevertheless, in a few dioceses the percentage of women appointed to official senior employee positions has increased, even significantly (above 50%). In other dioceses, however, the percentage has decreased or is very low (10%–11%). There remains much to do to ensure all dioceses, notwithstanding financial constraints, have at least equal numbers of women and men in all official senior employee positions. Otherwise the 'stained glass ceiling' will be a constant reminder that the Church is not a credible sign of the Kingdom of God and his righteousness.[47]

Pope Francis has made some positive statements about the place of women in the Church, but has been slow to take a strong stand to drive their active and meaningful engagement. The Church has not kept pace with the seismic shifts that have occurred in secular society, where most Australians generally expect women to be valued, oppose their subjugation and subservience, and are calling for concerted efforts to redress long-standing systemic disadvantage and injustice.

The Catholic Church is frequently seen to be impeding the contribution of women to its mission and, in some areas, the opportunities to take leadership positions have been reduced even further. It seems to have forgotten that Jesus treated women with openness, respect, acceptance and tenderness.

1.10 People and inequality

Inequality is a glaring sign of our times. It involves the unequal sharing of the wealth, land, resources and material goods of planet Earth among its people. In 2018, Oxfam concluded that 82% of the wealth generated in 2017 went to the richest 1% of the global population, that the 3.7 billion poorest half of the world's people saw no increase in their wealth, that the wealth of the ultra-rich (billionaires) had risen 6 times faster than the wages of ordinary workers, that 26 ultra-rich persons had the same wealth as the poorest 3.8 billion people combined, and that about half of the world's people lived on less than $8.26 (US$6.00) per day.[48] The causes of this inequality were identified as the erosion of workers' rights, the excessive influence of big business over government policy-making, and the relentless corporate drive to minimize costs in order to maximize returns to shareholders.[49]

... In 2018, Oxfam concluded that 82% of the wealth generated in 2017 went to the richest 1 per cent of the global population ...

Australia has experienced a quarter of a century of continuous economic growth, but the benefits of this good fortune have not been distributed equally. In our workplaces, conditions and security of employment have been eroded, while those who are unemployed subsist on incomes well below poverty levels.

A 2018 Roy Morgan Wealth Report found that:

i) the wealthiest 10% have an average per capita net wealth of over $2 million and hold 48.3% of Australia's net wealth;

ii) the share of Australia's net wealth held by the poorest half of Australians is 3.7% (down from 3.9% in 2007); and

iii) personal wealth is highly correlated to income level, with those earning over $130k p.a. having an average net wealth ($1.2 million) nearly five times those earning under $15k ($248k).[50]

Pope Francis has pointed out that:

> when nature is viewed solely as a source of profit and gain, this has serious consequences for society. This vision of 'might is right' has engendered immense inequality, injustice and acts of violence against the majority of humanity, since resources end up in the hands of the first comer or the most powerful: the winner takes all. Completely at odds with this model are the ideals of harmony, justice, fraternity and peace as proposed by Jesus.[51]

Australia is currently experiencing a housing crisis, and our Indigenous brothers and sisters struggle with economic and social burdens that most Australians cannot imagine.

1.11 People and climate change

A massive accumulation of largely incontestable scientific data from long-term research in multiple disciplines, has convinced most people to now accept that much of the change taking place in the Earth's climate is the result of human activity and that, if left unchecked, will certainly cause irreversible damage to the planet and the lives of people.

Australians, who make up just 0.33% of the world's population, generate about 1.3% of global greenhouse emissions. Per person, Australians have one of the highest emissions rates in the world, and in 2017 put 556 million tonnes of greenhouse gases into the atmosphere.[52]

The 2017 UN *Climate Change Report* states: "Climate change is the defining challenge of our time, yet it is still accelerating faster than our efforts to address it. Atmospheric levels of carbon dioxide are higher than they have been for 800,000 years, and they are increasing. So, too, are the catastrophic effects of our warming planet – extreme storms, droughts, fires, floods, melting ice and rising sea levels."[53]

In 2015, the nations of the world, recognising the urgency and magnitude of the challenge, adopted the goal of limiting global average temperature rise to a 1.5°C target, well below a dangerous 2°C. Nations are now agreed that urgent action and greatly increased ambition are needed – in emissions reductions and in promoting adaptation to current and future impacts of climate change – if a climate catastrophe is to be avoided. There is now no time, nor reason, to delay. The dogma that pollution and high emissions are the unavoidable cost of progress is dead. Failing to act will simply consign all of humanity to ever-worsening climate calamity.

Pope Francis addressed this issue in his 2015 Encyclical *Laudato Si'* where he said:

> If present trends continue, this century may well witness extraordinary climate change and an unprecedented destruction of ecosystems, with serious consequences for all of us … Climate change is a global problem with grave implications: environmental, social, economic, political, and for the distribution of goods. It represents one of the principal challenges facing humanity in our day. Its worst impact will probably be felt by developing countries in coming decades. Many of the poor live in areas particularly affected by phenomena related to warming, and their means of subsistence are largely dependent on natural reserves and eco-systemic services such as agriculture, fishing and forestry. They have no other financial activities or resources which can enable them to adapt to climate change or to face natural disasters, and their access to social services and protection is very limited.[54]

Unfortunately, he noted: "Many of those who possess more resources and economic or political power seem mostly to be concerned with masking the problems or concealing their symptoms, simply making efforts to reduce some of the negative impacts of climate change"[55], all the more reason why greater attention must be given to "the needs of the poor, the weak and the vulnerable, in a debate often dominated by more powerful interests"[56]. It is the poor who often end up paying the price of climate change. Cardinal Bo, the Archbishop of Yangon, observed in a recent reflection on certain excerpts from *Laudato Si'* that the Church must develop a coalition to combat the evil undercurrents of money and power: "The earth is on loan to us and we owe at least this much to international justice."[57]

1.12 People and institutions

In Australia, according to *The Age* "conflicts of interest and a lack of transparency and accountability have corroded community confidence in bedrock institutions including banks, churches, law enforcement, unions and professional sport." [58] Other institutions could be added to the list, even including parliaments. It is a tragic sign of our times.

Of most concern is the standing of Christian churches, particularly the Catholic Church, which is meant to be the sign of the Kingdom of God and the "light" to the nations. However, because of child sexual abuse within the institution and the systemic cover-up perpetrated by bishops, the Church is now perceived by many as a counter-sign of the Kingdom of God.

In its *Final Report*, the Royal Commission said this about religious institutions:

> More than 4,000 survivors in private sessions told us they were sexually abused as children in religious institutions in Australia. The abuse occurred in churches, presbyteries and rectories, confessionals, religious schools, orphanages and missions, and various other settings. We heard about child sexual abuse occurring in 1,691 different religious institutions. The sexual abuse took many forms. It was often accompanied by physical or emotional abuse. Most victims were aged between 10 and 14 years when the abuse first started. The perpetrators we heard about included priests, religious brothers and sisters, ministers, church elders, teachers in religious schools, workers in residential institutions, volunteers, youth group leaders and others.

We conducted 30 case studies on religious institutions. They revealed that many religious leaders knew about allegations of child sexual abuse yet failed to take effective action. Some ignored allegations and did not respond at all. Some treated alleged perpetrators leniently and failed to address the obvious risks they posed to children. Some concealed abuse and shielded perpetrators from accountability. Institutional reputations and individual perpetrators were prioritised over victims and their families. Religious leaders and institutions across Australia have acknowledged that children suffered sexual abuse while in their care. Many have also accepted that their responses to this abuse were inadequate. These failures are not confined to religious institutions. However, the failures of religious institutions are particularly troubling because these institutions have played, and continue to play, an integral and unique role in many children's lives. They have been key providers of education, health and social welfare services to children for many years. They have been among the most respected institutions in our society. The perpetrators of child sexual abuse in religious institutions were, in many cases, people that children and parents trusted the most and suspected the least.[59]

The Royal Commission found that 61.4% of children abused in religious institutions were abused in those belonging to the Catholic Church[60], and that of the 9025 priests who had worked in ministry during the 60-year period 1950-2010, a total of 507 were alleged perpetrators. Taking into account the duration of their ministry, the proportion of all priests who were alleged perpetrators was 7%: 7.9% of diocesan priests and 5.6% of religious priests. The proportion of religious brothers of some congregations who were alleged perpetrators was exceptionally high: 22% for Christian Brothers, 20.4% for Marist Brothers, 20.9% for Salesian Brothers, and 40.4% for St John of God Brothers.[61] The recent high-profile scandals of two cardinals of the Church have further depleted the standing of the institution.

1.13 Australia and the nuclear threat

Australians are all too aware of the threat of nuclear war. Australian military personnel were part of the occupation forces in Japan after the nuclear devastation of two of its cities. Of the 8 nations that currently have nuclear weapons – China, France, Russia, United Kingdom, United States, India, North Korea, Pakistan – four are in our region. Australia is now within the range of a nuclear strike by long-range intercontinental ballistic missiles. The current tensions between the nuclear-armed US and North Korea and the nuclear-armed India and Pakistan heighten the concerns.

Until 1949, when the US was the sole nuclear-weapon state, Australia supported an international control system with agreed nuclear weapons limitations and prohibitions. When five states gained nuclear weapons in 1960 – China, France, the Soviet Union, the United Kingdom, and the United States – Australia engaged in negotiating the Nuclear Non-Proliferation Treaty (NPT) to ban the transference of nuclear weapons between states, and to establish safeguards to prevent nuclear energy being diverted from peaceful uses to the production of weapons. Australia signed the treaty in 1970 and ratified it in 1973.

In 2007, an Australian organisation, the International Campaign to Abolish Nuclear Weapons (ICAN), set out to build a global movement to abolish nuclear weapons, and in 2017, through a coalition of non-government organisations in 100 countries, developed a UN-sponsored Treaty on the Prohibition of Nuclear Weapons (TPNW), intended to ban and eliminate nuclear weapons throughout the world. It prohibits nations from developing, testing, producing, manufacturing, transferring, possessing, stockpiling, using or threatening to use nuclear weapons, or allowing nuclear weapons to be stationed on their territory. It also prohibits nations from assisting, encouraging or inducing anyone to engage in any of these activities. The treaty was negotiated at the United Nations in July 2017, with the participation of more than 135 nations. It opened for signatures on 20 September 2017. It is permanent in nature, and will be legally binding on those nations that join it. The treaty will enter into legal force once 50 nations have signed and ratified it. Until now, nuclear weapons have been the sole weapons of mass destruction not subject to a comprehensive ban.

A nation that possesses nuclear weapons may join the treaty, so long as it agrees to destroy them in accordance with a legally binding, time-bound plan. Similarly, a nation that hosts another nation's nuclear weapons on its territory may join, so long as it agrees to remove them by a specified deadline. Nations are obliged to provide assistance to all victims of the use and testing of nuclear weapons and to take measures for the remediation of contaminated environments.

As an 'umbrella state' Australia does not produce or possess nuclear weapons, but claims to rely on US nuclear weapons for its defence under a policy of so-called "extended nuclear deterrence". Since the TPNW makes it unlawful for a state to base its national defence on an ally's nuclear weapons, to sign the TPNW would oblige Australia to renounce its nuclear umbrella.

The Australian community is divided on the TPNW. The Australian Government officially opposed the TPNW process and boycotted its negotiations.[62] Yet a November 2018 Ipsos public opinion poll found almost 80% of the public wanted Australia to join the TPNW which would further Australia's commitment to a nuclear-weapon-free world, a goal it has consistently endorsed and supported.

In 2017, Pope Francis stated:

> the escalation of the arms race continues unabated and the price of modernizing and developing weaponry, not only nuclear weapons, represents a considerable expense for nations. As a result, the real priorities facing our human family, such as the fight against poverty, the promotion of peace,

GETTING BACK ON MISSION

the undertaking of educational, ecological and healthcare projects, and the development of human rights, are relegated to second place."[63]

... Weapons of mass destruction, particularly nuclear weapons, create nothing but a false sense of security. They cannot constitute the basis for peaceful coexistence between members of the human family, which must rather be inspired by an ethics of solidarity ...

Nuclear weapons exist in the service of a mentality of fear that affects not only the parties in conflict but the entire human race. International relations cannot be held captive to military force, mutual intimidation, and the parading of stockpiles of arms. Weapons of mass destruction, particularly nuclear weapons, create nothing but a false sense of security. They cannot constitute the basis for peaceful coexistence between members of the human family, which must rather be inspired by an ethics of solidarity.[64]

The Catholic Church in Australia has never made a clear, forceful, and principled statement on the elimination of nuclear weapons.

1.14 Church communications

In 1973, Erin Hoffer observed that "in times of change learners inherit the earth; while the learned find themselves beautifully equipped to deal with a world that no longer exists". In this present time of change, the Catholic Church in Australia appears as the 'learned', often striking out against the secular media and trying to communicate to a world with which it is out of touch, and a world in which it has lost almost all respect. Instead of being an effective medium for communicating the Gospel message and effectively proclaiming the Kingdom of God, it has contaminated the message by its actions and omissions, and rendered itself less credible and relevant.

Resources do not produce effective communication, especially when the Church is out of touch and not listening. The messages emanating from the Church in Australia in recent times have often demonstrated a non-listening attitude and disrespect of its audience with obfuscation, less than honest responses, and some arrogance. And when bishops have made reactionary responses to legitimate calls for renewal and reform, they have put obstacles in the way of effective communication of the Gospel message and the credibility of the Church.

> ... The messages emanating from the Church in Australia in recent times have often demonstrated a non-listening attitude and disrespect of its audience with obfuscation, less than honest responses, and some arrogance ...

Effective communication is not about bombarding people with religious messages, but about willingness to be available to others, "patiently and respectfully engaging their questions and their doubts as they advance in their search for the truth and the meaning of human existence".[65] For the Church to communicate well, it has to "dialogue with people, be at their side, and accompany everyone along the way".[66]

Effective communication is far more than process, technique and spin. It has to be based on honesty, openness, warmth, respect and integrity: "the best antidotes to falsehoods are not strategies, but people: people who are not greedy but ready to listen, people who make the effort to engage in sincere dialogue so that the truth can emerge".[67] Gill Cann rightly observes: "poor communication inoculates the faithful rather than attracts them".[68]

1.15 The Catholic Church and Australia's First Peoples

Australia's First Peoples, who possibly numbered 315,000 to more than 1 million in 1788, now number over 761,000 and constitute 3% of the total Australian population.[69] Indigenous Catholics are also increasing, and at the 2016 census numbered 130,000, or 16% of the total Indigenous population, a significant increase from 81,265 in 1996.[70]

Until 1967 Australia's First Peoples were not counted in the national census. The recent 'Closing the Gap' reports indicate a continuing failure to address adequately the continuing disadvantages of our indigenous peoples.

In its early days, the Catholic Church in Australia was greatly concerned about the plight of indigenous peoples. Its advocacy on their behalf received various responses from government and from within the Church. Practical church efforts to support, protect and educate them were mostly made by religious orders of men and women in mission centres and remote areas.

Since the 1960s Catholic groups have given the indigenous peoples greater support and accompaniment in advancing their progress and taking their rightful place in Australian society. While progress has been slow but steady, Pope John Paul II's address at Alice Springs in 1986, highlighting their significance for the Church and for the maturity of the nation, was a landmark moment. Thereafter, there has been increased stress on Indigenous empowerment and agency, taking voice, and participating fully in social and cultural development.

Few Aboriginal persons have joined religious orders or become priests, though considerable numbers have been educated in Catholic schools, and a significant number of Indigenous leaders acknowledge the influence of Catholic social values and solidarity in their advocacy.

In most Catholic schools, Australia's First Peoples are given some recognition as the original inhabitants of this land through display of the Aboriginal or Torres Islander flag along with the Australian flag, ceremonial message sticks, or bollards and buildings painted in Indigenous colours or patterns. The history of dispossession and oppression is acknowledged, especially in ceremonies around 'Sorry Days' or events recognising 'native title'.

In recent years, Catholic Bishops and church agencies have encouraged the use of Indigenous symbols, paintings, dance and musical instruments in liturgical services, especially on significant occasions. The attitudes of many Australians to Indigenous cultures have changed as a result, and they increasingly recognise the unique and extraordinary values in Indigenous experience and culture, expressed by some in terms of The Dreaming.

> ... Many Indigenous people retain a strong spiritual sense of identity as belonging to their cultural group and especially to the country of their birth. Many have a sense of what might be called the 'spirit of their land', which relates readily to the Christian notion of the Holy Spirit ...

Many Indigenous people retain a strong spiritual sense of identity as belonging to their cultural group and especially to the country of their birth. Many have a sense of what might be called the 'spirit of their land', which relates readily to the Christian notion of the Holy Spirit. As a result of their own suffering over the recent centuries of dispossession and alienation in their own land, many also relate readily to the message of the Gospels, about Jesus who suffered unjustly for us all.

Most States and Territories have Aboriginal and Islander Catholic ministries which network through the National Aboriginal and Torres Strait Islander Catholic Council (NATSICC).

Melbourne has an Aboriginal Catholic Ministry, and a number of religious sisters and other volunteers help with pastoral work, fundraising and support activities for 700 Aboriginal children in schools (Opening the Doors program), and preparing liturgical events.

The work of the Aboriginal Catholic Ministry coordinators has had an extraordinary impact on Catholic and other schools, as well as civil events, promoting awareness of Aboriginal history and culture, and advocating for the Reconciliation process in Australia, especially through the FIRE (Friends Igniting Reconciliation through Education) Carrier program and the ceremonial 'message stick' introduced into many churches and schools and displayed in a public place of honour.

1.16 Other signs of the times

There are other signs of the times that we are aware of, and these are indicated and addressed in other places in our submission, particularly in Parts 3 and 4. We are particularly aware that there has been much progress in recent years in building closer ties, fellowship and understanding with other churches in Australia of the Christian faith, and in opening up a productive dialogue with our Australian brothers and sisters who follow other religious traditions and beliefs. We believe that the Plenary Council must be mindful of these signs when it convenes and discerns.

Some discussion questions:
- Do you believe the Catholic Church has gone 'off mission'? Why, or why not? (1.2)
- How do you understand the statement that 'God's mission has a Church', not vice versa? Is this difference significant?
- The Church is in a 'dynamic evolutionary process'. In what ways is this your experience? (1.3)
- If our parishes were *pilgrim* communities, as suggested by Vatican II, what would outsiders notice? (1.3)
- Vatican II encourages us to work with sisters and brothers in other Christian traditions to address the 'signs of the times'. Is this happening in your local area? Why/why not? Does it matter? (1.16)

Notes

1 International Theological Commission (2018) *Synodality and the Mission of the Church*. Retrieved from: http://www.vatican.va/roman_curia/congregations/cfaith/cti_documents/rc_cti_20180302_sinodalita_en.html
2 Vatican II, *Gaudium et Spes*, n. 3.
3 Mark 1:15; Matt, chapters 3-25; *Acts* 1:3.
4 Matt 6:9-13.
5 *Rom* 14:17.
6 Matt 5:2-10.
7 Pope John Paul II, *Redemptoris Missio*, 1991, n. 18.
8 Mark 1:1-8; *Ezekiel* 18:30-31.
9 *Rom* 8:19-25.
10 An expression coined by the late Bishop Michael Putney of Townsville (2001-2014).
11 Matt 6:33
12 *Evangelii Gaudium*, nn. 146, 171, 88, 272, 198.
13 *Gaudium et Spes*, n. 1.
14 Connolly, Noel, "The Kingdom of God: A vision to give meaning, direction and a sense of mission" in *Australian Journal of Mission Studies*, Vol.12, No. 1 (June 2018), pp. 48-54.
15 *Rev* 21:1.
16 Connolly, *op. cit.*, p. 49.
17 Vatican II, *Gaudium et Spes*, n. 4.
18 Vatican II, *Gaudium et Spes*, n. 3.
19 United Nations. (2017). Department of Economic and Social Affairs. Retrieved from https://www.un.org/development/desa/publications/world-population-prospects-the-2017-revision.html
20 Countries currently experiencing negative growth include Japan, Italy and Greece.
21 These are migrants who have sought long-term or permanent residence.
22 United Nations High Commission for Refugees, Global Trends: Forced Displacement in 2017, Geneva, June 2018. Retrieved from: https://www.unhcr.org/globaltrends2017/
23 Resettlement is the process of offering permanent residence status to refugees who cannot return to their home country for fear of continued persecution.
24 Australian Human Rights Commission. Retrieved from https://www.humanrights.gov.au/face-facts-asylum-seekers-and-refugees
25 Settlement Services International (2019). Retrieved from https://www.ssi.org.au/faqs/refugee-faqs/141-how-many-refugees-does-australia-settle-each-year
26 In 1800 no official count was made of the local indigenous peoples, but estimates of their pre-1788 numbers range from 315,000 to more than 1,000,000. Post-colonisation, their numbers decreased significantly. Cf. ABS, 1301.0 – Year Book Australia (1994), *Statistics on the Indigenous Peoples of Australia*. Though counts and estimates of the indigenous population were made at every national census from 1901, the figures were not included in the official count of the Australian population until 1971 following the repeal of Section 127 of the Commonwealth Constitution in 1967. At 30 June 2017, there were an estimated 761,000 Aboriginal and Torres Strait Islander people in Australia.

27   ABS, Population clock. Real time. Retrieved from http://www.abs.gov.au/
      ausstats/abs@.nsf/0/1647509ef7e25faaca2568a900154b63?OpenDocument

28   Megalogenis, George, "Australasia Rising", in *The Age Good Weekend*, 26
      January 2019.

29   ABS, Population Clock, 28 January 2019.

30   ABC News (2018). Retrieved from https://www.abc.net.au/news/2018-08-
      20/where-do-migrants-to-australia-come-from-chart/10133560 The UK
      (16,982) and NZ (8199) also supply large numbers.

31   Deakin University (2018), *The Worldviews of Generation Z, March 2018* study
      was conducted by researchers from the Australian National University,
      Deakin University and Monash University to uncover Australian
      teenagers' experiences and understanding of religion and diversity.
      The Australian Research Council funded study of "Young Australians'
      Perspectives on Religions and Non-Religious Worldviews" is an Australian
      Research Council funded project focused on teenagers' experiences and
      understandings of religious, spirituality, gender and sexual diversity, and
      comprised a nationally representative telephone survey of 1200 people aged
      13-18, supplemented by 11 focus groups with students in Years 9 and 10
      in three states. Retrieved from https://www.deakin.edu.au/about-deakin/
      media-releases/articles/study-finds-australian-teens-welcome-religious-
      diversity,-but-with-caution

32   The survey was conducted at the same time as the marriage equality postal
      survey.

33   ACBC, National Centre for Pastoral Research, *Social Profile of the Catholic
      Community in Australia based on the 2016 Australian Census,* Canberra, March
      2019. Cf. Table 1, p. 4.

34   ACBC, Pastoral Research Office, *Mass Attendance in Australia: A Critical
      Moment*, December 2013.

35   Gallup Polls, 1947 and 1960.

36   ACBC, Pastoral Research Office, *op. cit.* p. 1.

37   National Centre for Pastoral Research, Pastoral Research Online, Issue 44,
      April 2019, *2016 National Count of Attendance – National Summary.* Cf. pp.
      2-3.

38   Commonwealth Bureau of census and Statistics, 1961 Commonwealth
      Census, Vol. 8, pp. 42-49, Tables: Religion by Sex and Birthplace.

39   Gender Diversity Progress Report, Australian Institute of Company Directors,
      Sept – Dec 2018.

40   Bryant, W. & Bricknall, S. (2017), *Homicide in Australia 2012-2014: National
      Homicide Monitoring Program report.* Canberra: Australian Institute of
      Criminology. Retrieved from: https://bit.ly/2ozctxh.

41   Australian Bureau of Statistics. (2017). *Personal Safety Survey 2016.* ABS cat.
      no. 4906.0. Canberra: ABS. Retrieved from: http://www.abs.gov.au/ausstats/
      abs@.nsf/mf/4906.0

42   Australian Bureau of Statistics. (2017). *Personal Safety Survey 2016. ABS cat.
      no. 4906.0.* Canberra: ABS. Retrieved from: http://www.abs.gov.au/ausstats/
      abs@.nsf/mf/4906.0

43   AHRC (2018). *Everyone's business:* 4th *national survey on sexual harassment in
      Australian workplaces.* Retrieved from: https://whiteribbon.org/2Ea7Q6C

44   Australian Bureau of Statistics. (2017). *Personal Safety Survey 2016. ABS cat.
      no. 4906.0.* Canberra: ABS. Retrieved from: http://www.abs.gov.au/ausstats/
      abs@.nsf/mf/4906.0

45 Australian Bureau of Statistics. (2017). *Personal Safety Survey 2016. ABS cat. no. 4906.0.* Canberra: ABS. Retrieved from: http://www.abs.gov.au/ausstats/abs@.nsf/mf/4906.0

46 Women in STEMM Australia (2019) Retrieved from https://womeninscienceaust.org/about/

47 The word 'righteousness' means 'the quality of being morally correct and justifiable and may be considered synonymous with 'rightness'. In the Hebrew Bible, righteousness is one of the chief attributes of God, and in a man it is an attribute implying that a person's actions are justified and pleasing to God.

48 Oxfam, *Reward Work, Not Wealth*, London, 22 January 2018.

49 The Final Report of the Royal Commission into Misconduct in the Banking, Superannuation and Financial Services Industry, 4 February 2019, concurred with this: "First, in almost every case, the conduct in issue was driven not only by the relevant entity's pursuit of profit but also by individuals' pursuit of gain, whether in the form of remuneration for the individual or profit for the individual's business" (p. 1).

50 *Roy Morgan Wealth Report* (September 2018). Retrieved from http://www.roymorgan.com/findings/7733-wealth-inequality-in-australia-is-getting-worse-201809210554

51 Pope Francis, *Laudato Si'*, n. 82.

52 Australian Government, Department of the Environment and Energy, *2017 Review of Climate Change Policies,* December 2017, Canberra, p. 5.

53 United Nations, Climate Change Report, 2017. Cf. Foreword.

54 Pope Francis, *Laudato Si'*, 2015, n. 24-25.

55 *Ibid.* n. 26.

56 *Ibid.* n. 52.

57 Cardinal Bo (2018). L'Osservatore Romano. *Our moral obligation to save the planet Earth.* Retrieved from http://www.osservatoreromano.va/en/news/our-moral-obligation-save-planet-earth

58 *The Age,* 11 February 2019, p. 20

59 Royal Commission into Institutional Responses to Child Sexual Abuse, *Final Report: Preface and Summary*, 2017, pp. 43-44

60 Royal Commission, *Final Report*, December 2017. Final Information Update

61 Royal Commission into Institutional Responses to Child Sexual Abuse, *Proportion of priests and non-ordained religious subject to a claim of child sexual abuse 1950-2010*, February 2017.

62 International Human Rights Clinic (2018) *Australia and the Treaty on the Prohibition of Nuclear Weapons,* Harvard Law School. Retrieved from http://hrp.law.harvard.edu/wp-content/uploads/2018/12/Australia-TPNW-12-12-18 FINAL.pdf

63 Pope Francis, Address to the International Symposium on Prospects for a World Free of Nuclear Weapons and for Integral Disarmament, Rome, 10 November 2017.

64 Pope Francis, Message to the United Nations Conference to Negotiate a Legally Binding Instrument to Prohibit Nuclear Weapons, 27 March 2017

65 Pope Benedict XVI, *Message for the 47th World Communications Day*, 2013

66 Pope Francis, *Message for the 48th World Communication Day, Communication at the Service of an Authentic Culture of Encounter, 1 June 2014.*

67 Pope Francis, World Communication Day message, 24 January 2018.

68 Pastor Gill Cann, *Red Alert: Does the Future Have a Church?* Albatross Books, Australia, 2018.

69 Australian Institute of Health and Welfare. (2017). Retrieved from https://www.aihw.gov.au/reports/australias-welfare/australias-welfare-2017-in-brief/contents/indigenous-australians

70 ACBC, National Centre for Pastoral Research, *Social Profile of the Catholic Community in Australia based on the 2016 Australian Census,* Canberra, March 2019. Cf. Table 4, p. 5.

PART 2

PEOPLE OF GOD

The concept of the People of God is a central tenet of our tradition that time and again empowers and prompts the whole Church, particularly the laity, to act in our world to bring Christ's message of love and justice to all. It seems that there has never been a time as crucial as now for the faithful to speak out. This comprehensive document enables us to revisit and understand the rich chronology of our history and governance. St. Paul's charter of equality and freedom will drive our action for accountability, transparency and inclusion of all at this time in history.

- Marilyn Hatton, advocate for equality for women and all in the Catholic Church; founding Convener of the Australian Catholic Coalition for Church Reform and founding member of Catholics Speak Out and Concerned Catholics.

2.1 Israel: People of God and light to the nations

God's election of Israel as his "People" is a central concept in the Hebrew Scriptures: "And you shall be my people, and I will be your God."[1] The original Covenant was forged between God and Abraham[2], but later reaffirmed with the People of Israel[3]. God chose Israel to reflect his own holiness, his plan, his intention and his moral vision for humanity: "You are my witnesses, declares the Lord, and my servant whom I have chosen, so that you may know and believe me, and understand that I am he. Before me no God was formed, nor shall there be any after me. I, I am the Lord; and besides me there is no saviour."[4] "You shall be holy to me; for I the Lord am holy, and I have separated you from the other peoples to be mine."[5] Israel was to be "a light to the Nations".[6]

For a thousand years the prophets acted as the 'conscience of Israel' keeping its people true to its mission to be a "light to the Nations", shaking the people out of their complacency and false securities, and calling them back to fidelity to the Covenant; a focus far more important than their obsessive observance of the Mosaic Law and the Temple rituals.

During 900 years before and after Christ, Israel experienced a succession of traumatising events that profoundly altered its self-understanding, its connection with the world around it, and its relationship with God. These experiences caused Israel to develop strategies and structures to enshrine, protect and preserve its national identity and cultural integrity with a body of teaching, laws and regulations – developed by the Pharisees, scribes and Elders during the 3rd century BCE – which came to be known as the Halakah.

2.2 The Halakah

The Halakah was a collection of authoritative commentaries on the Torah that included interpretations, laws, regulations and customs that defined and safeguarded the distinctiveness of Israel's monotheism, the exclusiveness of Jewish identity and belief, as well as providing the cultural and ethical strategies needed for the survival of the people. It demanded that the Jewish people maintain a strictly symbiotic, intolerant and exclusionary ethos. The markers of national identity, its laws of separation including regulations for ritual and dietary purity were not dissimilar from the idea of 'apartheid'. The Halakah demanded strictly enforced exclusion on the basis of ethnicity, social status and gender, and its laws of moral and ritual distance applied not only to the relationship of Jews with their Gentile neighbours, but to a whole range of relationships among Jews themselves.

The Mishnah (200 CE), with its 613 Halakahic commandments and regulations, governed Jewish everyday life from birth to death and, at the time of Jesus, Jewish interpreters of the Torah engaged in fierce debates which defined much of Jesus' ministry and teaching. Jesus gained a reputation as a violator of most of the Halakah boundaries: "Now the tax collectors and sinners were drawing near to hear him. And the Pharisees and the scribes murmured, saying, 'This man receives sinners and eats with them'"[7], and was leading Israel astray.[8] The Jewish Sanhedrin determined that because of his 'blasphemies' Jesus deserved to die.[9]

With its constant and insistent demands, the Halakah had so dulled the hearts and minds of Israel that it became deaf to the voice of the prophets sent by God to call the Jewish people back to covenantal fidelity and right relationship with God: "Therefore I send you prophets and wise men and scribes, some of whom you will kill and crucify, and some you will flog in your synagogues and persecute from town to town."[10]

For Jesus, this killing and persecution of the prophets, the authentic teachers and keepers of its collective memory, demonstrated that Israel had gone 'off mission'. It had lost its vision, moral authority, its power to reflect the reign of God and, therefore, its true identity.

> ... The Reign (Kingdom) of God that Jesus taught was about God's pressing moral claim on all humanity, a claim that cut across all other ethical codes, whether Jewish Halakah or Gentile ethical humanism ...

The Reign (Kingdom) of God that Jesus taught was about God's pressing moral claim on all humanity, a claim that cut across all other ethical codes, whether Jewish Halakah or Gentile ethical humanism. The very idea of the Kingdom that Jesus preached implied a profound conversion of the human heart and a radical transformation of a person's outlook on life, so dramatically illustrated in the 'Beatitudes' and the moral imperatives of the Kingdom.[11]

2.3 The Gentile question

The Acts of the Apostles records the pivotal assembly at Jerusalem, where the apostles and the rest of the disciples came together to discern what God was asking of them in the face of the dilemma posed by the tension between the codified separatist and exclusivist Jewish Halakah and Jesus' command to preach the Gospel to the entire world. The Jerusalem decision was a compromise solution: it allowed the Halakah-abiding Jewish disciples to continue to frequent the Temple, and for the Gentile Christians to live without the restrictions of Jewish law.[12]

> ... 'inclusion' would be the essential and defining principle of Christian life and mission ...

The Jerusalem decision proved revolutionary, for it set a course for the entire Christian movement to move away decisively from a culture of symbiosis to one of osmosis. Thereafter, 'inclusion' would be the essential and defining principle of Christian life and mission, and the new People of God would be "the light of the world", a people called to holiness, and divinely sent to "all nations" that they might be the "universal sign of salvation".[13]

2.4 Paul's charter of equality and freedom

After his conversion, Paul's long period of reflection on the significance of Jesus' life, preaching, death and resurrection - not just for his fellow Jews, but for all humanity – led him to the revolutionary insight that, in the community of Jesus' followers, there could be no place for any determinisms based on ethnicity, social class and gender. For Paul, all persons reborn through Baptism into Christ belong to a community of free and equal human beings: "As many of you as were baptised into Christ, have clothed yourself with Christ. There is no longer Jew or Greek, no longer slave or free, there is no longer male and female, for all of you are one in Christ Jesus".[14]

> ... There is no longer Jew or Greek, no longer slave or free, there is no longer male and female, for all of you are one in Christ Jesus ...

This radically new and distinctive Christian understanding of society subverted the ancient cultures and social structures founded on inequality of gender, human dignity, and ethnicity. They could not contend with a community whose source of equality was realised in the humanity of Jesus.

2.5 Vatican II and the People of God

Vatican II gave new life to the great biblical notion of the People of God. God sanctifies and saves men and women, not as individuals but as "a people who would acknowledge him in truth and serve him in holiness".[15] The People of God enjoy the dignity and freedom of the children of God. The law that guides them is Christ's commandment of love, their goal is the Kingdom of God, and their mission is to be the light of the world. Vatican II taught:

Christ is the light to all the nations. Hence, this Sacred Synod, gathered in the Holy Spirit, eagerly desires to bring the light of Christ to all. By her relationship with Christ, the Church is like a sacrament, or sign of intimate union with God, and of the unity of all mankind; it is also an instrument for achieving such union and unity. Therefore, this Council desires to unfold more fully to the faithful of the Church and to the whole world its inner nature and universal mission with urgency. The eternal Father created the whole world to raise man to a participation in the divine life. God the Father offers to help us aim unto salvation.[16]

... By her relationship with Christ, the Church is like a sacrament, or sign of intimate union with God, and of the unity of all mankind; it is also an instrument for achieving such union and unity ...

The People of God throughout the world are made 'one' by the unity of the Father, Son and Spirit, and this *communion* expresses the core of the mystery of the Church: a relationship with God, and an invitation to each individual, through the Spirit, to participate in the communion of Father, Son and Spirit. It is a communion with God, with all others of Christ's faithful, and with the Church.[17]

One of the embarrassments for Vatican II is that, although it speaks about the 'People of God', the only theology of the laity – the largest part of the People of God – that was available was the 'Catholic Action' model, according to which lay women and men wishing to be involved in the evangelical mission of the Church, had to have a mandate from the hierarchy. They had to submit to its scrutiny, control and compliance, and be monitored by the clergy to make sure that their lay call to holiness came under the Episcopal mission 'to sanctify'. But a laity which had to be 'clergy-dependent' and closely watched was part of a distorted ecclesiology.[18]

Pius X taught a warped understanding of the hierarchical structure of the Church, with clergy reigning from above and laity below.

> It follows that the Church is essentially an unequal society, a society comprising two categories of persons: the Pastors and the flock, those who occupy a rank in the different degrees of the hierarchy and the multitude of the faithful. So distinct are these categories that only the pastoral body has the necessary right and authority for promoting the end of the society and directing all its members towards that end. The one duty of the multitude is to allow itself to be led, and, like a docile flock, to follow the Pastors.[19]

Pius XI went on to teach that Catholic action could only be authorised and understood as an extension of the mission of the hierarchy, with total control from above:

> Obeying our watchful and assiduous instructions ... it does not wish to be nor can be anything other than "the participation and the collaboration of the laity with the Apostolic Hierarchy".[20]

This pyramidal, authoritarian ecclesiology is the heartland of 'clericalism'. American theologian and historian, Russell Shaw, speaks of the domineering and elitist nature of clericalism and the destructive disequilibrium it has caused to the Church and its mission:

> Clericalism assumes that clerics not only are but also are *meant* to be the active, dominant elite in the Church, and laymen the passive, subservient mass. As a result, the laity is discouraged from taking seriously its responsibility for the Church's mission, and evangelization is neglected. So are efforts to influence the structures of secular society on behalf of the values of the Gospel, the evangelization of culture, as it is called. A large part of the program of the Second Vatican Council remains not only unaccomplished but also un-attempted.[21]

Bishop Vincent Nguyen Van Long singles out clericalism as the biggest obstacle to genuine Church reform with its trademark characteristics of secrecy, privilege, status and entitlements:

… Bishop Vincent Nguyen Van Long singles out clericalism as the biggest obstacle to genuine Church reform with its trademark characteristics of secrecy, privilege, status and entitlements …

> I see clericalism as a by-product of a certain model of Church informed or underpinned or sustained by a certain theology. I mean, it's no secret that we have been operating, at least under the two previous pontificates, from what I'd describe as a 'perfect society' model where there is a neat, almost divinely inspired, pecking order, and that pecking order is heavily tilted towards the ordained. So you have the pope, the cardinals, the bishops, religious, consecrated men and women, and the laity right at the bottom of the pyramid. I think we need to dismantle that model of Church. I think we really need to examine seriously that kind of model of Church where it promotes the superiority of the ordained and it facilitates that power imbalance between the ordained and the non-ordained, which in turn facilitates that attitude of clericalism.[22]

In 1963, French theologian Yves Congar OP, commenting on the failure of the clergy to understand that they are members of the one Church, not masters standing above the laity, wrote:

> We (the clergy) are still a long way from reaping the consequences of the rediscovery, which we have all made in principle, of the fact that the whole Church is a single people of God and that she is made up of the faithful as well as the clergy. We have an idea we feel implicitly and, without admitting it, unconsciously, that the Church is the clergy and that the faithful are only our clients and beneficiaries. This terrible concept has been built into so many of our structures and habits that it seems to be taken for granted and beyond change. It is a betrayal of the truth. A great deal still remains to be done to de-clericalise our conceptions of the Church (without jeopardizing her hierarchical structures), and to put the clergy back where they belong, in the place of member-servants.[23]

... The reforms that now have to be made encompass the Church's spirituality, culture and structures of governance, and will require a profound conversion from a narrow elitist clerical leadership to an ecclesiology of synodality, collegiality and inclusion of all ...

In the same way that Israel went 'off mission', so the Church has also gone 'off mission', regressing into the false security of its structures and behaviours that both Jesus and his earliest followers rejected. The reforms that now have to be made encompass the Church's spirituality, culture and structures of governance, and will require a profound conversion from a narrow elitist clerical leadership to an ecclesiology of synodality, collegiality and inclusion of all. And to begin, the leadership must take seriously its obligation to 'listen' and to renew the Church as a community of justice.

2.6 Theology of the Laity – *Sensus fidei fidelium*

Cardinal John Henry Newman had a particular understanding of the place and role of the laity in the Church which played a critical role in shaping two of Vatican II's most important documents: *Lumen Gentium* and *Gaudium et Spes*. His insights were most apparent in this statement:

> The holy People of God … the entire body of the faithful, anointed as they are by the Holy One, cannot err in matters of belief. They manifest this special property by means of the whole peoples' supernatural discernment in matters of faith when "from the Bishops down to the last of the lay faithful" they show universal agreement in matters of faith and morals. That discernment in matters of faith is aroused and sustained by the Spirit of truth. It is exercised under the guidance of the sacred teaching authority, in faithful and respectful obedience to which the people of God accepts that which is not just the word of [people] but truly the word of God. Through it, the people of God adheres unwaveringly to the faith given once and for all to the saints, penetrates it more deeply with right thinking, and applies it more fully in its life.[24]

For Newman, St Paul's notion of dynamic interdependence of functions of the living body[25] was central to his theology. He described the relationship between pastors and people as a "conspiracy of pastors and faithful"[26], in which, Christiansen observes, the faithful "should have a respected place justified by their proven witness to Christian orthodoxy"[27].

For Newman, "the voice of tradition may in certain cases express itself, not by Councils, nor Fathers, nor Bishops, but in the *communis fidelium sensus* or 'shared sense of the faithful'".[28] Today, this concept is more widely known as the *sensus fidei fidelium* or 'the sense of faith of the faithful' and is defined by the International Theological Commission as

> a sort of spiritual instinct that enables the believer to judge spontaneously whether a particular teaching or practice is or is not in conformity with the Gospel and with apostolic faith. It is intrinsically linked to the virtue of faith itself; it flows from, and is a property of, faith.[29]

Now, more pressingly than ever before, Australia's bishops have to understand that, as a result of the clerical child sexual abuse scandals, compounded by their systemic institutional dissemblance and cover-ups, they have lost their moral authority and compromised the very reason for their existence. A major corrective to the current crisis in the Church in Australia is urgently needed, to restore an equilibrium and sound health to a damaged community. As the Catholic community prepares for the Plenary Council 2020/21, it is imperative that the bishops listen closely to, and be informed by, what Newman called the 'common sense of the faithful': "I shall offend many men when I say, we must *look to the people*; our influence is to depend on *them,* yet the sacraments reside with us" (Newman's italics).[30]

... Australia's bishops have to understand that, as a result of the clerical child sexual abuse scandals, compounded by their systemic institutional dissemblance and cover-ups, they have lost their moral authority and compromised the very reason for their existence ...

2.7 Vatican II and the rights and duties of Christ's faithful

A major sign of the times since the 1937 4th Australasian Plenary Council has been a determination by the community of nations to identify a range of human rights, codify them through the United Nations in declarations, charters, treaties and conventions, and urge sovereign nation states, through binding legislation, to commit themselves to honour them.

The Second Vatican Council had a similar determination to defend human rights[31], and more specifically to identify the rights and responsibilities of Christ's faithful derived from baptism and their belonging to the People of God, to codify them and to promulgate them. It affirmed that all Christ's faithful have common rights and duties, each right implying a duty, and each duty a right. Their origin arises from the fundamental dignity of the human person as free and able to reason, and from God's plan of salvation for humanity: "Since all men and women possessed of a rational soul and created in the image of God have the same nature and the same origin, and since they have been redeemed by Christ and enjoy the same divine calling and destiny, the basic equality which they all share needs to be increasingly recognised."[32]

... "Since all men and women possessed of a rational soul and created in the image of God have the same nature and the same origin, and since they have been redeemed by Christ and enjoy the same divine calling and destiny, the basic equality which they all share needs to be increasingly recognised" ...

2.8 *Lex Ecclesiae Fundamentalis* and *Justice in the World*

Vatican II recognised that the Church is not a perfect society, complete in and of itself, nor analogous to the civil state. It exists as a visible, organised society for one purpose only: to fulfil God's mission entrusted to it by Christ. All rights and duties of Christ's faithful must, therefore, be understood in the accomplishment of that mission, and interpreted in the relationship between the individual and God, Christ, and the Christian community. Vatican II called this relationship '*communio*'.

Some rights and duties reflect the fundamental dignity derived from baptism and incorporation into the Body of Christ: the right to privacy, good name and reputation (C. 220), to freedom from coercion in choosing a state of life (C. 219), to proclaim the Gospel (C. 211), to promote and sustain apostolic action (C. 216), to spiritual assistance from the sacraments and Word of God (C. 213), to worship, and to follow one's own spiritual life (C. 214); and the duty of Christian obedience (C. 212 §1), and to lead a holy life (C. 210). Other rights and duties derive from the same dignity but reflect the organised structure of the Church and the variety of functions and vocations in the community: the right to express one's needs, desires and opinions (C. 212 §2), to a Christian education (C. 217), to academic freedom of inquiry and expression (C. 218), to associate (C. 215), and to defend one's rights and be judged with equity (C. 221 §§1-2); and the duty to provide for the Church's needs and to promote social justice (C. 222).

Those with authority and power to govern have a duty to make the faithful aware of their rights, and to provide the structures and opportunities for the faithful to exercise their rights freely and without impediment.[33]

Vatican II strongly encouraged Catholics to join with their fellow Christians in searching for ways to achieve unity in belief and worship and to cooperate actively in the proclamation of the Gospel. There is now a new sense of urgency in this search, as the signs of the times indicate an upsurge in violence, terrorism, social upheaval, divisions of all kinds, the threat of mass destruction, and war.

Integral to the faith of the People of God is the conviction that the credibility of its life and mission depends on inner unity and its message of inclusion. Jesus prayed for unity among his followers and unity in their mission.[34] Unity among Christians and the search for common ground between Christians and the followers of other faiths are not options, they are essential.[35]

> ... Those with authority and power to govern have a duty to make the faithful aware of their rights, and to provide the structures and opportunities for the faithful to exercise their rights freely and without impediment ...

Following Vatican II, Paul VI urged the development of a Fundamental Law of the Church (*Lex Ecclesiae Fundamentalis*) envisioned as a moral guide for the interpretation and implementation of the new *Code of Canon Law.*

In 1971, the World Synod of Bishops discussed, debated and adopted a significant portion of the work already completed, and in its final document, titled *Justice in the World,* the Synod Fathers noted:

> Of itself it does not belong to the Church, insofar as she is a religious and hierarchical community, to offer concrete solutions in the social, economic and political spheres for justice in the world. Her mission involves defending and promoting the dignity and fundamental rights of the human person.[36]

One of that document's most important principles concerns the credibility of the Church, challenging all the faithful to live lives of integrity, congruence, and evangelical transparency:

While the Church is bound to give witness to justice, she recognises that anyone who ventures to speak to people about justice must first be just in their eyes. Hence we must undertake an examination of the modes of acting and of the possessions and lifestyle found within the Church herself.[37]

A final draft of the *Lex Ecclesiae Fundamentalis* was circulated in 1980, and although approved by a specially convened international commission, the whole project was abandoned without explanation. Paul VI never approved or promulgated it, but several of its elements, and key principles from *Justice in the World,* were incorporated in Part II – The People of God – of the 1983 *Code of Canon Law.*

2.9 Charter of Rights and Responsibilities for Christ's Faithful

Catholics for Renewal believes that it is now time for the Church in Australia, through the Plenary Council 2020/21, to draw up and promulgate an Australian Catholic Charter of Rights and Responsibilities that should inform the culture and governance of every Catholic organisation and institution in the nation.

A model for this type of Charter, to help local parishes prepare for the Plenary Council, was recently prepared by the Yarra Deanery of the Archdiocese of Melbourne in collaboration with *Catholics for Renewal*, and a copy is attached in Appendix 3.

We note here[38], as an example of the need for such a Charter, the considerable distress caused to people of LGBTIQ sexual orientation by the teaching in the *Catechism of the Catholic Church* regarding 'chastity and homosexuality'[39]. The *Catechism* relies on a limited interpretation of Sacred Scripture presenting homosexual acts as "acts of grave depravity" and claims that tradition declares that "homosexual acts are intrinsically disordered." It further states that homosexual acts "do not proceed from a genuine affective

> *... Catholics for Renewal* **believes that it is now time for the Church in Australia, through the Plenary Council 2020/21, to draw up and promulgate an Australian Catholic Charter of Rights and Responsibilities that should inform the culture and governance of every Catholic organisation and institution in the nation ...**

and sexual complementarity", and describes homosexual tendencies and inclinations as "objectively disordered".

However, the *Catechism* also notes that those of homosexual orientation "must be accepted with respect, compassion, and sensitivity" and that "every sign of unjust discrimination in their regard should be avoided", a Christian position that applies of course to all people, but is inconsistent with the discriminatory impact of the other provisions within the Catechism about homosexual people. That mutual respect is reflected in modern society, as illustrated by marriage equality legislation passed by Australian and other parliaments throughout the world.

We **recommend** that these provisions in the Catholic Catechism be reviewed urgently in light of modern understanding of God-given human sexuality.

2.10 Recommendations

Recommendation 2.1:

that the Plenary Council 2020/21 develop a Charter of Rights and Duties for Christ's Faithful in Australia, based on those set out in the 1983 *Code of Canon Law*, particularly Canons 210-223, augmented by those contained in the Synod of Bishops document *Justice in the World,* and updated using the fresh insights contained in Pope Francis's Apostolic Exhortations *Evangelii Gaudium* (2013) and *Episcopalis communio* (2018), his Encyclical Letter *Laudato Si'* (2015), the Directory for the Pastoral Ministry of Bishops (*Apostolorum successors,* 2004)[40], and the most recent documents of the International Theological Commission (2014, 2018)[41].

Recommendation 2.2:

that the Charter incorporates the right of Australian Catholics to have made available to them by their diocesan bishops all the canonical structures recommended by Vatican II, and other necessary avenues for effective pastoral dialogue, so that they can express their needs and desires with freedom and confidence.[42]

Recommendation 2.3:

that the Charter incorporates the right of Christ's faithful to expect their diocesan bishops, as a matter of course, and in order to fulfil their missionary obligation, as stressed by Pope Francis, to:

i) "listen to everyone and not simply to those who would tell them what [they] would like to hear";

ii) "be bold and creative in rethinking the goals, structures, style, and methods of evangelization in their respective communities";

iii) ensure that proposals of goals will not prove illusory by including "an adequate communal search for the means of achieving them"; and

iv) "not walk alone, but rely on [all the faithful] as brothers and sisters under [their] leadership, in a wise and realistic pastoral discernment."[43]

Recommendation 2.4:

that the Charter incorporates the right of all persons (and groups) who have suffered abuse or injustice at the hands of an ordained cleric, professed religious or church-employed person, to receive just redress.

Recommendation 2.5:

that the Charter incorporates the right of all the faithful to know:

i) the quality of pastoral ministry they are entitled to receive from their pastors;

ii) the standards of ethical conduct their pastors will uphold and follow;

iii) what mechanisms will be put in place to guarantee accountability and transparency; and

iv) what actions will be taken to ensure gender balance throughout the Church.

Recommendation 2.6:

that the Charter incorporates the right of every Australian bishop, priest, religious or layperson accused of doctrinal error and/or failure of leadership, to be afforded due process and a fair trial in accord with the standards of Australian civil justice.

Recommendation 2.7:

that the Charter incorporates the right of Christ's faithful in Australia to be invited to express their opinion when new bishops are to be selected and appointed, reappointed, and to be moved, and that a new process be drawn up to ensure this is enabled.[44]

Recommendation 2.8:

that the Charter incorporates the right of Christ's faithful in parishes to be recognised as living communities of faith, and be consulted whenever there is a proposal to divide, merge, amalgamate, cluster, or close a parish.

Recommendation 2.9:

that the Charter be officially promulgated, published in print and digital format, be widely disseminated on all official Catholic Church websites, and be displayed in print at the entrance of every church, Catholic educational, health and welfare institution throughout the nation.

... The Catechism relies on a limited interpretation of Sacred Scripture presenting homosexual acts as "acts of grave depravity" and claims that tradition declares that "homosexual acts are intrinsically disordered". ...

Recommendation 2.10:

that the Plenary Council request the Holy See to review urgently the provisions of the Catechism regarding homosexual people in light of modern understanding of God-given human sexuality.

Some discussion questions:

- Vatican II states that God sanctifies and saves us, not as individuals, but *as a people*. To what extent do you believe that parish communities grasp this radical shift? (2.5)
- This section explores reasons for the development of *clericalism*. Consider the quotes provided and discuss your responses. (2.5)
- In what ways is the laity called, or obliged, to challenge church hierarchy and exercise leadership? (2.6- 8, see also 4.6)
- How could the pyramidal structure which positions the laity at the bottom be inverted? What cultural change and first steps would be required?
- Take time to consider well the recommendations for developing a Charter of Rights and responsibilities for Christ's faithful in Australia. Discuss the value of such a Charter. (2.1)

Notes

1   *Jer* 30:22; *Deut* 7:6.
2   *Gen* 12:2.
3   *Exodus* 34:10; *Deut* 30; *Joshua* 8:30-35; 24.
4   *Isaiah* 43:10-11.
5   *Levs* 20:26.
6   *Isaiah* 49:6.
7   *Lk* 15:1-2; *Mark* 3:1-6; *Jn* 9:16.
8   *Lk* 23:14; *Jn* 7:12.
9   Matt 26:66.
10 Matt 23:34ff.
11 Matt 5
12 *Acts* 11.
13 Matt 5:14-16; Vatican II, *Lumen Gentium*, n. 48.
14 *Gal* 3:27-28; *1 Cor* 12:12-13; *2 Cor* 5:17.
15 *Lumen Gentium*, n. 6.
16 *Lumen Gentium*, n. 1-2.
17 Timbs, D. *A People not a Pyramid. Christianity. Leadership in a Society of Equals. Pt I.* Retrieved from: http://www.catholicsforrenewal.org/A%20People%20not%20a%20Pyramid.%20Split%201%20&%202-2-1.pdf
18 Shaw, R. (2013) Clericalism: A football team with only coaches and no players. Retrieved from: https://www.catholicworldreport.com/2013/12/23/clericalism-a-football-team-with-only-coaches-and-no-players/
19 Pius X. (1905) *Vehementer Nos.* Retrieved from http://w2.vatican.va/content/pius-x/en/encyclicals/documents/hf_p-x_enc_11021906_vehementer-nos.html
20 Pius XI. (1931) *Non Abbiamo Bisogno, On Catholic Action in Italy.* Retrieved from: http://w2.vatican.va/content/pius-xi/en/encyclicals/documents/hf_p-xi_enc_29061931_non-abbiamo-bisogno.html
21 Russell Shaw, *To Hunt, to Shoot, to Entertain.* San Francisco: Ignatius Press, 1993, 13.
22 V. Long (2017) *Australian Catholics.* Retrieved from: https://australiancatholics.com.au/article.aspx?aeid=50654
23 Yves Congar, *Power and Poverty in the Church. The Renewal and Understanding of Service* Mahwah, NJ: Paulist Press, 2016 (1963), p. 139.
24 Vatican II, *Lumen Gentium*, n. 12.
25 *1 Cor* 12.
26 Drew Christiansen, "A Conspiracy of Bishops and Faithful: Reading Newman's 'On Consulting the Faithful' today," *America Magazine*, September 27, 2010. Retrieved from https://www.americamagazine.org/issue/748/article/conspiracy-bishops-and-faithful
27 Ibid.
28 Rush, O. (2001). *Sensus Fidei: Faith making sense of Revelation.* Retrieved from http://cdn.theologicalstudies.net/62/62.2/62.2.1.pdf
29 International Theological Commission (2014). *Sensus Fidei in the life of the Church.* Retrieved from http://www.vatican.va/roman_curia/congregations/cfaith/cti_documents/rc_cti_20140610_sensus-fidei_en.html
30 Sharkey, M. *Newman on the Laity.* Retrieved from http://www.ewtn.com/library/Theology/NEWMNLAY.HTM
31 2nd Ordinary Assembly of the Synod of Bishops. (1971). *Justice in the World.* n. 37: "Of itself it does not belong to the Church, insofar as she is a religious and hierarchical community, to offer concrete solutions in the social, economic

and political spheres for justice in the world. Her mission involves defending and promoting the dignity and fundamental rights of the human person." Retrieved from https://www1.villanova.edu/content/dam/villanova/mission/JusticeIntheWorld1971.pdf

32 Vatican II, *Gaudium et Spes*, n. 29

33 Cf. Coriden, J. (1990) *"What became of the Bill of Rights?'* in *CLSAP* 52, 47-60. Coriden notes that despite the rights set out in the Code, difficulties remain in implementation for many reasons: lack of information, lack of protections, lack of access to procedures, lack of support from bishops and clergy, and complex terminology. Cf. Beal, J et al. *New Commentary on the Code of Canon Law*, Paulist Press, NY, 2000, p. 257. Beal argues that the implications of communion need further development especially for structures.

34 *Jn* 17

35 Vatican II, *Unitatis – redintegatio*, 1964, Decree on Ecumenism: Retrieved from:http://www.vatican.va/archive/hist_councils/ii_vatican_council/documents/vat-ii_decree_19641121_unitatis-redintegratio_en.html

36 *Op. cit., Justice in the World*, n. 37

37 *Op. cit., Justice in the World*, n. 40

38 This paragraph was not included in the original submission submitted to meet the Ash Wednesday 2019 deadline and has now been forwarded separately to the Plenary Council secretariat.

39 *Catechism of the Catholic Church*, nn 2357-9: Chastity and homosexuality
    2357 Homosexuality refers to relations between men or between women who experience an exclusive or predominant sexual attraction toward persons of the same sex. It has taken a great variety of forms through the centuries and in different cultures. Its psychological genesis remains largely unexplained. Basing itself on Sacred Scripture, which presents homosexual acts as acts of grave depravity,[141] tradition has always declared that "homosexual acts are intrinsically disordered."[142] They are contrary to the natural law. They close the sexual act to the gift of life. They do not proceed from a genuine affective and sexual complementarity. Under no circumstances can they be approved.
    2358 The number of men and women who have deep-seated homosexual tendencies is not negligible. This inclination, which is objectively disordered, constitutes for most of them a trial. They must be accepted with respect, compassion, and sensitivity. Every sign of unjust discrimination in their regard should be avoided. These persons are called to fulfill God's will in their lives and, if they are Christians, to unite to the sacrifice of the Lord's Cross the difficulties they may encounter from their condition.
    2359 Homosexual persons are called to chastity. By the virtues of self-mastery that teach them inner freedom, at times by the support of disinterested friendship, by prayer and sacramental grace, they can and should gradually and resolutely approach Christian perfection.

40 Congregation for Bishops (2004) Retrieved from http://www.vatican.va/roman_curia/congregations/cbishops/documents/rc_con_cbishops_doc_20040222_apostolorum-successores_en.html

41 International Theological Commission, *Sensus fidei in the life of the Church* (2014); *Synodality in the life and mission of the Church* (2018)

42 Pope Francis, *Evangelii Gaudium*, n. 31; *Episcopalis communio*,

43 Ibid. n. 33

44 Cf. Also, our Recommendations 3.12 and 4.9-4.13

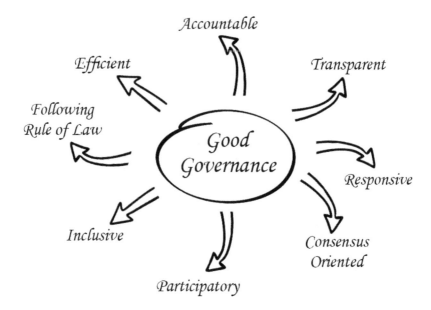

PART 3

CHURCH GOVERNANCE

Both the Royal Commission and the Truth Justice and Healing Council called for urgent review and renewal of the Church's governance structures and practices. Without fundamental change of the kind advocated in the following chapter, many in the Church will remain alienated. The culture will continue to be one of a male patriarchy, disinterested in the people of the Church, dismissive of the role that women can play; and will have shown itself to have learned very little from the recommendations of the Royal Commission. We can only pray that this book, the work of the Royal Commission and the Plenary Council will lead to substantial changes in culture, governance and renewal.

- Elizabeth Proust, Deputy Chair of the Truth Justice and Healing Council, former Chair of Australian Institute of Company Directors.

3.1 The meaning of governance

Governance encompasses the leadership, authority, accountability, culture and control of an organisation enabling the achievement of the organisation's mission. Good governance requires high levels of accountability, transparency and inclusion. It never discriminates on the basis of gender or other diversity, always respecting civil law, due process and natural justice.

A well-accepted definition of corporate governance is:

the process by which organisations are directed, controlled and held to account [encompassing] authority, accountability, stewardship, leadership, direction and control exercised in the organisation.[1]

Governance involves collaboration in pursuit of a common mission or purpose, whether spiritual or secular. It is the means by which people collaborate using their God-given abilities to achieve a purpose.

... Governance involves collaboration in pursuit of a common mission or purpose, whether spiritual or secular. It is the means by which people collaborate using their God-given abilities to achieve a purpose ...

Governance can be effective or ineffective, or even dysfunctional if those with the responsibility to govern are unaccountable and autocratic. Good governance is accountable, transparent and inclusive; it is primarily concerned with effective leadership focussed, in the case of the Church, on the mission given the Church by Jesus.

The autocratic nature of the Catholic Church's governance has in itself discouraged any reflection on its efficacy. The faithful, clerics and lay, have subserviently accepted autocratic governance systems dating from the revival of Roman law in the middle-ages and the absolute monarchies of Europe in the 16th and 17th centuries. These dysfunctional arrangements of entrenched privilege and autocracy have done much damage to the Church's mission and culture, begetting a culture that is in many respects the antithesis of Christ-likeness and prejudicial to the Church's God-given mission, as exposed by the Australian Royal Commission into Institutional Responses to Child Sexual Abuse. That culture, commonly referred to as clericalism, has been thoroughly inculcated into all the faithful and consequently has blinded the faithful to its very existence and to the Church's rejection of the servant-leadership modelled by Jesus.

... good secular governance normally rejects all discrimination, supported by values that often have their foundations in Christian teaching, values that ironically are not always visible in the culture of the global institutional Church ...

Good governance is also dependent on good leadership and a shared culture which ensure that all in the organisation are committed to the organisation's mission. Above all, good governance creates and maintains an organisational culture which facilitates that collaborative work towards a common goal. Effective governance requires forward planning and reporting against progress towards mission. This calls for a focus on mission, analysis of past performance, regular reading of the current signs of the times, lawful and ethical behaviour, due process, natural justice, and careful scrutiny of likely and foreseeable events.

It is notable that good secular governance normally rejects all discrimination, supported by values that often have their foundations in Christian teaching, values that ironically are not always visible in the culture of the global institutional Church – again a situation exposed by the Royal Commission. There can be no higher purpose than the mission of the Church bringing all the people of God into the communion of the Father, Son, and Spirit. It behoves the Church's leaders to ensure that the Church is governed in accordance with the best of human skills. It is a lamentable fact that the form of governance adopted by the Church over many centuries, and currently in force, is in so many respects not in accord with the Church's specific teachings, particularly on the roles of its leaders and of the People of God.

Good governance recognises and accords with the principle of subsidiarity, as advocated by Pope Pius XI who stated that:

> it is an injustice and at the same time a grave evil and disturbance of right order to assign to a greater and higher association what lesser and subordinate organisations can do.[2]

All decision-making should take place at the most appropriate level of an organisation, the Church included, to ensure justice and informed decision-making. Success or failure in the governance of the Church depends first of all on the quality of its life of faith, hope and charity. It was the quality of the life of the early Christian communities that was the dynamism which drew people into their membership, as reflected in Tertullian's quote from a pagan Roman, "See how these Christians love each other."[3]

Clerical child sexual abuse and its cover-up is a failure of governance through a failure of love by our Christian communities around the world. It was the trust of Church authorities in the existing doctrines and unaccountable and autocratic structures of the Church rather than in the call of the Spirit that led to their protection of the institution over the wellbeing of children. Attempts at reform will not succeed if we do not make our priority the renewal of our lives of faith, hope and charity.

3.2 Church authority

Governance requires authority, and a source for that authority. Ultimate authority to govern can come from a variety of sources, e.g. the people in a democratic society; shareholders in a public corporation; members in an incorporated association; or from God in the case of the Church.

Authority exists in the Church to support the Church's mission, and the modes of governance in which it is expressed must accord with the divine love revealed in Christ. All ministry in the Church is modelled on the example of the Good Shepherd.[4] All authority to govern in the Church comes from Jesus Christ for the purposes of propagating his teachings. Jesus received that authority from the Father:

> ...Authority exists in the Church to support the Church's mission, and the modes of governance in which it is expressed must accord with the divine love revealed in Christ...

> Then Jesus came to them and said, "All authority in heaven and earth has been given to me. Go therefore and make disciples of all nations, baptising them in the name of the Father, and of the Son, and of the Holy Spirit."[5]

Jesus handed to Peter and the other Apostles the power and authority to govern the Church:

> I will give you the keys of the kingdom of heaven, and whatever you bind on earth will be bound in heaven, and whatever you loose on earth will be loosed in heaven.[6]

Peter and the Apostles exercised the authority they had received from Jesus in various ways: they chose a replacement apostle for

Judas Iscariot, preached authoritatively, baptised, worked miracles and signs, testified to the resurrection of Jesus, laid hands on (ordained) the first deacons, founded new churches, and made a critical and synodal decision about the mission to the Gentiles at the Council of Jerusalem (Acts 15:1-35).

The Apostles did not always agree (Gal 2:1-21), and Paul even "opposed Peter to his face, because he stood self-condemned" (*Gal* 2:11). But there was always the 'brotherhood', the 'fellowship' (*koinonia*) of apostles and disciples of the Lord, the community of the 'faithful', united in charity for a common purpose (Acts 2:42-47).

While the Apostles received a special mandate from Jesus, all Christ's faithful through baptism share in the priesthood of Jesus with its ministry of teaching, sanctifying and governing; ministerial priesthood differs through possession of 'sacred power.'[7] Within ministerial priesthood there are bishops (with fullness of Orders) "for whom priests are assistants"[8]. Episcopal ordination confers triple offices of teaching, sanctifying and governing. Priests share with bishops the priesthood of Christ but depend on bishops for exercise of their power.

...there are many good governance provisions in the Code that are not reflected in the actual governance practices of the Church...

The *Code of Canon Law*[9] codifies the exercise of authority in the Church including some principles of governance, having regard to divine law, scripture, tradition and the ecumenical councils, particularly Vatican II, and also regard to secular governance principles. The Code contains norms relating to sacred power to govern, who can exercise it, how and when it can be exercised, and the structures and processes through which it can be exercised. It is a regrettable fact that there are many good governance provisions in the Code that are not reflected in the actual governance practices of the Church.

The power of governance is identified as legislative, executive and judicial (C. 135), and the pope, diocesan bishops and some others can exercise and (in certain situations) delegate executive power

(CC. 134-144); there are some limitations on the executive power of bishops. Canon 127 provides that a superior is not to act contrary to advice from legally constituted groups whom he is required to consult "without what is, in his or her judgement, an overriding reason", and C. 212 §3 acknowledges "the right, indeed at times the duty, in keeping with their knowledge, competence and position, to manifest to the sacred Pastors their views on matters which concern the good of the Church (and) ... the right also to make their views known to others of Christ's faithful."

There is significant provision for consultation with the people of God in the exercise of authority, e.g. C. 461 provides for diocesan synods (including laity) to be held "when the diocesan Bishop ... judges that the circumstances suggest it", and Canon 511 requires every diocese to establish a diocesan pastoral council "in so far as pastoral circumstances suggest it." Canon 512 provides that pastoral council members be "selected in such a way that the council truly reflects the entire portion of the people of God which constitutes the diocese".

> ... Collegial governance, mandated by Vatican II, Canon Law, Scripture and Tradition, is perverted by the reservation of authority on important matters to the hierarchy and by the cloaking of the exercise of that authority in excessive secrecy ...

Vatican II specifically called for the "venerable institution of synods and councils (to) flourish with fresh vigour".[10]

In practice, important canonical provisions have not been implemented by many bishops. In particular, there have been very few diocesan synods held in Australian dioceses and there are very few diocesan pastoral councils which, if canon law is to be respected, begs the question: What "circumstances" are there in so many dioceses that "suggest" that synods and councils are not needed?

Collegial governance, mandated by Vatican II, Canon Law, Scripture and Tradition, is perverted by the reservation of authority on important matters to the hierarchy and by the cloaking of the exercise of that authority in excessive secrecy. A specific example of this perversion which has inflicted egregious harm on the faithful has been the recent controversy regarding a canonical prohibition through the pontifical secret on the reporting of clerical child sexual abuse. The Royal Commission has recommended that:

> The Australian Catholic Bishops Conference should request the Holy See to amend canon law so that the pontifical secret does not apply to any aspect of allegations or canonical disciplinary processes relating to child sexual abuse. (Recommendation 16.10.)

The Australian Catholic Bishops Conference (ACBC) response stated:

> The pontifical secret does not in any way inhibit a bishop or religious leader from reporting instances of child sexual abuse to civil authorities.

... Collegial governance of the Church is prejudiced by Canon 129 which focusses "the power of governance" on the ordained, i.e. ordained males (c. 129 §1), with the lay faithful, women and men, only permitted to 'cooperate' in the exercise of that power ...

This response of the Australian bishops conflicts not only with the findings of the Royal Commission, but also other sources including two United Nations Committees and three other independent commissions of investigation, as well as earlier statements from the Roman Curia.[11] *Catholics for Renewal* believes that the Australian bishops should refer the matter to the Holy See to confirm that the pontifical secret does not prevent reporting to the civil authorities regardless of whether there are mandatory criminal reporting laws in the State concerned, not a difficult request if their response to the Royal Commission is correct.

Further, given the Royal Commission's considered view that knowledge of child sexual abusers at large should be provided to civil police, the Holy See should be asked to go further and issue a clear instruction that Church authorities be required to report knowledge of child sexual abusers at large.[12]

Failure to remove any restriction on Church personnel reporting such knowledge to the civil authorities would be to perpetuate this perversion of collegial governance of the Church.

Collegial governance of the Church is prejudiced by Canon 129 which focusses "the power of governance" on the ordained, i.e. ordained males (C. 129 §1), with the lay faithful, women and men, only permitted to 'cooperate' in the exercise of that power:

> §1. Those who have received sacred orders are qualified, according to the norm of the prescripts of the law, for the power of governance, which exists in the Church by divine institution and is also called the power of jurisdiction.

> §2. Lay members of the Christian faithful can cooperate in the exercise of this same power according to the norm of law.

Notwithstanding this canon, some authorities have appointed other than ordained clerics to positions that could be seen as having governance authority beyond 'cooperation', a practice that should be welcomed as better reflecting the teachings of Vatican II. Among canonists, this has long been a contentious provision that, read literally, affects the capacity of any non-ordained woman or man to hold an office of governance, thus excluding well-qualified members of the laity from exercising the power of 'governance', a function clearly not dependent on, or particularly related to ordination.

The provision suggests further exclusion of women from governance of the Church, as women are already banned from any exercise of authority associated with ordination. The situation of women in the governance of the Church is discussed further below. We **recommend** that the Holy See be requested to repeal Canon 129.

3.3 Governance and power in the Church

Governance in the Church must accord with the teachings of Jesus and promulgate those teachings by practice and example. All – bishops, priests and the lay faithful – must ensure that their behaviour models good governance, for the sake of the Kingdom. Canon 208 states:

> there is a genuine equality of dignity and action among all of Christ's faithful. Because of this equality they all contribute, each according to his or her own condition and office, to the building up of the Body of Christ.

Bishops and priests have a responsibility to fully inform Christ's faithful of their rights and responsibilities and to explain them properly, regularly, and clearly. They must provide Christ's faithful with the opportunities to exercise freely their rights and responsibilities.

Jesus taught a particular way of governing, a way of love and humility:

> You know that among the Gentiles those whom they recognise as their rulers lord it over them, and their great ones are tyrants over them. But it is not so among you (Mark 10:42-43a).

> So those who are last now will be first then, and those who are first will be last (Matt 20:16).

> It shall not be this way among you. Instead, whoever wants to become great among you must be your servant (Matt 20:26).

Jesus condemned hypocrisy, endorsed openness and transparency, rejected rules as ends in themselves, and set the highest standard of governance for his times, and the principles and values he taught apply to governance in our times. He condemned the practices of the Pharisees, such as their excessive emphasis on the payment of tithes while neglecting "the weightier matters of the law: justice and mercy and faith" (Matt 23:28).

> ...Jesus condemned hypocrisy, endorsed openness and transparency, rejected rules as ends in themselves, and set the highest standard of governance for his times, and the principles and values he taught apply to governance in our times...

Accountability, transparency and inclusion are the critical elements of good governance that should guide the leaders of the Church in ensuring appropriate structures, practices and culture in the pursuit of the Church's God-given mission, particularly the principles of subsidiarity and synodality.

Accountability: Canon law provisions for accountability focus on diocesan bishops' accountability to the Pope and collegial accountability. Local bishops generally exercise authority in their dioceses without accountability, transparency or inclusion. Such autocracy is at odds with Christ-like leadership, with the synodal principles of the Church since New Testament times, and indeed with the principles of good governance. Fifty years ago, Vatican II reminded bishops of the need to listen to the laity on important matters, and consider what they had to say.[13] Pope Francis constantly reminds bishops of this in the context of the synodal approach, also stressed by Vatican II. This broad notion of accountability has been recently repeated more forcefully by the Holy See in the contexts of clerical child sexual abuse and synodality.[14] When secular corporate governance fails, organisational leaders can be held accountable by shareholders and governments. The People of God are entitled to expect, and good decision-making demands, that there be structures and practices at every level of their church for expressing their opinions and informing decision-making processes, and for holding decision-makers accountable.

Transparency: The norm of openness and transparency also has strong support in the biblical tradition: "Let your word be 'Yes, Yes', or 'No, No'; anything more than this comes from the evil one" (Matt 5:37), and "everyone who does wicked things hates the light and does not come to the light, lest his works should be exposed" (Jn 3:19-20). Transparency ensures good process and enables accountability, whereas secrecy enables incompetence, fraud and deception. Transparency also reinforces inclusion whereas secrecy excludes the people of God from the business of God's Church.

Archbishop Coleridge, now President of the ACBC, told the Royal Commission: "I think that we haven't yet embraced adequately a transparency that is appropriate and even necessary for an unusual community of communities like the Catholic Church."

> ...Archbishop Coleridge, now President of the ACBC, told the Royal Commission: "I think that we haven't yet embraced adequately a transparency that is appropriate and even necessary for an unusual community of communities like the Catholic Church."...

Inclusion: Inclusion is a moral value that evolves over time. St Paul's teaching that "there is no longer Jew or Greek, there is no longer slave or free, there is no longer male and female, for all of you are one in Christ Jesus" (Gal 3:28) is a prophetic statement of what must come – the Kingdom of God – rather than a description of the state of things in his time. In our time and culture Paul's prophecy is yearning for fulfilment, and the value of inclusion has reached a new stage in its evolution. Vatican II made no distinction between the roles of men and women in discerning the content of the faith. Nor did Pope Francis distinguish their roles when he stated that bishops must not "propose goals without an adequate communal search for the means of achieving them", otherwise they "will inevitably prove illusory".[15]

Inclusion is based on respect for the God-given talents of all in decision-making, a rejection of the notion of autocracy that a leader can decide without reference to others with relevant knowledge, skills and experience. There can be neither subsidiarity nor synodality without inclusion. Inclusion of all clearly precludes any discrimination on the grounds of gender or diversity, rather demanding that all be included in the Church's governance.

Subsidiarity: Vatican II wanted the principle of subsidiarity to permeate all governance, both ecclesial and civil.[16] This principle aims to locate decision-making as close as possible to those who will be affected by the decisions made. This requires decision-making at the lowest level appropriate – using national episcopal conferences, parish and diocesan pastoral councils, diocesan and particular synods (plenary and provincial) – to ensure that church laws are most appropriately suited to the place, circumstance, and the needs of the times.

Individuals and communities should be allowed to act on their full human potential and live in a dignified manner. For Pope Francis, "excessive centralisation, rather than proving helpful, complicates the Church's life and her missionary outreach."[17] The Australian Church has experienced painfully inappropriate centralisation of authority in the difficulty met by both bishops and religious superiors in dismissing convicted paedophiles from the priesthood or their religious orders.

Synodality: A close relation of subsidiarity, synodality was linked to co-responsibility by Vatican II and is reinforced by the listening implicit in these principles. Pope Francis has observed:[18]
- the journey of synodality is the journey that God wants from his church in the third millennium
- a synodal church is a listening church, aware that listening is more than hearing – a reciprocal listening in which each one has something to learn
- how could we speak about the family without engaging families themselves, listening to their joys and their hopes, their sorrows and their anguish?

Archbishop Charles Scicluna, one of the planners for the Pope's Vatican meeting of presidents of the world's bishops' conferences meeting in February 2019, recently said: "We bishops need to adopt a synodal approach. We cannot do it alone in our community, we need also to empower the laypeople, the laity, in order to help us be good stewards."[19] The synodality of the Plenary Council should reflect good governance in action.

The Church's current governance is dysfunctional as exposed by crises in Australia and universally, and demonstrated through autocracy and secrecy, a lack of both accountability and inclusion. The Church is failing to meet the expectations of Jesus' teachings, the teaching of Vatican II, or best human practice, thus compromising decision-making and performance. Poor governance has led to grave errors in the exercise of authority, shown conclusively by the scandal of clerical child sexual abuse, particularly the institutional support for protection of paedophiles at the expense of children.

> ... Poor governance has led to grave errors in the exercise of authority, shown conclusively by the scandal of clerical child sexual abuse, particularly the institutional support for protection of paedophiles at the expense of children ...

There can be no doubt about the institutional culpability of the Church in light of the Royal Commission's report.[19b] The question of individual culpability of particular bishops raises matters for individual judgment, but the institutional culpability has been unquestionably determined.

The Royal Commission concluded that the Church, in its anxiety to preserve its reputation, power and wealth, protected paedophile priests and religious from civil prosecution, minimised the significance of such abuse to the governance of the institution, and resisted stoutly efforts of victims to seek redress. Such responses by the Church to a scandal which is comparable to the well-chronicled and grotesque Reformation-era abuses, reflect institutional self-service and self-protection rather than the service of the vulnerable. Any analysis of the moral paralysis which underlies this response reveals dysfunctional modes of governance.

Resistance to calls to reform the Church's governance on the grounds of divinely guaranteed indefectibility of its hierarchy must be recognised as presumptuous. An historical Church, as *Lumen*

Gentium proclaims it to be[20], is one whose mission in every respect including its governance practices is bound by the conditions of life in this world. God expects us to be accountable for our behaviour and to use our human gifts fully in doing all God's work, particularly the work of God's Church.

Reform of the Church's governance is urgent, both in Australia and universally, a situation established beyond doubt by the Royal Commission. We **recommend** that the Plenary Council should commit to necessary reforms in Australia and advise the Holy See of the need for urgent reform universally, including a range of changes to Canon Law.

3.4 The Royal Commission and governance

The evidence and findings of the Royal Commission into Institutional Responses to Child Sexual Abuse have exposed an autocratic system of governance in the Church at odds with a community based on the values of Jesus; a leadership obsessed with its status more than its mission, with a clericalist culture based on the unquestioned and exclusive authority of male celibates. Those leaders are increasingly elderly, often inadequately formed for leadership roles, and commonly showing little respect for the views of an informed and articulate faithful.

The Royal Commission found bishops, authorized to govern with sacred power, who did not exercise their duty of care for the Church's own children, and who, even when knowing that innocent children were being sexually abused, did not protect them. It would seem from the Report of the Royal Commission that many bishops had a distorted understanding of the Church's mission, trusted unaccountable and autocratic Church structures rather than the words of Jesus and the call of the Spirit, and relied on a governance regime so unfit for purpose that they failed to deal with the crisis and address its root causes.

In the end, instead of protecting the children, the institutional Church chose to protect the abusers, cover-up their crimes, work to safeguard the reputation of the institution, and show little or no compassion or justice to the children and their families. It was a failure of monumental proportions.

On the specific issue of governance, the Royal Commission's Recommendation 16.7 stated that:

> The Australian Catholic Bishops Conference should conduct a national review of the governance and management structures of dioceses and parishes, including in relation to issues of transparency, accountability, consultation and the participation of lay men and women. This review should draw from the approaches to governance of Catholic health, community services and education agencies.

This key recommendation was strongly endorsed by the ACBC's highly regarded Truth Justice and Healing Council (TJHC), which drew the ACBC's attention to the Royal Commission's findings that:

- the powers of governance held by individual diocesan bishops and provincials are not subject to adequate checks and balances;
- diocesan bishops have not been sufficiently accountable and there has been no requirement for their decisions to be made transparent or subject to due process.

The TJHC described the Royal Commission's findings as "damning of the Church's decision-making and accountability" and concluded that "the case for an independent review along the lines recommended by the Commission is compelling."[21] The Council advised the ACBC that the review "should be progressed as a matter of urgency and within a broader assessment of the effectiveness of governance and lay participation generally in the Church."

> ... The Council advised the ACBC that the review "should be progressed as a matter of urgency and within a broader assessment of the effectiveness of governance and lay participation generally in the Church." ...

The TJHC specifically recommended that:

- the ACBC delegate the conduct of the review to the ACBC's Implementation Advisory Group to establish the terms of reference in accordance with the framework of analysis used by the Royal Commission;
- the review team should include both corporate and canon law experts, plus a recognised authority on ecclesiology;

- an extensive consultation process be conducted; and
- the review be completed by mid-2019 with results made public during the lead up to the Plenary Council.

The ACBC and Catholic Religious Australia effectively rejected that considered advice of their own Truth Justice and Healing Council, including their call for urgent action. Rather, the bishops commissioned from their Implementation Advisory Group, without timelines, some alternative and preliminary advice:

- regarding the kind of review that might best fulfil the intentions of the Recommendation in light both of Catholic ecclesiology and approaches to:
- the governance of Church agencies;
- processes of consultation with experts to shape the review;
- the terms of reference;
- potential reviewers; and
- an achievable timeline, mindful of the extent of the task which would engage 28 Latin Rite dioceses, 5 Eastern Rite dioceses/eparchies, 2 ordinariates and 1 personal prelature, comprised of 1394 parishes throughout Australia.

The ACBC essentially set aside the TJHC's recommendation and ignored its perceptive identification of the need for "a broader assessment of the effectiveness of governance and lay participation generally in the Church".

The ACBC misleadingly described its response to this key recommendation of the Royal Commission as "accepted in principle", while deferring and modifying its consideration. Through that response, the ACBC has denied the Plenary Council the benefit of considered advice on this critical issue of the governance of dioceses and parishes.

It would seem that the Australian bishops do not recognise the imperative for review of the governance of their dioceses and parishes. We **recommend** that the ACBC immediately expedite implementation of the Royal Commission's Recommendation 16.7 with results made public during the lead up to the Plenary Council.[22]

3.5 The culture of clericalism

Clericalism has been recently described as "an oligarchic and condescending system devoted to the preservation of its own power regardless of the price".[23]

The Royal Commission reported in detail on the culture of 'clericalism' which has corrupted church governance. Good governance goes beyond structure, power and rules to the culture of the hierarchy and even the faithful generally, their attributes and dispositions[24], both as individuals and as institution. The morality of both members and institution is seen both in their actions, and in the values, attributes and dispositions they bring to their work.

Ultimately, an organisation's leadership and culture will determine the efficacy of its governance, even with sound structures and practices in place. The prevailing culture of clericalism in the Catholic Church distorts its governance, already inadequate owing to autocratic, unaccountable and inadequate structures and practices. Pope Francis recently reiterated:

> I have said many times that a perversion of the church today is clericalism.[25]

Various secular authorities around the world have condemned clericalism in the Church, and the reports of the two recent Australian inquiries – the Victorian Parliamentary Inquiry into the Handling of Child Abuse by Religious and Other Organisations (2012-2013) and

... The morality of both members and institution is seen both in their actions, and in the values, attributes and dispositions they bring to their work ...

the Royal Commission into Institutional Responses to Child Sexual Abuse (2012-2017) – exposed the Church's eagerness to preserve its power and wealth, to protect abuser priests and religious for the sake of the Church's own reputation, to resist fair and just redress, and to deny the connection between the abuse and the Church's dysfunctional governance.

The toxic culture of clericalism is central to the Church's poor governance, which is further prejudiced by structures and practices, and particularly by the failure of leaders to be accountable and inclusive. Clericalism explains why bishops and other clerics were, and are, unwilling to have structures and systems in place which will make them accountable; for clericalism attributes supposedly superior personal qualities to the ordained and to office-holders acculturated into a mindset of personal superiority. Amongst other things, the notion of 'clericalism' implies that, merely by entering the clerical state, the cleric attains a divinely personal superiority entitling him (sic) to a higher institutional status and authority than non-clerics, consequent privilege within the Church and deference from non-clerics, and an *ex officio* presumption of greater holiness than non-clerics.[26]

> ...The toxic culture of clericalism is central to the Church's poor governance, which is further prejudiced by structures and practices, and particularly by the failure of leaders to be accountable and inclusive ...

The clericalist culture has also infected the non-ordained (laity), long educated into excessive deference to the ordained and unquestioning respect for their authority and teaching. Often this has led the laity to consider their own views, although often better informed by superior knowledge, skills and experience, to be inferior to the views of the ordained, simply because of their respect for the sacred office of the ordained.

Leadership drives culture, and the culture of the Church should reflect Christ-like values and morality in structures, practices and decision-making which promote living the Good News. Regrettably, the practices of the hierarchy do not accord with good governance and responsible leadership, concepts which are fundamental to the Church's divine mission. This reflects seminary training, clerical formation, and bishop selection which has inadequate regard for the responsible exercise of authority through leadership.

The dysfunctional culture of the Church rejects notions of leadership that detract in any way from the unfettered ability of its clerical leaders to exercise authority without consultation or accountability. This thinking seems to be based on a presumptuous faith that God is in the business of protecting Church leaders from error even when they fail to respect the best of human practices.

Bishops and clergy need to be in touch with the people of the Church in providing informed leadership, always responsible for applying Christian values to the issues facing society and ensuring that they have listened to the people of the Church.

The Church exists for one purpose only: to continue God's mission which Jesus gave it. A culture that detracts from this has to be rejected and eradicated. Clericalism puts a distance between the ordained and the non-ordained, and even magnifies it. Good governance does the opposite, and brings clergy and laity closer together and engaged in their common mission. Good bishops are not remote, but 'smell of the sheep'[27]. They make themselves accountable to their people, are open with them, are humble and are at their service. Good bishops listen and hear.

We **recommend** new structures and practices that facilitate engagement and transparency, and a more consultative and discriminating process for selecting bishops, for their appointment and re-appointment, and for ensuring their accountability to the people of God.

3.6 Women and church governance

Historically, in our wider society, women have been subjugated and dismissed as inferior to men. Educational, career and social opportunities have not paralleled those of men. While disparity remains in relation to gendered violence, human trafficking, and equal pay for equal work, there has been a paradigmatic shift to recognise the equality of women in recent decades.

It is now accepted that women have the right to the opportunities and pathways that have always been afforded to men. In modern times, the United Nations has declared all are born free and equal in dignity and rights.[28] In the spirit of Christ, the Church should be at the forefront of championing those rights and dismantling discrimination.

> ... women are not "qualified ... for the power of governance" (C. 129.1) because they cannot receive sacred orders that are deemed a prerequisite ...

Sadly, the Catholic Church is one of the last bastions of male domination. The subservience of women in the Catholic Church is apparent in the portrayal of women as mere 'handmaidens' and 'helpmates'; and is also apparent in customs, traditions and power structures. Put simply, women are not "qualified ... for the power of governance" (C. 129.1) because they cannot receive sacred orders that are deemed a prerequisite. In so doing, the magisterium has effectively institutionalised discrimination.

We categorically refute the widely promulgated view that the difference between women and men in the religious sphere "can be explained in large part by maternal duties".[29] The biological determinism implicit in this perspective is the very premise responsible for much of the historical discrimination against women. In contemporary society, women with and without children assume senior positions in industry and government, academia, and the professions, and there is no logical reason this should not occur in the Catholic Church as it does in other Christian traditions.

Male domination and misogyny should be foreign to the Church founded by Christ; indeed, the Church should lead the way in promoting the equality of women and men in every area of its mission and ministry, and banishing all forms of discrimination within its community.[30]

Mary McAleese observed that:

> paradoxically, it is the questioning voices of educated Catholic women which the Church hierarchy simply cannot cope with and scorns rather than engages in dialogue. The Church which regularly criticizes the secular world for its failure to deliver on human rights has almost no culture of critiquing itself. It has a hostility to internal criticism which fosters blinkered servility and which borders on institutional idolatry.[31]

Today's Church should look to Jesus as a model of how men can surround themselves with women (Luke 8, 2-3) exercising responsible roles.

The traditional notions of women as only nurturers must not be used as a rationale for excluding women from positions of leadership, and higher responsibilities. The exclusion of women from having a significant role in governance within the Church is an issue of justice and equality.[32] Unless women are included at the highest levels, good governance will not be possible.

There is a tendency to equate inclusion of women in the Church as resting solely with the case for the ordination of women priests. *Catholics for Renewal* asserts that this reductionist approach is an attempt to obfuscate core issues. The ordination of women is one of several ways the Church could ameliorate structural inequality. There are three tiers where the Church could redress the failure to include women in governance mechanisms, the first of which requires no change in canon law and could be implemented immediately:

i)   the appointment of women by the Pope to head a number of Vatican dicasteries (say 50%);

ii) the admission of women to the diaconate; and

iii) the ordination of women to the priesthood.

We **recommend** accordingly below.

In a comprehensive analysis of scripture, the Pontifical Biblical Commission found no theological evidence which would preclude women from being ordained as priests.[33] The Church's own tradition does not support the teaching that women are incapable of being validly ordained.

> ...The Church must scrutinise the signs of the times and see the recognition of women's rights throughout the entire secular world as a sign to the Church that it must revise this ban on women's ordination ...

The exclusion of women from the priesthood has no foundation in scripture; this is a man-made construct where patriarchy is assumed to be the unassailable 'norm', a view so blinkered it fails to give credence to any other perspective as the defining characteristic of a dominant hegemony. The Church must scrutinise the signs of the times and see the recognition of women's rights throughout the entire secular world as a sign to the Church that it must revise this ban on women's ordination.

It is imperative the Church redresses the inequality of women and the hypocrisy of institutionalised discrimination. Vatican II asserted that:

> with respect to the fundamental rights of the person, every type of discrimination, whether social or cultural, whether based on sex, race, colour, social condition, language or religion, is to be overcome and eradicated as contrary to God's intent.[34]

At this unprecedented juncture, the faithful expects the Church to catalyse change. We want to see the prevailing culture overhauled to become one which embraces diversity in decision-making, reflected meaningfully in governance structures as outlined above. In the meantime, the institutional Church's dysfunctional governance continues to suffer from the institutionalised disadvantage of single-sex control, an effective denial of the God-given benefits of gender balance in decision-making, ironically benefits that have been identified and harvested by the secular world. Exclusion of women from Church governance is an issue of both justice and good governance.

The force of the demand for equality from both women and men should be regarded as one of the most compelling signs of our own times. It goes to the heart of the Kingdom of God, to God's mission, and to the Good News. In neglecting the equality of women, we betray our mission as the expression in history of Christ's love for all.

3.7 Conclusion

The Australian Catholic Bishops Conference has focused on very necessary processes to protect children but has failed to grasp the contextual imperative to reform dysfunctional governance and culture. That dysfunctional governance and culture enabled the immoral decision-making that aggravated the scandal of clerical child sexual abuse, and that governance continues to subvert the Church's God-given mission. The Australian Church must implement without further delay the Royal Commission's recommendation for a national review of the governance and management structures of dioceses and parishes.

As recommended by the Truth Justice and Healing Council, that review should be conducted as a matter of urgency. Inertia should not be used as a tool of management. The review needs to be independent and conducted by persons who have established their objective credentials. The review must inform the Plenary Council, and also the Holy See, on the need for universal reform. The review cannot await the Plenary Council 2020/21, and the Plenary Council must not serve as an excuse for resisting the urgent responses required to the present governance crisis facing the Church.

… The Australian Catholic Bishops Conference has focused on very necessary processes to protect children but has failed to grasp the contextual imperative to reform dysfunctional governance and culture. That dysfunctional governance and culture enabled the immoral decision-making that aggravated the scandal of clerical child sexual abuse …

The Catholic Church can no longer sustain the defence offered in evidence to the Royal Commission, namely the discredited assertion that "the faults (exposed in the Commission's examination of clerical child sexual abuse) overwhelmingly have been more personal faults, personal failures, rather than structures"[35] – the 'few bad apples' defence. The dysfunctional governance of the Church is systemic.

In both canon law and common duty, all Catholics have a moral obligation as members of the faithful to accept responsibility for the state of their church's dysfunctional governance and to hold their leaders accountable. Good governance – accountability, transparency and inclusion – must replace the autocracy and associated clericalist culture that has been responsible for evil in the Church. We recommend accordingly below.

In August 2018, Pope Francis released across the world a personal response to the scandal of clerical child sexual abuse in the form of a letter 'To the People of God'[36], in which he asked for a profound transformation of hierarchical and priestly culture. He stated:

> It is impossible to think of a conversion of our activity as a Church that does not include the active participation of all the members of God's People.

Pope Francis' letter condemns as crimes, "the abuse of power and the abuse of conscience perpetrated by a significant number of clerics and consecrated persons" and calls for a "solidarity that summons us to fight all forms of corruption, especially spiritual corruption". Francis acknowledges and condemns the Church's pervasive culture of toxic clericalism. He acknowledges that the Church has "delayed in applying these actions and sanctions that are so necessary".

However, while acknowledging the presence of "filth", "pride", and "self-complacency" among the Church's leaders, Francis fails to identify steps that need to be taken to reform the governance structure and culture that have nurtured this evil. Many of the "actions and sanctions that are so necessary" were set out in the Royal Commission's final report of December 2017, in the form of recommendations that go far beyond the procedural changes for child safety with which the leaders of the Church seem preoccupied.

Procedures and practices will be of limited effect if not reinforced by Church law, leadership, structures and culture. Changes to procedures and practices without reformed governance are little more than a cynical attempt to avoid accountability.[37]

Early in his pontificate, Pope Francis offered in his first apostolic exhortation the prospect of reform, consistent with the needs identified in this paper, in speaking of his 'dream' of:

> a missionary impulse capable of transforming everything, so that the Church's customs, ways of doing things, times and schedules, language and structures can be suitably channelled for the evangelisation of today's world rather than for her self-preservation.[38]

Six years on, little change has been effected but that need for transforming the church's customs and ways of doing things – its governance – has been strikingly confirmed. Significant changes in the Church will need to occur quickly after the conclusion of the Plenary Council if our bishops are to keep faith with the people of God.

... Many of the proposals we recommend below could be adopted by decision of the ACBC to apply in Australia forthwith, to correct existing failures immediately ...

Many of the proposals we recommend below could be adopted by decision of the ACBC to apply in Australia forthwith, to correct existing failures immediately. The Plenary Council would then be in a better position to consider more complex matters raised by the Australian faithful.

Our proposals lay a structural foundation for accountability and inclusion, necessarily accompanied by transparency, subsidiarity, co-responsibility, and synodality in the governance of the church, and for reform of the culture of clericalism. Such structural and cultural change requires urgent leadership from the most senior levels.

3.8 Recommendations

Our recommendations on Church Governance comprise three groups:

A – those requiring **immediate implementation pre-Council**

B – those requiring **determination by the Plenary Council**

C – those outside the direct competence of the Plenary Council requiring referral by the Council to the Holy See:

A Recommendations requiring immediate implementation pre-Council;

Recommendation 3.1:

> that each diocesan bishop, prior to the first session of the Council, convene a diocesan synod or assembly or other means of engagement and dialogue to ascertain the *sensus fidei* of the faithful in his care; and that these synods/assemblies be accepted as an integral part of preparing the Plenary Council agenda. At this diocesan synod/assembly, the diocesan bishop should seek guidance on how to select the non-religious lay faithful who will represent the diocese at the Plenary Council 2020/21.[39]

Recommendation 3.2:

> that the ACBC immediately expedite implementation of the Royal Commission's Recommendation 16.7 that the ACBC conduct a national review of the governance and management structures of dioceses and parishes with results to be made public during the lead up to the Plenary Council. This review should

valuably inform considerations of the Plenary Council and ensure a more thorough appreciation of these critical governance issues.

B Recommendations requiring determination by the Plenary Council:

Recommendation 3.3:

that the Plenary Council legislate that each diocesan bishop must establish a diocesan pastoral council, and that its membership is to be gender balanced and reflect the diversity of the faithful in the diocese. Vatican II intended that diocesan pastoral councils support and guide bishops in their pastoral ministry. The International Theological Commission has stated that "the diocesan pastoral council proposes itself as the permanent structure most favourable to the implementation of synodality in the particular church."[40] The selection process for members of this council should not only follow the canonical guidelines (C. 512) but be based on merit and independence, comprising members of the faithful committed to "carry forward the work of Christ himself under the lead of the befriending Spirit".[41]

Recommendation 3.4:

that the Plenary Council legislate that each parish priest must establish a parish pastoral council, and that its membership is to include men and women, and to attempt to represent the diversity of the faithful in the parish.

Recommendation 3.5:

that the Plenary Council legislate that at least once every five years, each diocesan bishop must convene a diocesan synod, recognising that a diocesan synod is the "instrument 'par excellence' for assisting the bishop to order his diocese", representing "the summit of diocesan participation structures", and occupying "a place of primary importance."[42] Moreover, when its membership reflects the diversity of vocations, ministries, charisms, skills, social backgrounds and geographical origins of the faithful within the diocese, it is an 'event of grace'. At least half those called to be synod members should be non-religious lay men and women balanced in their numbers.[43]

Recommendation 3.6:

that the Plenary Council legislate that each diocesan bishop convene a diocesan assembly between diocesan synods as an alternative less restrictive means of engaging the faithful. The International Theological Commission states that a diocesan assembly expresses and promotes communion and co-responsibility and contributes to the planning of integrated pastoral care and its evaluation. As such, a diocesan assembly is important to the synodal journey of a particular church and can serve as the ordinary preparation for a diocesan synod and also a plenary council.[44]

Recommendation 3.7:

that the Plenary Council legislate that a plenary council must be convened by the Australian Episcopal Conference at least once every fifteen years, and that at least one third of those to be called are non-religious laypersons with gender equality.

Recommendation 3.8:

that the Plenary Council legislate that each diocesan bishop be required to prepare in a synodal manner, with the clergy and laity of his diocese, a diocesan pastoral plan, to cover a forward period of no less than 5 years. The legislation should require regular reviews and updating before it expires. The pastoral plan must be circulated widely and online as a public document.

Recommendation 3.9:

that the Plenary Council legislate that each diocesan bishop be required to prepare and publish an annual report on the state of his diocese, and that it include information on:

i)   the implementation of the diocesan pastoral plan;

ii)   membership of the diocesan pastoral council and presbyteral council;

iii) Catholic education (primary, secondary, tertiary);

iv)   Mass attendance and reception of the sacraments;

v)   Rite of Christian Initiation of Adults (RCIA);

vi)   health, aged care and welfare activities;

vii) the financial situation (Profit & Loss Statement, Balance Sheet) of the diocese;

viii) state of the clergy and seminarians;

ix)   employees of the diocese;

x)   bishop's personal appraisal of the pastoral and other challenges/risks currently being faced;

xi)   decisions made or proposals being considered to address them; and

xii) significant achievements and developments.

Recommendation 3.10:

that the Plenary Council legislate that each parish priest, in consultation with his parish pastoral and financial councils, is to prepare and publish an annual report on the pastoral and financial state of the parish.

Recommendation 3.11:

that the Plenary Council legislate that bishops and presbyters are to be held accountable for their pastoral, administrative and financial decisions.

Recommendation 3.12:

that the Plenary Council develop a more suitable, inclusive and open process for the selection of bishops in Australia, having regard to Recommendations 4.9 – 4.13 below. Explicit in the qualities required of the candidate should be his qualifications and skills to lead and to govern. The process for selection should be transparent and public, with due regard for necessary confidentiality.[45]

Recommendation 3.13:

that the Plenary Council develop a professional formation program for bishops and parish pastors to ensure that they have the necessary skills for:

i) leadership based on Christian values;

ii) listening to the *sensus fidei fidelium*;

iii) commitment to gender equality; and

iv) an understanding of Australian standards of best practice for good governance.

Recommendation 3.14:

that the Plenary Council commit to gender balance in the leadership of the Church, starting with women with appropriate skills and qualifications being appointed to senior executive positions in all dioceses.

C Recommendations outside the direct competence of the Plenary Council requiring referral by the Council to the Holy See

Recommendation 3.15:

that the 1983 *Code of Canon Law* be amended to:

i) Repeal Canon 129;

ii) require the Quinquennial Report, prepared by each diocesan bishop on the state of the diocese entrusted to him (C. 399), to include information necessary to establish compliance with best-practice standards of accountability, transparency and inclusion;

iii) allow an unredacted copy of each Quinquennial Report to be kept in the secret archives of the diocese, with access to legitimate researchers after say 20 years;

iv) ensure that any bishop accused of a failure in his governance of the diocese entrusted to him, be accorded a fair trial with due process; namely, with notification of the charges made against him, with access to the names of his accusers and the details of their accusations, with access to legal counsel, and with the opportunity to question his accusers under oath in an official court of law;

v) ensure that the pontifical secret does not prevent reporting to the civil authorities of child sexual abusers at large, regardless of whether there are mandatory criminal reporting laws in the State concerned; and

vi) require Church authorities to report knowledge of child sexual abusers at large regardless of whether there are mandatory criminal reporting laws in the State concerned (with exemptions for jurisdictions where human rights are at risk).

Recommendation 3.16:

that the Holy See commit to gender balance in the leadership of the Church at all levels.

Recommendation 3.17:

that the Holy See recognise the equality of women by appointing suitable and competent women as the prefect and secretary of a number of dicasteries of the Holy See (say half of all dicasteries).

Recommendation 3.18:

that the Holy See be asked to take note of the *sensus fidei fidelium* in Australia with regard to the ordination of women to the priesthood and to the diaconate; and that it review the Church's position regarding women and the sacrament of Holy Orders, commencing with the Order of Diaconate.

Recommendation 3.19:

that the Holy See be asked to ensure regular turnover of clerical staff in its various dicasteries; that those appointed be lay and clerical persons selected from across the world; and that they be persons who have 'the smell of the sheep'[46] and are fully committed to accountability to Christ's mission, who actively seek to be informed by the *sensus fidei fidelium*, and who have a lively culture of pastoral awareness and sensitivity.[47]

Recommendation 3.20:

that the Holy See be asked to remove the requirement of compulsory celibacy for diocesan priests,[48] noting that:

i) married priests currently minister in Australia;

ii) the compulsory nature of the celibacy discipline denies the faithful of ministers they need; and

iii) it blights the ministry of some priests who do not have the gift of celibacy.

Recommendation 3.21:

that the Holy See consider changes to the period of appointment and tenure of bishops in Australia[49] which would include:

i) the introduction of initial appointments by the Bishop of Rome for a 5-year period for all diocesan and titular bishops;

ii) the introduction of re-appointments for 5-year periods, subject to the individual bishop satisfying a review and assessment of his pastoral ministry and governance by the priests and faithful of his diocese;

iii) a transparent and accountable review and assessment process which respects the confidentiality of the participants and the reputation of the bishop;[50]

iv) the review and assessment process to be initiated and conducted by the Apostolic Nuncio;

v) the compiled report on the assessment to be sent to the Holy See by the Apostolic Nuncio; and

vi) the individual bishop subject to review to be given a copy of the report sent to the Holy See.

Some discussion questions:

- *The People of God are entitled to expect, and good decision-making demands, that there be structures and practices at every level of their church for expressing their opinions and informing decision-making processes, and for holding decision-makers accountable.* Discuss this statement. Is it your experience? (3.3)

- In relation to the causes of clerical sexual abuse, is it enough for the church to develop and implement child-safe policies and procedures? Why? (3.4)

- What are the implications for not including women in decision-making processes and leadership positions within the church? (3.6)

- Pope Francis is trying to bring about a *synodal* church. From reading this document why is *synodality* so important for us? (3.3)

- Does your diocese have a *Diocesan Pastoral Council*? If so, are you aware of its current work and composition? How might a well-functioning DPC promote diocesan mission? (3.2-3)

Notes

1   Joint Committee of Public Accounts and Audit, *Report 372, Corporate Governance and Accountability Arrangements for Commonwealth Government Business Enterprises*, (Canberra, Canprint, 1999), p. 7.

2   Pope Pius XI, *Quadragesimo Anno*,1931, n. 79

3   Tertullian, *Apologeticus, ch 39.*

4   Church Administration Handbook, St Paul's, Canberra, 2011, p. 50

5   Matt 28:18

6   Matt 16:19

7   Vatican II, *Lumen Gentium (Dogmatic Constitution on the Church),* 1965, n. 10

8   Vatican II, *Lumen Gentium,* n. 21

9   *The Code of Canon Law in English Translation,* prepared by The Canon Law Society of Great Britain and Ireland in association with The Canon Law Society of Australia and New Zealand and The Canadian Canon Law Society, 1983, Collins Liturgical, Sydney

10 Vatican II, *Christus Dominus,* 28 October 1965, n. 36

11 Tapsell, K. (2019). *The Australian Church Response to the Royal Commission Final Report on the Pontifical Secret* in Pearls and Irritations. Retrieved from https://johnmenadue.com/kieran-tapsell-the-australian-church-response-to-the-royal-commission-final-report-on-the-pontifical-secret/

12 Subsequent to this submission's lodgement, Pope Francis promulgated a *motu proprio* (an Apostolic Letter) entitled *Vos estis lux mundi* ('You are the light of the world') on 9 May 2019 which established new procedural rules to combat sexual abuse and purportedly to ensure that bishops and religious superiors are held accountable for their actions. The rules seem regrettably limited in their likely effect – see Keiran Tapsell, *Pope Francis and the Closed Door Syndrome* in Pearls and Irritations, 21 May 2019, included in Supplements (3) and retrieved from https://johnmenadue.com/kieran-tapsell-pope-francis-and-the-closed-door-syndrome/

13 Vatican II, *Lumen Gentium,* n. 37

14 International Theological Commission, *Synodality in the Life and Mission of the Church* Internazionale, CT 2018, *La Sinodalità Nella Vita e Nella Missione Della Chiesa,* Rome.

15 Pope Francis, *Evangelii Gaudium,* n. 33

16 *Declaration on Christian Education,* n. 3; *Gaudium et Spes (Pastoral Constitution on the Church in the Modern World,* 1965, n. 86

17 Pope Francis, *Evangelii Gaudium,* 24 Nov. 2013, n. 32

18 *Address of His Holiness Pope Francis.* (October 2015) Ceremony Commemorating the 50th Anniversary of the Institution of the Synod of Bishops. Retrieved from *http://w2.vatican.va/content/francesco/en/speeches/2015/october/documents/papa-francesco_20151017_50-anniversario-sinodo.html*

19 Sweetser, T. P. (2019) "What do U.S. Catholics think about Pope Francis and the sexual abuse crisis? " in *America Magazine.* Retrieved from https://www.americamagazine.org/faith/2019/01/03/what-do-us-catholics-think-about-pope-francis-and-sexual-abuse-crisis?utm_source=Newsletters&utm_campaign=d2d2b6fcd7-DAILY_CAMPAIGN_2019_1_3&utm_medium=email&utm_term=0_0fe8ed70be-d2d2b6fcd7-58556297

19b The institutional Church's dysfunctional governance is at last beginning to be acknowledged publicly by some Church leaders. Dr Hans Zollner SJ, recently stated that "the Church as an institution is in question, by the state and by the People of God." The Record, 27 June 2019, reported on a talk to staff of the Archdiocese of Perth at the Newman Sienna Centre, Doubleview, on Monday 24 June, by Dr Zollner, arguably the major advisor in the Vatican on clerical child sexual abuse, a member of the Vatican's Pontifical Commission for the Protection of Minors, consultor to the Congregation for the Clergy, President of the Centre for Child Protection, and Vice Rector of Pontifical Gregorian University in Rome. https://www.therecord.com.au/news/local/exclusive-vatican-expert-gives-insight-into-abuse-crises/ retrieved 6 June 2019

20 Vatican II, *Lumen Gentium*, n. 1 : "… the Church is in Christ like a sacrament or as a sign and instrument both of a very closely knit union with God and of the unity of the whole human race"; and n. 9: "While it transcends all limits of time and confines of race, the Church is destined to extend to all regions of the earth and so enters into the history of mankind."

21 Truth Justice and Healing Council. (2018) *The Royal Commission's recommendations, and responses from the Truth Justice and Healing Council*. p. 198. Retrieved from http://www.tjhcouncil.org.au/img/pdf/TJHC-Volume-2.pdf

22 Subsequent to this submission's lodgement, the ACBC and CRA announced 1 May 2009 the establishment of a panel of experts to conduct a national review of the governance and management structures of Catholic dioceses and parishes, including in relation to issues of transparency, accountability, consultation and lay participation as "another step in our serious response to the Royal Commission and will help establish a way forward for the Church into the future". The panel has been asked for an interim report by the end of October and a final report in the first half of 2020. This initiative is welcomed and seemingly in accord with our recommendation (see 3.2 below). The ACBC/CRA media release is at Supplements (2) and may be accessed directly at: https://www.catholic.org.au/acbc-media/media-centre/media-releases-new/2189-respected-leaders-named-to-conduct-church-governance-review/file)

23 Martel, F. (2019) *In The Closet Of The Vatican: Power, Homosexuality, Hypocrisy*, Bloomsbury Continuum; 2019 quoted in NCR, Feb 21, 2019, *Duplicity, hypocrisy of the prelates exposed in Martel's 'Closet' book* by Cozzens, D. Retrieved from https://www.ncronline.org/news/opinion/duplicity-hypocrisy-prelates-exposed-martels-closet-book?clickSource=email

24 Charles E. Curran, *Directions in Fundamental Moral Theology* (Dublin: Gill & Macmillan,1986), 63

25 Faggioli, Massimo, *From Collegiality to Synodality* - Pope Francis's Post-Vatican II Reform, Commonweal, 23 November 2018

26 This sentence provides additional comment on clericalism not included in the submission as lodged.

27 Glatz, C. (2013) *Pope Francis: Priests should be "Shepherds living with the smell of the sheep"*, The Catholic Telegraph. Retrieved from https://www.thecatholictelegraph.com/pope-francis-priests-should-be-shepherds-living-with-the-smell-of-the-sheep/13439

28 Universal Declaration of Human Rights (1948) Article 1.

29 Hauke, M., *Women in the Priesthood? A Systematic Analysis in the Light of the Order of Creation and Redemption*, San Francisco, Ignatius Press, 1986, p. 209

30 Vatican II, Gaudium et Spes, n. 29

31 Mary McAleese, International Women's Day Address, Rome, 8 March 2018.

32 Some tentative, possibly token, steps have been taken in a number of dioceses and in the Holy See towards greater involvement of women in Church governance, cf: Christopher Lamb, "Pope appoints four women to top Synod jobs" in *The Tablet*, 24 May 2019. Retrieved from https://www.thetablet.co.uk/author/15/christopher-lamb

33 Swidler, A. & Swidler, L. (eds.) *Women Priests*, Paulist Press, 1977, pp. 338-346.

34 Vatican II, *Gaudium et Spes*, n. 29

35 Royal Commission into Institutional Responses to Child Sexual Abuse, Transcript of G Pell, Case Studies 28 and 35, 29 February 2016 at 16186:21-28

36 His Holiness Pope Francis. (Aug 2018). *Letter to the People of God*. Retrieved from https://www.vaticannews.va/en/pope/news/2018-08/pope-francis-letter-people-of-god-sexual-abuse.html

37 Subsequent to the lodgement of Plenary Council submissions, Catholic Professional Standards Limited published the National Catholic Safeguarding Standards, 30 May 2019. Retrieved from https://www.cpsltd.org.au/safe-church/national-catholic-safeguarding-standards/ Retrieved from

38 Pope Francis. *Evangelii Gaudium – Apostolic Exhortation on the Proclamation of the Gospel in Today's World*. (Rome: Vatican/St Paul's Publications, 2013), 28

39 Cf. Also, our Recommendation 5.8

40 International Theological Commission. (2018) *Synodality and the Mission of the Church*, n. 81. Retrieved from http://www.vatican.va/roman_curia/congregations/cfaith/cti_documents/rc_cti_20180302_sinodalita_en.html

41 Vatican II, *Gaudium et Spes*, n. 3

42 *Successores Apostolorum*, n. 67; n. 166

43 Cf. *Instruction on Diocesan Synods*, 1997

44 International Theological Commission, *Synodality and the Mission of the Church*, Rome, 2018, n.82

45 Cf. Also, our Recommendations 2.7 and 4.9-4.13

46 Glatz, C. (2013) *Pope Francis: Priests should be "Shepherds living with the smell of the sheep"*, The Catholic Telegraph. Retrieved from https://www.thecatholictelegraph.com/pope-francis-priests-should-be-shepherds-living-with-the-smell-of-the-sheep/13439

47 *ibidem*

48 Note: Australia's National Council of Priests recently called for optional celibacy and married priests, and planned to take the issues to the Vatican – see Joanne McCarthy *We live in joyful hope: Plan to allow married Catholic priests,* Sydney Morning Herald, 16 September 2018. Retrieved from https://www.smh.com.au/national/we-live-in-joyful-hope-plan-to-allow-married-catholic-priests-20180916-p5042e.html

49 Cf. Recommendation 3.12 for a more inclusive and open process for the selection of bishops in Australia, and the importance of qualifications and skills to lead and to govern.

50 Cf. Also, our Recommendations 3.3-3.1

PART 4

PASTORAL LEADERSHIP AND PARISH MINISTRY

As Pope Francis reminded us, we are living in a change of era, not just an era of change, and we need to listen attentively to the Holy Spirit whispering in the hearts of all believers and seekers. The whole Church is called to be a sacrament of God walking with us, reflecting God's total commitment to human wellbeing, in this world and the next. 'Getting back on mission' offers a practical vision of how to rebuild our church, recognising the crises we face, and urging us to adapt our pastoral responses and structures so we are more truly Good News for the world.

- Bruce Duncan CSsR, founding Director of the Yarra Institute for Religion and Social Policy and of Social Policy Connections, lecturer in history and social justice at Yarra Theological Union.

4.1 The sacraments and signs of the times

Vatican II stated that "the human race has passed from a rather static concept of reality to a more dynamic, evolutionary one [and] that in consequence there has arisen a new set of problems, a series as important as can be, calling for new efforts at analysis and synthesis".[1] These new efforts at analysis and synthesis have to be directed at the sacraments as to other areas of belief, and re-interpreted in accord with the 'signs of the times' if their full significance is to be made intelligible to the People of God in every time and place.[2] Any new synthesis also has to see the sacraments as signs of God's continuing saving action in human history, made visible to Christ's faithful at critical points in their lives: moments of intense encounter with the action of God drawing them as individuals and as part of the human race to their destiny as "my sons and daughters".[3] The sacraments equip Christians to see the remnants of the original chaos in the world, and to push back the boundaries of that chaos by their life in Christ.

... signs of God's continuing saving action in human history, made visible to Christ's faithful at critical points in their lives ...

The significance of the sacraments as 'signs' is that they provide divinely guaranteed effectiveness, which will only be understood when it is realised that the sacraments are, by the power of the Word of God uttered by the minister, God's saving action in the process of creative evolution and human history. They are not mere rituals.

In a recent (2018) survey[4] of Catholic bishops and priests in Australia, 85% said that "conducting worship and administering the sacraments" was by far their most important active role,[5] with their next most important roles being "administering the work of the local church" (43%) and "teaching people about the Christian faith" (41%).

However, in a clear sign of mismatch, the same Catholic pastors said that they believed they were spending more time and effort than they should on "conducting worship and administering the sacraments" and that they would be better serving the people in their care by putting more time and effort into "teaching the faith" and "offering prayer and being a spiritual role model".

Clearly, in relation to sacramental ministry there are problems: some priests and faithful see the power of the sacraments as flowing from some miraculous power of the priest, and some priests also experience frustration in their ministry because they see it as consisting largely in ritual performances. Resolution of these problems will lie in better education, and we therefore **recommend** that the Plenary Council review the role of the ministers of the sacraments to ensure that the priorities of their ministry reflect a sound understanding of the relationship between Word, sacrament and ministry.

4.2 The Sacraments of Initiation: Baptism, Confirmation, Eucharist

Baptism, Confirmation and Eucharist are the three interrelated sacraments of initiation. All three are required for full Christian initiation (C. 842).

Baptism is the gateway to the sacraments. Through baptism, freely accepted, a person is freed from sin, reborn as a child of God, configured to Christ and incorporated into the community of the Church. Baptism also confers rights and responsibilities (cf. Part 2) but, above all, the virtues of faith, hope and charity, which equip the Christian for ecclesial life and call on them to live the faith, to trust in God, and to express the power of the life born of hope and love.[6]

Confirmation strengthens the baptised person and obliges them to be a witness of Christ by word and deed and to defend the faith. It enriches the baptised person by the gift of the Spirit and binds that person more perfectly to the Church (C. 879).

The Eucharist is the "most august sacrament" through which the Church continually grows and lives. The Eucharistic sacrifice is the summit and source of all worship and Christian life. It signifies and makes real the unity of the People of God and brings about the building up of the body of Christ. It is the sacrament of the Church's *communio*. All the other sacraments and all the works of the apostolate are connected to the Eucharist and ordered to it (C. 879). If the Eucharist is ceasing to attract participants, or even to hold those initiated to full membership of the Church, this is a sign that the present quality of our community life of faith, hope and love is failing to radiate the love of God. The empirical evidence (Table 4.1) indicates some of these failings.

In Australia over the last 16 years the reception of the sacraments of initiation has not kept pace with the growth (+5.8%) of the Catholic population. In fact, there has been a noticeable downturn in baptisms of infants and children under the age of 7 years (-17.1%), in baptisms for persons aged over 7 years (-4.1%), in confirmations (-11.8%), and in first communions (16.9%). These signs of the times cannot be ignored if God's mission is to be fulfilled.

FIGURE 4.1: AUSTRALIAN CATHOLIC POPULATION AND REGULAR MASS ATTENDERS: 1947-2016

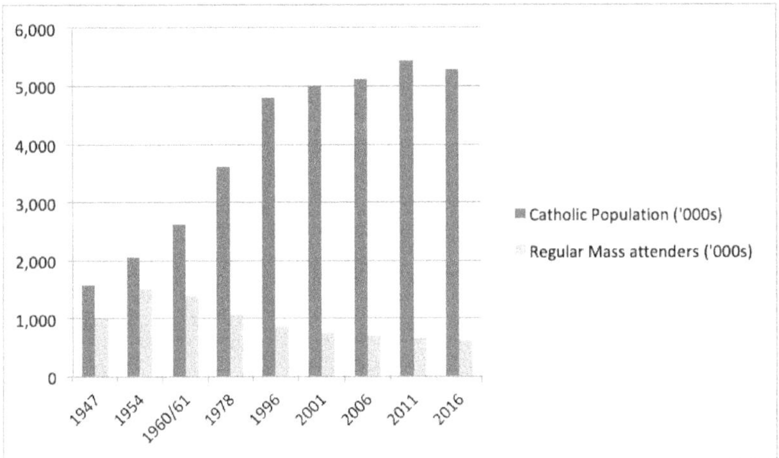

Sources: ABS Census Data, 1961, 1996, 2001, 2006; *Catholic Church Life Survey* 1996 and 2001; *National Church Life Survey* 2001 and 2006; *National Count of Attendance 2006*; CROPP, 1978; Mol, 1985; O'Farrell, p. 428, Gallup Polls, 1947, 1960, 1976 (Note: Gallup Poll rates have tended to be higher than actual attendance rates); Robert Dixon, Stephen Reid and Marilyn Chee, *Mass Attendance in Australia: A Critical Moment*, ACBC, 2013, cf. Table 3, page 7. Retrieved from https://ncpr.catholic.org.au/national-count-of-attendance/; and ACBC, NCPR, *2016 National Count of Attendance − National Summary. Retrieved from* https://ncpr.catholic.org.au/wp-content/uploads/2019/04/Pastoral-Research-Online-Edition-44-April-2019.pdf

It also has to be pointed out that many of the 4,444 claimants of sexual abuse by priests in Catholic institutions were children who had been baptised by their abusers, and that the bishops who had confirmed them were the bishops who denied them justice and protected their abuser priests. Such a perversion of the life that the sacrament of Confirmation is meant to signify has led to a corresponding perversion of its intended effect: rather than functioning as a sacrament of initiation to the Christian community, it is now being referred to as "the sacrament of departure", for many young people depart or disaffiliate from the Church shortly after receiving this sacrament.

In 1954, 74% of all Australian Catholics (1.53 million) regularly participated in the Eucharistic celebration. Since then, fewer and fewer have been regularly participating, and results from the 2016 National Attendance Count show a new low figure (Figure 4.1).

The *2016 National Count of Attendance7* data, published in April 2019 (Table 4.2), show that the total number of average regular weekly Mass attenders fell from 662,376 (12.2% of all Catholics) in 2011 to 623,356 (11.8% of all Catholics) in 2016, a decrease of 39,020 attenders (-5.9 %).

The 2016 National Count of Attendance, which also shows average total weekly attendance numbers and rates for individual dioceses (Table 4.2), indicates that the rate of attendance in 17 territorial dioceses was less than 10%, and in 7 dioceses was less than 8%: Cairns (7.0%), Geraldton (7.1%), Hobart (6.7%), Maitland-Newcastle (6.8%), Rockhampton (7.5%), Townsville (7.0%), and Wilcannia-Forbes (7.8%). Between 2006 and 2016 attendance numbers declined in 24 of the 28 territorial dioceses, in some quite significantly: Adelaide (-17%), Armidale (-25%), Ballarat (-31%), Bathurst (-32%), Brisbane (-19%), Broken Bay (-23%), Canberra & Goulburn (-22%), Hobart (-24%), Lismore (-28%), Maitland-Newcastle (-33%), Port Pirie (-24%), Rockhampton (-22%), Sandhurst (-25%), Toowoomba (-36%), Wagga Wagga (-23%), Wilcannia-Forbes (-35%), and Wollongong (-19%). The most substantial numerical declines since 2006 were in the major cities of Adelaide (-5,745), Brisbane (-13,384), Melbourne (-16,789), and Sydney (-9,945). In only 4 dioceses since 2006 were there improvements in attendance rates: Bunbury (+16%), Darwin (+45%), Perth (+7%), and Sale (+1%), with only Darwin (+ 1,854) and Perth (+ 3,670) showing significant numerical increases.

The reasons why so many Catholics have stopped attending Mass was researched by the ACBC Pastoral Projects Office (PPO) in 2007,[8] which found there was no single definitive reason, but a combination of factors: some Church-centred, some participant centred, and often both intertwined. It concluded that there are actions that the Church could take which would reduce the likelihood of current Mass attenders joining the ranks of those who have stopped attending, and even increase the chances of some returning. But if no action were taken, current Mass attenders would likely follow the path of those who had already disappeared.[9]

Not to be underestimated as a further reason why so many Catholics have ceased to attend Mass has to be the impact of the revelations by the Royal Commission and the Victorian Parliamentary Inquiry concerning clerical child sexual abuse and the cover-up of that abuse by some bishops.

We **recommend** that the Plenary Council thoroughly examine the empirical evidence of the reception of the sacraments to: i) identify the failures in the life of the community to which it attests; and ii) address the causes of and remedies for those failures.

We **recommend** that the Plenary Council re-examine the pastoral strategies recommended by the ACBC Pastoral Projects Office in 2007 and legislate for appropriate action at diocesan and parish level.

We **recommend** that all adult catechumens, before being baptised, be given a copy of the proposed Charter of Rights and Duties for Christ's Faithful in Australia and have it explained to them.

We **recommend** that bishops who confer the sacrament of Confirmation be more mindful of the gifts of the Spirit received in the sacrament, particularly wisdom, knowledge and understanding, and understand that they have a duty to respect those gifts in the confirmed and to listen to what Christ's faithful have to say.

4.3 Sacrament of Penance or Reconciliation

The sacrament of Penance has to be understood in the evolutionary perspective embraced by Vatican II and interpreted in accord with the signs of the times.

Throughout space, time and human history there has been a divinely driven process of evolution wherein God, in an overflow of Trinitarian love, draws order out of original chaos.[10] In that process the power of God's love draws all Creation towards ultimate perfection. To Israel and Christ's faithful, God's saving action by calling God's People to be a sign of that destiny, the Kingdom of God.

> For the creation waits with eager longing for the revealing of the children of God; for the creation was subjected to futility, not of its own will but by the will of the one who subjected it, in hope that the creation itself will be set free from its bondage to decay and will obtain the freedom of the glory of the children of God. We know that the whole creation has been groaning in labour pains until now; and not only the creation, but we ourselves, who have the first fruits of the Spirit, groan inwardly while we wait for adoption, the redemption of our bodies.[11]

Evolution takes time. In nature, chance determines the outcome; in human affairs it is choice.

God's love is the power which draws God's People to perfection, yet the power of choice enables humans to pull against the power of love. Christians call this 'sin'. Human affairs have always been tainted by sin and its effects, but the power of God is winning the battle with sin: Christ rose from the dead and sent the Spirit upon the world, who acts through human beings, not in their place.

The sacrament of Penance signifies the action of God's forgiving love upon his People and the human race when they have resisted the pull of his love, and failed to extend the reach of that love to all the situations of their lives – from the most personal to the international. It signifies that, no matter how great our failures, they do not have the last word on what we become – whether as individuals or as a people.

Today in Australia, very few Catholics avail themselves of the sacrament of Penance. This has been the situation for several decades. The abandonment of this sacrament must be recognised as a failure on the part of the believing community to interpret its meaning and adapt its form in the manner necessary to draw people to it. Either they do not recognise their need for forgiveness and the world's need for redemption from chaotic situations, or they do not see it as the source of that forgiveness and redemption. New analysis is required.

> …**Today in Australia, very few Catholics avail themselves of the sacrament of Penance. This has been the situation for several decades. The abandonment of this sacrament must be recognised as a failure on the part of the believing community to interpret its meaning and adapt its form in the manner necessary to draw people to it**…

Vatican II recommended that "the rite and formulas for the sacrament of penance are to be revised so that they give more luminous expression to both the nature and effect of the sacrament".[12] After the Council three distinct 'rites' were established: i) the First Rite of Reconciliation for individual penitents with personal confession and absolution; ii) the Second Rite for several penitents with personal (private) confession and absolution; and iii) the Third Rite for several penitents, with 'general' confession and general absolution.[13]

It was clear that this sacrament had to be reformed to meet the signs of the times, but resistance came from the hierarchy itself. In

1998 a document titled *Statement of Conclusions,* purporting to be an official statement on the state of the Church in Australia and a blueprint for its future, claimed that its chief weakness was a "crisis of faith" stemming from "the tolerance characteristic of Australian society". It asserted that there was a "diminished sense of sin among the laity", that "as guardians of the sacraments, the bishops were to take action against the introduction of 'spurious elements' in the liturgy", that "individual confession is the 'sole ordinary means' by which one is reconciled with God", and that "the Third Rite of Reconciliation was 'illegitimate' and had to be eliminated".[14]

This document was the product of a group within the hierarchy who regarded such reforms as inconsistent with the Tradition of the Church, and set out to overturn, wherever they could, reforms already in place. The work of these so-called 'traditionalists' is universally recognised and their efforts at resisting reform of the sacrament were successful. For many years after the Third Rite was established it was authorized for use throughout Australia and was widely participated in by large numbers during Advent and Lent. However, at the behest of the traditionalists within the hierarchy in 1998, the *Statement of Conclusions* forbade the Third Rite from further use in Australia.

Contrary to a 'new synthesis' conception of sin as part of the original chaos persisting in the world, as well as human contributions to that chaos, the *Statement of Conclusions* emphasised only the 'individual' nature of sin – as distinct from structural injustice and immorality – and appropriately it was not universally received by Australian Catholics. It provoked a strong reaction from their *sensus fidei* and an *Open Letter* to the Australian bishops from 75 priests and religious in 1999 said that terminating the Third Rite had closed down a 'profound and transforming experience' in the life of the Church.[15]

Canon law provides that all those who are entrusted with the care of souls by virtue of office are obliged to make the sacrament of reconciliation available to the faithful when they reasonably request to make their confession (C. 986). At present, in Australia, only the First Rite is generally available. The use of the Third Rite is restricted to emergencies and other special circumstances. We believe that many Catholics in Australia are reasonably seeking to have their confessions heard and that those with the care of their souls are not making adequate provision for this.

We **recommend** that the Plenary Council legislate to restore the use of the Third Rite of Reconciliation in the Church in Australia to at least twice each year, during Lent and Advent, and that this Rite be properly explained to Christ's faithful.

The recent Royal Commission reported that it heard of priests misusing the practice of religious confession to facilitate abuse or to silence victims. It found that "the practice of the sacrament of Reconciliation contributed to both the occurrence of child sexual abuse in the Catholic Church and to inadequate institutional response to abuse"[16], that some Church leaders viewed child sexual abuse as a sin to be dealt with through private absolution and penance rather than as a crime to be reported to police, that the sacrament enabled perpetrators to resolve their sense of guilt without fear of being reported, that the sacrament created a situation where children were alone with a priest, and that some children experienced sexual abuse perpetrated by Catholic priests in the confessional.[17]

> …**We recommend that the Plenary Council legislate to restore the use of the Third Rite of Reconciliation in the Church in Australia to at least twice each year, during Lent and Advent, and that this Rite be properly explained to Christ's faithful**…

We concur with all the Royal Commission's findings and support all its relevant recommendations, namely:

Recommendations 16.26: "The Australian Catholic Bishops Conference should consult with the Holy See, and make public any advice received, in order to clarify whether: a) information received from a child during the sacrament of reconciliation that they have been sexually abused is covered by the seal of confession; and b) if a person confesses during the sacrament of reconciliation to perpetrating child sexual abuse, absolution can and should be withheld until they report themselves to civil authorities."

Recommendation 16.48: "Religious institutions which have a rite of religious confession for children should implement a policy that requires the rite only be conducted in an open space within the clear line of sight of another adult. The policy should specify that, if another adult is not available, the rite of religious confession for the child should not be performed."

The Royal Commission also recommended in its *Criminal Justice Report* (August 2017) that each state and territory government should legislate a criminal offence for failure to report matters that may involve child sexual abuse offences; and that the offence should extend to knowledge gained on the basis of information disclosed in a religious confession.[18]

Our primary concern is that if a known child sexual abuser is at large in the community, that abuser constitutes a grave danger to children. We therefore **recommend** that, in order to ensure that no child sexual abusers are left unidentified and at large in the community, the Plenary Council should carefully examine the seal of confession as it currently operates in the First Rite[19], with a view to: i) maintaining its essential purpose while conforming to civil laws requiring reporting knowledge of child sexual abusers at large obtained in a sacramental confession; and ii) mandating that absolution be deferred, conditional on the abuser penitent self-reporting the crime(s) committed to the civil authorities of the jurisdiction where the crime(s) was committed and providing proof of the self-reporting.

We further **recommend** that the sexual abuse of a child or minor[20] be declared a 'reserved sin' with absolution reserved to a diocesan bishop; and that absolution be deferred, conditional on the abuser penitent self-reporting the crime(s) committed to the civil authorities of the jurisdiction where the crime(s) was committed and providing proof of the self-reporting.[21]

4.4 Sacrament of Holy Orders

Through baptism all participate in the one priesthood of Christ, some in the common priesthood, others in the ministerial priesthood conferred by consecration or ordination. Those who are ordained are called 'clerics'; those who are not ordained are called 'laity'. The sacrament of Holy Orders confers sacred power to govern. Though their priesthood differs in essence and degree, Vatican II describes both laity and clergy as participating in the one priesthood of Christ.[22]

Canon 1009 distinguishes three grades of Orders: the episcopate, the priesthood, and the diaconate; Canon 1024 states that "only a baptised male can validly receive sacred ordination". Some lay men and women also consecrate their lives to God by vows of poverty, chastity and obedience for the sake of the Kingdom of God. They are not ordained and are called 'religious'. Some ordained clerics are also religious.

The program of formation for the priesthood should present the sacrament of Holy Orders, like all the other sacraments, as a sign of the action of God in history for the salvation of his people. The priesthood is fundamentally a call to the service of God's people, not an individual calling to a particular 'office' with rank and privilege. Any change brought about in the individual by the sacrament should not be conceived as an 'ontological change' – a change in his being – but change in his relationship to God and

> ...The priesthood is fundamentally a call to the service of God's people, not an individual calling to a particular 'office' with rank and privilege...

the community. Ordination designates him as a leader 'within' the community in the ministry of the Word, of which the sacramental ministry is an expression.

The view of priesthood as a personal gift or calling, with ontological change at ordination, develops and promotes the mindset and culture of clericalism, which presents the priest as elevated above and separated from laypersons, even distinguishing him ontologically from other lay members of Christ's faithful. That view imparts to candidates for the priesthood a defective sense of self, inadequate psychosexual development, a sense of entitlement, and an inflexible adherence to a theology of separation and hierarchical superiority.

We **recommend** that the program of formation must instil a mindset that: i) welcomes collaborative and co-responsible lay and ordained ministries; ii) respects the inherent value of lay ministry; and iii) does not view ordained persons as superior in status to laypersons.

4.5 Bishops and the Episcopate

At Vatican II, and subsequently, the theology and legislation around bishops, particularly in regard to collegiality, synodality, and governance, has undergone and continues to undergo significant development.[23]

We **recommend** that the Plenary Council legislate to ensure that all priests, permanent deacons, religious and non-religious lay members of Christ's faithful in a diocese are given the opportunity to have a co-responsible and participatory role in the selection of their own bishop(s).

> ...that the Plenary Council encourage the co-responsible participation of Christ's faithful in the selection process of their own bishop(s)...

We **recommend** that the Plenary Council encourage the co-responsible participation of Christ's faithful in the selection process of their own bishop(s).

We **recommend** that the Plenary Council legislate to ensure that the Apostolic Nuncio, as part of his responsibility, must seek out and welcome any recommendation or expression of concern from Christ's faithful in a particular diocese in regard to the selection or appointment of a new bishop to that diocese.

We **recommend** that the Plenary Council legislate to make it obligatory for the Apostolic Nuncio to advise Christ's faithful in a particular diocese when the selection process for the bishop(s) of their diocese is to begin and end, and to invite their participation.

We **recommend** that all metropolitan archbishops and diocesan bishops encourage and facilitate the participation of Christ's faithful in any new selection process whenever they seek the appointment of a new auxiliary bishop.

We **recommend** that bishops be persons of prayer, humility, faith and courage, live close to the people committed to their care, and be true pastors, leaders, and agents of renewal for the sake of the Kingdom of God.[24]

We **recommend** that all bishops develop and adopt a mindset of pastoral ministry which LISTENS carefully and constantly to the *sensus fidei* of Christ's faithful in their diocese, learn to govern with synodality, co-responsibility, accountability, transparency, inclusion, and subsidiarity, and embrace women as equals.

We **recommend** that all bishops engage:

i) a professional supervisor to 'look over' or 'oversee' how they personally approach and conduct their ministry; and

ii) a regular spiritual director.

4.6 Priests and priesthood

The 1998 *Statement of Conclusions* insisted that there "must be greater clarity to preserve the authentic identity of priests", for "blurring of lines between clergy and laity has led to adverse consequences"; "priests must play their part in affirming their special identity" by "giving greater attention to pious practices" and "retrieving for themselves those tasks entrusted to the laity but rightly belonging to the ordained clergy."[25]

In 2009, however, Pope Benedict XVI said that "too many of the baptised do not feel part of the ecclesial community and live on its margins, and that it is necessary to improve pastoral structures so that the co-responsibility of all the members of the People of God in their entirety is gradually promoted, with respect for the vocations and respective roles of consecrated persons and the laity. This demands a change in mindset, particularly concerning lay people. They must no longer be viewed as 'collaborators' of the clergy, but truly recognised as 'co-responsible' for the Church's being and action."[26]

... There can be no place for 'elites' in the Christian community. One of the greatest evils currently present in the Catholic Church is 'clericalism'. It resides not only in clerics but also in laypersons ...

The Church fulfils its mission through the ministries and charisms of all Christ's faithful. All must collaborate closely and without competition in the 'common task', each participating according to their 'proper' role. Collaboration and the ecclesial nature of all ministries – clerical and lay – must not distinguish between the ordained and non-ordained as between professionals and amateurs.[27] There can be no place for 'elites' in the Christian community. One of the greatest evils currently present in the Catholic Church is 'clericalism'. It resides not only in clerics but also in laypersons.

4.6.1 Clericalism

The Royal Commission (2012-17) found that within the Catholic Church there exists a culture of 'clericalism' – the idealisation of the priesthood, and by extension, the idealisation of the Catholic Church. It is based on the 'dangerous' [sic] theological notion that at ordination the priest undergoes an 'ontological change' making him 'sacred' and different to ordinary human beings, and permanently a priest. It is linked to a sense of entitlement, superiority and exclusion, exaggerated levels of unregulated power and trust, and ultimately the abuse of power. It nurtures ideas that the Catholic Church is autonomous and self-sufficient, and that child sexual abuse by clergy is a matter to be dealt with internally and in secret. It is at the centre of a tightly interconnected cluster of factors contributing to child sexual abuse, and which the perpetrators and those in positions of authority were able to, and did, exploit.

Due to clericalism, some bishops and religious superiors identified with the perpetrators rather than the innocent child victims and their families, and sometimes even denied that their priests and religious were capable of abuse. Clericalism even led bishops and religious superiors to perpetrate a cover-up to avoid public scandal and to protect the Church's reputation and the status of the priesthood.[28]

Clericalism has also played a critical role in governance.

We **recommend** that priests and bishops retain close ties with their own family members, and with colleagues and parishioners who will support them outside their professional and ministerial roles, and tell them what they need to hear, not what they want to hear.

We **recommend** that priests and bishops allow some trusted persons into their personal lives as close friends – including but not limited to brother priests – who know them well, who will be honest with them and keep them grounded, and who will always be there for them.

4.6.2 Selection, screening and initial formation of candidates for the priesthood

During the 1960s, candidates in formation for the priesthood (diocesan and religious) peaked at almost 1400 across Australia. The Royal Commission found that prior to the 1970s, the screening and selection process of candidates, as well as their initial formation for celibacy and pastoral ministry, was inadequate and increased the risk of child sexual abuse. The formation took place in segregated, regimented, monastic and clericalist environments, was based on obedience and conformity, and was likely to have been detrimental to psycho-sexual maturity and to have produced priests and religious who were cognitively rigid.

Post the 1970s there were improvements, but largely *ad hoc* and inconsistent. During that period, the number of candidates for the diocesan and religious priesthood dropped sharply and, since 2000, has remained in the range of 200–300 (Figure 4.2).

FIGURE 4.2: ALL SEMINARIANS (DIOCESAN AND RELIGIOUS), AUSTRALIA, 1835-2017

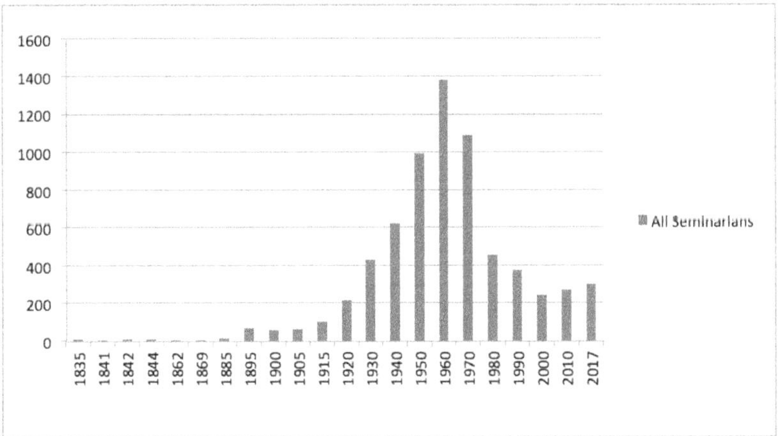

Source: Official Catholic Directories, various titles and various years

Many Australian seminaries have also closed. In 1971 there were 58 major and minor seminaries. Today there are just 23 major seminaries, including 10 diocesan (2 belonging to the Neocatechumenal Way), and 13 religious orders.[29] In the diocesan seminaries, over half the candidates were born in countries outside Australia; in the religious seminaries, the proportion is probably higher.

The Royal Commission made four recommendations regarding the selection, screening and formation of candidates for the priesthood. We fully concur with all four:

Recommendation 16.20: "In order to promote healthy lives for those who choose to be celibate, the Australian Catholic Bishops Conference and all Catholic religious institutes in Australia should further develop, regularly evaluate and continually improve, their processes for selecting, screening and training of candidates for the clergy and religious life, and their processes of ongoing formation, support and supervision of clergy and religious."

Recommendation 16.21: "The Australian Catholic Bishops Conference and Catholic Religious Australia should establish a national protocol for screening candidates before and during seminary or religious formation, as well as before ordination or the profession of religious vows".

Recommendation 16.22: "The Australian Catholic Bishops Conference and Catholic Religious Australia should establish a mechanism to ensure that diocesan bishops and religious superiors draw upon broad-ranging professional advice in their decision-making, including from staff from seminaries or houses of formation, psychologists, senior clergy and religious, and lay people, in relation to the admission of individuals to: a) seminaries and houses of religious formation; and b) ordination and/or profession of vows".

Recommendation 16.23: "In relation to guideline documents for the formation of priests and religious: a) The Australian Catholic Bishops Conference should review and revise the *Ratio nationalis institutionis sacerdotalis: Programme for priestly formation* (current version December 2015), and all other guideline documents relating to the formation of priests, permanent deacons, and those in pastoral ministry, to explicitly address the issue of child sexual abuse by clergy and best practice in relation to its prevention; and b) all Catholic religious institutes in Australia should review and revise their particular norms and guideline documents relating to the formation of priests, religious brothers, and religious sisters, to explicitly address the issue of child sexual abuse and best practice in relation to its prevention".

Recommendation 16.24: "The Australian Catholic Bishops Conference and Catholic Religious Australia should conduct a national review of current models of initial formation to ensure that they promote pastoral effectiveness, (including in relation to child safety and pastoral responses to victims and survivors) and protect against the development of clericalist attitudes".

To these recommendations we add the following[30]:

We **recommend** that the review of the *National Program of Priestly Formation* be immediate, independent, and comprehensive, with particular focus on the systemic factors related to: i) initial selection and ongoing assessment of candidates for the priesthood; ii) adequate personal and psychosexual development and integration; and iii) initial and on-going professional education and formation for pastoral ministry.

We **recommend** that candidates seeking admission to the program of formation for the priesthood should:

i)   be at least 24 years of age;
ii)   have gained a university degree or trade qualification;
iii) have worked for three years in their chosen field or trade;
iv)   have demonstrated financial independence; and
v)   have demonstrated a capacity for independent living.

We **recommend** that a National Protocol for the Assessment of Candidates for the Priesthood be immediately developed and adopted. It should include:

i)   having access to a highly skilled, multi-disciplinary team of professionals external to seminary staff, with extensive expertise in clinical psychiatry and psychology and a comprehensive understanding of the sub-cultures of religious life and diocesan priesthood;

ii) using this team for the initial and on-going assessment of candidates for the priesthood (and religious life);

iii) establishing a training and mentoring program for selected clinicians to become members of this team; and

iv) a clear statement of the pre-requisites for candidates for formation for the priesthood.

We **recommend** that, during their formation for the diocesan priesthood, seminarians remain living, for the most part, in the community, and preferably in non-institutional settings with a model to be developed.

We **recommend** that all staff involved in the formation of candidates for the priesthood must have an adequate and accurate self-knowledge, a high level of professional training and substantial pastoral experience.

We **recommend** that the personal, professional and pastoral formation of priests be holistic, ongoing and reviewable, covering their relational, psychological, emotional, and spiritual development. They must be trained to understand that they will be accountable to pre-determined standards of ethical behaviour set out in an official code of conduct.

We **recommend** that priests and bishops always approach and conduct their ministry with humility and in the spirit of service, according to Gospel values and for the building up of the Kingdom of God.

4.6.3 Celibacy

The Royal Commission concluded that compulsory celibacy for clerics and vowed celibacy for religious was not a direct cause of child sexual abuse, but was a contributory factor, especially when combined with other risk factors. It found that the risk is elevated when celibate male clergy and religious have privileged access to children in certain types of institutions, including schools, residential institutions and parishes.

The Royal Commission also found that celibacy is often implicated in emotional isolation, loneliness, depression and mental illness, and may contribute to various forms of psycho-sexual dysfunction, including psycho-sexual immaturity. For many priests and religious it is an unattainable ideal that leads to 'double lives' and a culture of secrecy and hypocrisy. In some cases it led some priests and religious to overlook the violations of celibacy by their colleagues and/or to minimise the child sexual abuse of those colleagues as forgivable moral lapses.

... celibacy is often implicated in emotional isolation, loneliness, depression and mental illness, and may contribute to various forms of psycho-sexual dysfunction, including psycho-sexual immaturity ...

The Royal Commission made two recommendations relating to celibacy:

Recommendation 16.18: "The Australian Catholic Bishops Conference should request the Holy See to consider introducing voluntary celibacy for diocesan clergy."

Recommendation 16.19: "All Catholic religious institutes in Australia, in consultation with their international leadership and the Holy See as required, should implement measures to address the risks of harm to children and the potential psychological and sexual dysfunction associated with a celibate rule of religious life. This should include consideration of whether and how existing models of religious life could be modified to facilitate alternative forms of association, shorter terms of celibate commitment, and/or voluntary celibacy (where that is consistent with the form of association that has been chosen)".

We concur with both recommendations.

We further **recommend** that those candidates who voluntarily embrace celibacy for the sake of the Kingdom of God, be fully informed of the loss of generativity it involves, guided in how to embrace and grieve for this loss, and how to live celibacy creatively and lovingly.[31]

Pope Francis appears unlikely to change the discipline of compulsory celibacy for diocesan priests, for he recently said: "When it comes to the Latin Rite, a phrase of St. Paul VI comes to mind: 'I would rather give my life than to change the law on celibacy.'

Personally, I believe that celibacy is a gift to the Church. I'm not in agreement with allowing optional celibacy. No!"[32]

While we respect Pope Francis's position, we still agree with the Royal Commission. We are also supportive of Vatican II's insight that "the human race has passed from a rather static concept of reality to a more dynamic, evolutionary one, [and] in consequence, there has arisen a new series of problems, a series as important as can be, calling for new effort of analysis and synthesis".[33] We regard mandatory priestly celibacy as one of these problems.

The Royal Commission is not the sole entity which has highlighted the problems associated with compulsory celibacy for priests of the Latin Rite. To argue that compulsory celibacy for all priests is a gift to the Church, when it was found to be a 'contributing factor'[34] to the abuse of children, is to persist in the synthesis of the past, rather than to make a new synthesis on what state of life is most appropriate to its ministers of the Word now. On the evidence of the Royal Commission and many other sources, compulsory celibacy should be removed and choice afforded to all candidates for ordained ministry. Such a choice would not remove or demean the 'gift' of celibacy, but by the act of acceptance, highlight its character as a gift.

... The protest of Christ's faithful against compulsory priestly celibacy cannot be repeated too often ...

The protest of Christ's faithful against compulsory priestly celibacy cannot be repeated too often, nor can the evidence of its original less worthy purposes – such as the protection of church property from inheritance by the children of priests – be sacralised away by the 'gift' defence. The willingness of today's Church to adapt its doctrines and disciplines to the pastoral needs of our times faces few greater tests than this.

4.6.4 Ordination of *viri probati*

At the same time as Pope Francis closed the door to optional celibacy, he indicated that he might be open to the possibility of allowing so-called *viri probati* – mature married men of deep faith and proven virtue, and natural leaders who have the respect of their community – to be ordained to the priesthood. However, he would only consider this where there was a grave shortage of priests and a need for the Eucharist and the sacraments: "there could only be a possibility in these far, faraway places, I think about the islands in the Pacific; it's something to think about when there's a pastoral need, there the shepherd has to think about the faithful".[35]

As a first step in the process of removing the reservation of priestly ministry to celibate men, this proposal has value. Australia is a 'faraway place in the Pacific', and in many dioceses there is a grave shortage of priests and a need for the Eucharist and the sacraments. In some dioceses, especially those in rural and outback Australia, many communities are extremely isolated and remote, and can be quite dangerous for male celibate priests in terms of loneliness and temptations.[36] Moreover, any early resolution to the shortage of priests, especially locally-born and raised, appears far away.

The issue of ordaining *viri probati* will almost certainly arise at the Pan-Amazonian Synod planned for October 2019. The preparatory document for that synod, circulated in June 2018, asks for frank and bold proposals in relation to ministries and liturgy. The Holy See has already indicated that the reflections of this synod will go far beyond the Amazon region and relate to the whole church.[37] They should certainly relate to Australia.

Two thoughtful and theologically sound models for the ordination and ministry of *viri probati* have been circulating for some time: one by Bishop Fritz Lobinger, former bishop of an African tribal land diocese; the other by Bishop Emeritus Erin Krautler of the Amazonian diocese of Xingu, Brazil.

We **recommend** that the Australian Plenary Council take particular note of the outcomes of the Pan-Amazonian Synod, especially as it relates to the ordination of *viri probati*.

We also **recommend** that the Plenary Council reflect seriously on the grave shortage of priests in certain dioceses and the impediments hindering the faithful from frequent access to the Eucharist and the other sacraments, and legislate to permit the ordinaries of such dioceses, in consultation and collaboration with the Australian Catholic Bishops Conference, to put forward to the Holy See concrete proposals for the ordination to the priesthood of suitable and mature married men of deep faith and proven virtue, who are natural leaders and have the support and respect of their communities.[38]

We further **recommend** that, if after a period of trial, the ministry of married priests proves successful and acceptable to the clergy and other faithful in the dioceses where it exists, a later plenary council should review the situation and, if opportune, recommend that the presence and ministry of married priests be accepted as a normal and permanent part of priestly ministry throughout Australia.

4.6.5 Ordination of women to the priesthood

In 1975, in a response to the Anglican Archbishop of Canterbury, Pope Paul VI stated that "it is not admissible to ordain women to the priesthood for very fundamental reasons", including Christ choosing his Apostles only from among men, the constant practice of the Church, and the constant teaching that the exclusion of women from the priesthood is in accord with God's plan".[39]

In 1976, when the issue resurfaced, Paul VI instructed the Congregation for the Doctrine of the Faith (CDF) to restate and expound the Church's traditional teaching, which it did through the Declaration *Inter Insigniores*, approved by the Pope, stating that the Church "does not consider herself authorised to admit women to priestly ordination".[40]

... Pope Paul VI stated that "it is not admissible to ordain women to the priesthood for very fundamental reasons" ...

In 1977 the Pontifical Biblical Commission also reviewed the scriptural basis for excluding women from the priesthood.[41] It found that the first Christian communities at Jerusalem, Antioch, and Ephesus were always directed or presided over by men exercising the apostolic power, variously called presbyters, prophets, teachers, and bishops (*episcopoi*), and concluded that the leadership role was always held by men and that the hierarchical order had a masculine character from the beginning. However, it also found that certain women made a positive collaboration in service to the Christian communities. It concluded that the primordial role of the 'leaders' in the early Christian communities was to preach and teach, and to keep the communities true to the teaching of the Apostles. But nowhere could it find them being charged with a special power to celebrate the Eucharist or to forgive sinners. However, because of the relationship between the administration of the sacraments and the hierarchy, it was accepted that the sacraments not be separated from the hierarchy.

There is no record in the New Testament of the administration of the sacraments being entrusted to women.[42] Nevertheless, women were entrusted to baptise.[43] Why then could they not also be entrusted with the Eucharist and Reconciliation? The Pontifical Biblical Commission concluded that "the New Testament by itself alone will not permit us to settle in a clear way, and once and for all, the problem of the possible accession of women to the presbyterate", but since the church hierarchy is entrusted with the sacramental economy, it may be that the hierarchy is able to entrust the ministries of Eucharist and Reconciliation to women in light of circumstances, without going against Christ's original intentions. In fact, this is what happened during the Communist era in Czechoslovakia (1948-1989), when four women were validly and lawfully ordained to the priesthood.[44]

In his 1994 Apostolic Letter *Ordinatio Sacerdotalis*, Pope John Paul II, in an attempt to close down all debate on the issue by "virtue of my ministry of confirming the brethren", stated: "I declare that the Church has no authority whatsoever to confer priestly ordination on women and that this judgment is to be definitely held by all the Church's faithful".[45] The following year the head of the Congregation for the Doctrine of the Faith, Cardinal Ratzinger, ruled that the teaching on an exclusively male priesthood had been "set forth infallibly".

In 2012, Pope Benedict XVI (formerly Cardinal Ratzinger) restated the Church's ban on the ordination of women to the priesthood and warned that he would not tolerate disobedience by clerics on fundamental teachings.[46] In March 2018, Pope Francis also said that the door to allowing women to be ordained to the priesthood "is closed".[47]

Nevertheless, the debate continues, and many Catholic clerics, religious, and laypersons continue to advocate for a change to what they perceive as discipline, not doctrine. Sister Joan Chittister has written: "The Church that preaches the equality of women but does nothing to demonstrate it within its own structures is dangerously close to repeating the theological errors that underlay centuries of Church-sanctioned slavery."[48]

A recent study concluded that a "*consensus fidelium* does not exist" with respect to the ordination of women or married men, and that it may take a long time for such a consensus to emerge.[49] The argument that women cannot be ordained priests because the Church has never done so is a persistence in an understanding of 'tradition' that was superseded in Vatican II. Pope Benedict XVI referred to 'the continuity of the life of the Church' and, more precisely, two typologies of social doctrine: one pre-conciliar, and one post-conciliar, differing one from the other, but a 'single, coherent and at the same time ever new, teaching'. Italian theologian, Carlo Molari, explains:

> The concrete form of the continuity between past and present does not lie in the meanings of the doctrines believed, but rather in the very saving events to which that faith refers. The meaning of those events manifests itself through the experience of the believers in that faith. It is in this way also that the present enters the interpretation [of Tradition and the faith to which its bears witness]. [50]

Fidelity to the 'living tradition' of the Church would require at least that the doctrine prohibiting the ordination of women be reconsidered in this light.

We **recommend** that the discussion and study of women's ordination to the priesthood not be shut down, but allowed to continue, as it is an issue which calls for new efforts of analysis and synthesis within the context of a more dynamic and evolutionary concept of reality.[51]

We **recommend** that the Plenary Council, although it cannot legislate on this issue, respectfully listens to the *sensus fidei* of Christ's faithful in Australia on the matter, and reports in full what it hears to the Holy See.

4.7 Deacons, the Diaconate and women

The diaconate is the third of the three grades of the sacrament of Holy Orders. For centuries the diaconate was reserved to men who were proceeding to priesthood, and they were ordained as 'transitional' deacons. Vatican II reinstated the permanent diaconate, but only for males, both celibate and married (C. 1031).

In 2009 Pope Benedict XVI added a third paragraph to Canon 1009: "those constituted in the order of the episcopate or the presbyterate receive the mission and capacity to act in the person of Christ the Head, whereas deacons are empowered to serve the People of God in the ministries of the liturgy, the word and charity".[52] This change effectively cut off the diaconate from any direct connection with the *sacerdotium,* which remains the exclusive reserve of bishops and presbyters. Ironically, however, this distinction between the 'sacerdotal' priest and bishop and the 'non-sacerdotal' deacon, may have opened the door to the ordination of women deacons, but it also closes the door to any possibility of women – if ordained as deacons – ever proceeding to the *sacerdotium* or rank of priest.

St Paul associated women with many different charismatic ministries (*diaconies*) of the Church, including prophecy, service, and apostolic work.[53] In the liturgy they have a place as prophetesses.[54] Some, such as Lydia, the mother of Mark, Prisca, Evodia and Syntyche, offer their houses for the meetings of the local communities.[55] Phoebe is explicitly described by Paul as a "deacon" of the church of Cenchrae and the "benefactor of many and myself as well".[56]

The 3rd century *Didascalia Apostolorum* says that "the deaconess should be honoured by you as a symbol of the Holy Spirit"[57], for at that time, in the Syriac-speaking churches, the 'widow' was almost synonymous with the 'deaconess' and was "required to go into the houses of the heathen where there are believing women, to visit those who are sick, to minister to them that are in need, and to bathe those who have begun to recover from sickness." In the *Constitutiones Apostolorum* the deaconess "does not bless, and she does not fulfil any of the things that priests and deacons do, but she looks after the doors and attends the priests during the baptism of women, for the sake of decency".[58]

Since Vatican II, the admittance of women to the diaconate, like the ordination of women to the priesthood, has been an issue which cannot be silenced. The International Theological Commission (ITC) examined the issue in 2002[59] and concluded that while the ministry of deaconesses did exist, it had developed unevenly in different parts of the Church. But it was not perceived as simply the feminine equivalent of the male diaconate, but as an ecclesial function exercised by women. There is mention of it being conferred by an imposition of hands[60] and the ordination ceremonies of women deacons being identical to those for male deacons.[61]

> ... Since Vatican II, the admittance of women to the diaconate, like the ordination of women to the priesthood, has been an issue which cannot be silenced ...

From the 10th century deaconesses were only named in connection with charitable institutions, and from the 12th century they had become nuns living in monasteries, involved only in education, medical care and parish service. Abbesses, though not ordained, were sometimes called deaconesses. The ITC concluded that: i) the deaconesses mentioned in the ancient Church were not purely and simply equivalent to the deacons; ii) the unity of the sacrament of Holy Orders is strongly underlined by ecclesial tradition and in the teaching of the Magisterium; and iii) it pertains to the ministry of discernment to pronounce authoritatively on this question.

In 2013 Pope Francis stated that "the Church acknowledges the indispensable contribution which women make to society through their sensitivity, intuition and other distinctive skill sets which they, more than men, possess", and acknowledged that there remains a need "to create still broader opportunities for a more incisive female presence in the Church."[62] Indeed, "demands that the legitimate rights of women be respected, based on the firm conviction that men and women are equal in dignity, present the Church with profound and challenging questions which cannot be lightly evaded."[63]

The question of ordaining women as deacons was raised again at the 2015 Synod of Bishops on the Family and subsequently in 2016, and to probe these questions further Pope Francis established a special Study Commission to review the theology and history of the order of deacon and examine whether women might be permitted to serve as deacons in the Church.[64] While the Commission, which concluded its report in January 2019, did not make recommendations, one of its members, recently stated that he "hope[s] that the Church will not be denied what it needs" and that "the Church needs more [people in] ministry".[65]

We agree, and believe that just as Vatican II authorised the restoration of the permanent diaconate for suitable and mature married men and young celibate men, to provide diaconal ministry "for the life of the Church", especially in certain areas where provision is difficult,[66] so today the diaconate for suitable and mature single, married and widowed women should be restored to provide diaconal ministry for the life of the Church.

We understand that a decision to restore the diaconate for women will be controversial, and that not all bishops would wish to have women deacons among their diocesan ministers.[67] However, they would have to justify *coram Domino* (*in the presence of the Lord*) why they choose to deny the faithful placed in their care the ministry of the diaconate simply because the minister is a woman.

Others are also concerned that the restoration of the permanent diaconate for women will block all momentum for the ordination of women to the priesthood. We believe that they are two quite separate issues and should not be conflated.[68]

We support the restoration of the permanent diaconate for women. We think that a mixed-gender clergy is desirable, for it is better when men and women work together in ministry. We also think that Christ's faithful in many particular churches are ready to receive and welcome women deacons and the ministries they will offer. We also believe that when the faithful recognise their ministries are those of service, not power, there will likely be, within a short time, a rethinking of priesthood.

Should Pope Francis decide during his pontificate[69] to restore the permanent diaconate for women we make the following recommendations:

We **recommend** that the Plenary Council or the Australian Catholic Bishops Conference legislate or make provision, with the approval of the Holy See, for the ordination of suitable and mature single, married, single and widowed women to the permanent diaconate and appointment for this ministry.

We **recommend** that each diocesan bishop, after consulting his Council of Priests and his Diocesan Pastoral Council, should convene a diocesan synod to hear the *sensus fidei* of faithful of the diocese on this matter, and make his decision in the Spirit based on the needs of the diocese and what he has heard.

We **recommend** that the Plenary Council or the ACBC develop suitable criteria for the selection and screening of suitable female candidates for this ministry, and a suitable program with active mentorship for their initial and on-going formation.

We **recommend** that the Plenary Council or the ACBC develop and implement a suitable program for the preparation and education of the faithful of the dioceses where women deacons are introduced, so that their ministry will be welcomed and appreciated.

We **recommend** that the approved ministries of women deacons include:

i) the solemn conferral of Baptism;
ii) keeping and dispensing the Eucharist;
iii) assisting at and blessing marriages in the name of the Church;
iv) bringing Viaticum to the sick and dying;
v) reading and explaining the Sacred Scriptures to the faithful;
vi) instructing and exhorting the faithful;
vii) presiding at the worship and prayer of the faithful;
viii) administering the sacramentals;
ix) officiating at funeral and burial services.[70]

4.8 Matrimony

In the dynamic perspective called for by Vatican II, the sacrament of Matrimony is intended to manifest the saving action of God at work in the mutual love of the spouses. In a recent Exhortation, Pope Francis said: "When a man and a woman celebrate the sacrament of Matrimony, God, so to speak, is mirrored in them: he stamps upon them the shape and the indelible character of his own love. Marriage is the icon of the presence of God's love amongst us."[71]

... The divine love which drives the entire process of creative evolution, and human history within it, has marriage as its icon. Yet, fewer and fewer Catholic couples see it as such and many choose not to confer this sacrament on each other with a liturgical celebration ...

The divine love which drives the entire process of creative evolution, and human history within it, has marriage as its icon. Yet, fewer and fewer Catholic couples see it as such and many choose not to confer this sacrament on each other with a liturgical celebration. The causes and remedies of this failure of our life as a believing community demand rigorous examination.

In Australia over the past 16 years, fewer and fewer Catholics have celebrated their marriage in a Catholic church with a Catholic liturgical celebration, either when both are Catholics (-45.5%) or when one partner is a Catholic and the other a baptised non–Catholic (-56.1%). Between 2001 and 2017, total marriages celebrated with the rites of the Catholic Church have decreased by 50.7 per cent (Table 4.3).

The 2016 Commonwealth Census data on the marital status of Catholics aged 15 years and over (4.2 million) revealed that just on half were married (slightly more men than women), that 11.2% were separated or divorced (far more women than men), that 5.8% were widowed (far more women than men), and that one third had never married (Table 4.4). In 1996, more Catholics were married (53.3%), fewer were divorced or separated (8.9%), fewer had never married (31.8%), and 6% were widowed. Of all widowed Catholics in 2016, 81% were female.

In 2016, there were 118,401 marriages registered in Australia, an increase (4.2%) on the previous year, but not as high as the peak year of 2012. Since 1996 marriages have increasingly been performed by marriage celebrants, and in 2016 they performed more than 3 out of 4 marriages (76.4%). Of the 27,901 marriages conducted by a minister of religion, 8,593 (30.8%) were with Catholic rites.

…The vast majority (80.8%) of couples who registered their marriage in 2016 had cohabited prior to their marriage …

Statistics also show that many people today do not accept the Church's strict prohibition on premarital sex. This suggests that in a world characterised by incessant change, people are unwilling to make a lasting commitment without first testing the waters. The vast majority (80.8%) of couples who registered their marriage in 2016 had cohabited prior to their marriage, marginally down (81.0%) from 2015. Couples who had cohabited before marriage were slightly older than those who had not. The median age in 2016 for grooms and brides born in Australia was 31.8 years and 29.7 years respectively.

There can be no doubt that Pope Paul VI's 1968 encyclical *Humanae Vitae* marked a turning point in the faithful's reception of Catholic teaching on sexual morality and marriage. After Vatican II, many Catholic married couples felt that the Church's teaching on birth control could and would change. *Humanae Vitae* left many feeling betrayed, altering their relationship with the hierarchy, but also making them realize that they could disagree with the Pope on non infallible issues and still remain good Catholics.[72] In 1963, 70% of Catholics accepted the Pope's teaching authority without question. By 1974 just 42% accepted it, and by 1999 more than 70% of US Catholics believed you could be a good Catholic without obeying the Pope's teaching on birth control. In Australia in 2011, of 543 Catholic priests surveyed on the statement "It is always a sin for married couples to use artificial birth control", 68% disagreed, 19% agreed, 11% were undecided, and 2% did not respond.[73]

The Commonwealth's earlier definition of marriage as a union between a man and a woman has also been rejected by many of the faithful. In November 2017, the Commonwealth Government conducted the Australian Marriage Law Postal Survey to gauge popular support for changing the *Marriage Act* (to marriage being a union between two people). It was preceded by a hurtful campaign in which the leadership of the Catholic Church took a very strong and public position opposing the survey question: "Should the law be changed to allow same-sex couples to marry?" The result of the survey was 7.8 million (61.6%) in favour of change, and 4.9 million (38.4%) opposed, with just 36,686 votes (0.29%) invalid or blank. The voting by Catholics was similar to the general vote, suggesting that the 'susceptibilities' of Catholics on marriage equality and traditional attitudes to LGBITQ+ persons had changed markedly.[74] The Plenary Council cannot honestly avoid asking itself whether the rejection by a significant number of the faithful of this, and of the other teachings of the Church on sexual morality and marriage, is not an expression of the *sensus fidelium* on the signs of the times.

... The Commonwealth's earlier definition of marriage as a union between a man and a woman has also been rejected by many of the faithful...

There is no impediment to lay Catholics registering and acting as civil marriage celebrants. However, the ACBC has instructed lay Catholic civil celebrants that they must not say any prayers or give blessings, lest people might mistake the civil celebration for the form of a Catholic wedding.[75] We do not agree with this instruction, when today more young people are choosing to marry without a priest and not in a church.[76]

We **recommend** that the ACBC support lay Catholic civil celebrants and encourage them to include prayers and blessings in the marriage services of Catholics if and when the Catholic spouse(s) request(s) them.

We **recommend** that more Catholic ministers be available to young people when they are preparing for marriage, and to accompany them at their time of great happiness and as they set out on their marriage journey.

We **recommend** that the Plenary Council legislate to allow diocesan bishops to give lay Catholic male and female civil marriage celebrants the authority to witness marriages in the name of the Church.[77]

We **recommend** that the Plenary Council legislate to allow people to be married in parks and gardens, in the bush, on beaches, or wherever they feel the presence of God is more powerfully present, and to simplify the system for granting permission (e.g. delegating authority to Parish Priests and Administrators).[78]

4.9 Sacred Liturgy

In its *Constitution on the Sacred Liturgy*, Vatican II said it had "special reason for judging it its duty to provide for the renewal and fostering of the liturgy"[79] for it is the "outstanding means by which the faithful can express in their lives, and manifest to others, the mystery of Christ and the real nature of the true Church."[80] In the liturgy the experience of the People of God of the saving action of God in their history is illuminated for them by the preaching of the Word, and given its fullest possible earthly expression in the celebration of the relevant rituals.

...Some priests emulate pre-Vatican II understandings, causing many of Christ's faithful to move from their local parish to 'lifeline' parishes where they can find a real sense of community and belonging to the People of God...

In certain dioceses, particularly those in rural areas, there are many clergy whose seminary formation has not put them in touch with the mind of Vatican II or subsequent liturgical developments. Some priests emulate pre-Vatican II understandings, causing many of Christ's faithful to move from their local parish to 'lifeline' parishes where they can find a real sense of community and belonging to the People of God.[81]

In many Australian parishes, large numbers of older Catholics who still attend Mass are unaware of the liturgical vision of Vatican II[82] and accept the *status quo*. Young Catholics, however, abandoned lifeless liturgies and worship long ago.

At present, there are few competent liturgists in Australia. Prior to 1996, liturgical formation and celebration in some dioceses was vibrant. Today, professional training in sacred liturgy is rare, and this lack in having deleterious effects on liturgical life.

Massimo Faggioli[83] maintains that there is an essential complementary relationship between Vatican II's document on the liturgy (*Sacrosanctum Concilium*) and the life of the church. The call to be the People of God has to be experienced in liturgy, where Christ is present in the gathered assembly. Many Eucharistic liturgies still focus on the altar, rarely inviting worshippers to engage in full, active, and conscious communal participation. Much worship takes the form of a 'corridor of God', not the worship of God's interconnected people sharing liturgical roles in an assembled community.

… The standard of most parish homilies, in content and delivery, is also highly questionable, and with many overseas-sourced priests, homilies are frequently unintelligible …

In rural Australia much worship remains purely devotional and of a bygone era. The liturgy of Vatican II is yet to arrive, and the people are deprived of sacred spaces that can nurture their living faith. Schoolchildren, corralled into church Masses, often sit bored and uninvolved, and no one asks: Is this just? Is this what it means to be God's living people? Often, already 'unchurched', the sacramental and liturgical experience passes them by, and prime opportunities to truly form faith seekers are lost.

Many priests and bishops have no interest in sacred spaces. But where beautiful sacred spaces have been created, especially with local architects, artists and artisans, worship and liturgy have been transformed and the sense of being a gathered people has flourished.

Liturgical music is also at a crossroads, with tension increasing between new forms of music akin to the evangelical style, and music that nurtures faith in the Catholic tradition. Some liturgists have expressed concern and discernment is now needed.

The so-called 'new translation' of liturgical texts into English has resulted in great angst in Australia and worldwide and many believe it is inappropriate for good liturgical worship.

The standard of most parish homilies, in content and delivery, is also highly questionable, and with many overseas-sourced priests, homilies are frequently unintelligible.

Recognising that the People of God assembled for worship have a right to liturgical texts, forms and spaces which nourish, support and deepen their faith and sense of community, we make the following recommendations:

We **recommend** that the Plenary Council make an unequivocal national commitment to widespread liturgical education in the spirit and principles of *Sacrosanctum Concilium*.

We **recommend** that the Plenary Council make a similar commitment to immediately establish a professional training program for liturgists in the spirit of Vatican II throughout Australia, with the aim of having them develop, promote and implement meaningful liturgical reform in all dioceses.

We **recommend** that the Plenary Council reawakens in parishes and dioceses throughout Australia a passion for the Rite of Christian Initiation of Adults (RCIA) which is true to the Vatican II spirit.

We **recommend** that the Plenary Council seeks to ensure that parish communities have meaningful liturgies, supported by quality resources, especially for baptism, liturgical presiding, and homiletics.

We **recommend** that the Plenary Council strongly encourage the creation and renewal of sacred spaces in the spirit of Vatican II.

We **recommend** that all formation programs for candidates for the priesthood and diaconate include professional training in Vatican II liturgical teaching[84] and the best of contemporary liturgical insights.

We **recommend** that all diocesan bishops and superiors of religious institutes provide adequate and ongoing training in Vatican II liturgical celebration and homiletics for all their priests and deacons – especially those sourced from overseas – who are engaged in parish ministry and experience difficulty in communicating. The training must include pastoral eloquence, speech therapy, accent modification, voice production, and homiletics.

We **recommend** that diocesan bishops and superiors of religious institutes take steps to identify their priests and deacons who are experiencing difficulty in providing the faithful with balanced and dignified liturgical celebrations and easily understood and scripture-related homilies.

We **recommend** that on an annual basis, a professionally prepared qualitative and quantitative survey be conducted anonymously in every parish and church throughout the nation, with an adequate sample of respondents, to assess the pastoral effectiveness of priests and deacons. Those surveyed are to be shown the results and offered the opportunity for further professional development.

We **recommend** that there be an urgent retraining of all clerics – including overseas-trained priests – whose liturgical understanding and practices, especially in homiletics, are not in tune with Vatican II, or suited to the needs of the local worshipping community. This is necessary for the sake of the clerics themselves, but above all in justice to the people of God.

We **recommend** that the Plenary Council legislate for the conduct of a regular and thorough review of liturgical music to ensure that it is suited to our times and Australian culture.

We **recommend** that the Plenary Council legislate for the urgent and ongoing review of the liturgical texts, including a reconsideration of previous texts which were prepared using a synodal process.

We **recommend** that the Plenary Council carefully examine how the spirituality, sacred rituals, dance, music and customs of Australia's First Peoples might be more effectively incorporated into Australian liturgical celebrations and worship.

4.10 Parish ministry in crisis

In 2011, an independent research report on Catholic parish ministry in Australia concluded that all the evidence, at an institutional level, suggested that this ministry was facing a real and huge disaster.[85] The evidence, gathered from the official data[86] on Australia's 28 territorial dioceses in 2010, with their 1282 parishes and 1523 priests, was convincing:

- One in four Australian parishes was without a full-time resident priest.
- Very few new parishes were being established.
- 184 existing parishes had been merged since 1994.
- Since 1995 local home-grown vocations to the priesthood had been few.
- The average age of priests ministering in parishes was 60 years and rising.
- Only 600 locally-born priests were likely to be available for parish ministry by 2025.
- An annual average net shortfall of 40 locally-born priests was likely over the next 15 years.
- Starting in 1997, parish ministry had become increasingly reliant on priests sourced from overseas.
- Parishes were generally having to care for an increasing number of Catholics, from an average 3481 Catholics per parish in 2000 to an average 4368 in 2010 (+25%).
- Just 13.8% of Catholics regularly attended Mass in 2006.[87]
- Fewer students from poorer and Catholic families were enrolled in Catholic schools.

Three years later, the situation had further deteriorated. Of the 1293 territorial parishes listed in the 2013/14 *Official Catholic Directory*,[88] just 821 had a full-time resident priest not shared with another parish (63.5%); 428 parishes had to share a priest (33.1%); and 20 parishes had no priest (1.5%).

Since 1986, when the last two dioceses (Parramatta and Broken Bay) were established, the number of parishes in the 28 territorial dioceses has decreased by 159 (-11%): from 1427 in 1986 to 1268 in 2017 (Table 4.5). Almost all this has been due to restructuring of some kind: merging, amalgamation or clustering of parishes. Very few new parishes have been erected, despite the Catholic population increasing from 3.8 million in 1986 to 5.3 million in 2016 (+39.5%).

4.11 Shortage of priests for parish ministry

The underlying cause of the reduction and restructuring of parishes has been the unavailability of priests for active and full-time parish ministry, particularly autochthonous[89] or local Australian-born priests. The total number of priests – diocesan and religious – in Australia peaked at 3861 in 1980 and has since decreased to 2951 at the close of 2017.[90] However, of the 2718 diocesan and religious priests residing in the 28 territorial dioceses in 2017, only 1321 (48.6%) were actively engaged in parish ministry, the vast majority of the others having retired due to age.[91] Two-thirds of all those active in parish ministry (877) in 2017 were diocesan priests, and one third (444) religious priests. [92]

The ratio of Catholics to priests has also changed significantly over the past 60 years. In 1950 there was, on average, one priest for every 543 Catholics across the nation. At the close of 2017, that average was one priest for every 1825 Catholics (Figure 4.3). But if only the priests active in parish ministry are taken into consideration, it would be one priest for every 4000 Catholics.

Australian-born priests now constitute less than half of all priests engaged full-time in parish ministry. The dioceses with the highest percentage in 2017 were Wollongong (88%), Ballarat (85%), and Wagga Wagga (79%).

The prospect of obtaining more locally-born priests is bleak. In Part 4 we outlined the situation with seminarians in Australia, explaining that numbers have been locked in the range of 200–300 for over 20 years, and that over half of all current seminarians are overseas-born (Figure 4.2).

FIGURE 4.3: TOTAL PRIESTS IN AUSTRALIA AND CATHOLICS PER PRIEST, 1820-2017

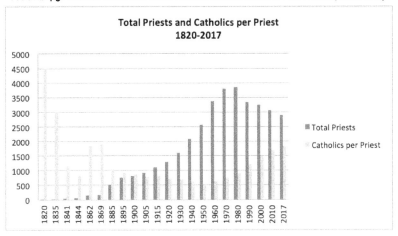

Source: Official Catholic directories, various titles and years.

Note: 1. Catholics per priest is based on total priests, both active and retired. If the ratio in territorial dioceses in 2017 was based on active full-time priests in parish ministry, there would be one priest for every 4070 Catholics.

More significant is that, by 2023, it is likely that there will be less than 450 Australian-born diocesan priests still ministering full-time in Australia's territorial parishes. Of the 517 Australian-born diocesan priests still active in full-time parish ministry, as many as 120 will reach retirement age (75 years) over the next 5 years (2017-2022), and another 50 over the following 5 year period (2023 to 2027).[93] In the 5-year period 2013-2017, only 46 Australian-born diocesan priests were ordained and, if this trend continues, only half the Australian-born diocesan priests who retire will be replaced, and the territorial dioceses will become even more reliant on priests sourced from overseas.

> ... by 2023, it is likely that there will be less than 450 Australian-born diocesan priests still ministering full-time in Australia's territorial parishes ...

Vatican II stated that "in order that the ministry of salvation be more suitably carried out, each diocese should regularly have clergy of at least sufficient number and quality for the proper care of the

People of God[94]". There is a clear obligation on every diocesan bishop to have sufficient priests, locally-born (preferably) or sourced from outside Australia, to provide regular parish ministry.

A 2011 survey of 543 Australian-born priests found almost half (47.4%) agreed that their workload had become excessive, especially in the rural dioceses, where they were expected to care for two or more parishes far apart on a regular basis.[95]

4.12 Overseas-sourced priests

The Church in Australia has always been reliant to some degree on priests sourced from churches outside the country. Until the 1960s there was still a significant number of Irish-born priests, diocesan and religious, working in parish ministry. However, for a period of about 30 years (1950-1980) increasing numbers of Australian-born priests not only moved the Church in Australia towards self-sufficiency, but a significant number of those priests (as well as religious sisters and brothers) were sent to other countries as 'foreign' missionaries. In 1972, there were 365 Australian priests ministering overseas, mostly in Asia and the Pacific, and another 63 ministering in remote parts of Australia to its First Peoples.

But beginning in the mid-1960s, and extending into the 1990s, many priests began to leave priestly ministry. A trickle at first, it soon became a mass exodus, with possibly 100,000 priests worldwide leaving priestly ministry. Many who wanted to marry with the permission of the Church, petitioned for formal laicisation; others just left. Over a period of 30 years, possibly 2000 Australian-born priests left ministry, putting a great strain on priestly resources. At the same time, vocations to the priesthood dried up, and fresh sources of Australian-born priests were in short supply. At the same time, the Catholic population swelled: from 2.1 million in 1960 to 4.1 million in 1990 (Figure 1.3).

> … But beginning in the mid-1960s, and extending into the 1990s, many priests began to leave priestly ministry. A trickle at first, it soon became a mass exodus, with possibly 100,000 priests worldwide leaving priestly ministry …

With a ban on married priests in the Latin Church, and Vatican II having encouraged bishops to be generous with sharing their priests with other churches where there was a shortage of priests,[96] Australia's bishops moved quickly to source the needed priests from churches outside Australia. For most of them this was viewed as a temporary band-aid solution for a problem that they believed would soon pass, and for this reason no long-term policy plans or implications were researched or considered.

An agreement on temporary visas was struck by the ACBC with the Commonwealth Government in 1997, and a confidential system of short-term contractual arrangements (3-5 years and renewable) put in place with the sending bishop or religious congregation in the overseas country to ensure a reliable supply. Arrangements for recruiting overseas-born seminarians were also negotiated by some dioceses.

By 2003 the overseas-born priests working in the parishes of the Australian territorial dioceses constituted around 5% of all priests working in this ministry. By 2009, they numbered 300-340 (20%-23%), by 2013 their number was around 560 (37%), and at December 2017, there were 676, representing 51% of all priests in parish ministry.[97] In seven dioceses the overseas-born priests represent over 60% of all priests in parishes, and in three dioceses 70% or more (Table 4.6).

Fifty-four overseas dioceses supply the 676 priests who currently minister in the parishes of the 28 Australian territorial dioceses. The largest numbers come from India (184 priests), the Philippines (93) Vietnam (88), Nigeria (49), Poland (57) and Italy (24). The priests are evenly split between diocesan and religious (Table 4.6).

In 2005-2008 the ACBC approved a 2-stage acculturation program for the newly arrived overseas-born priests. It operates nationally and is intended to make the priests feel welcome and appreciated, and to introduce them to Australian culture and church culture. Many, if not most, of the priests have arrived with a 'missionary' purpose to assist a church with a grave shortage of priests.

As yet, there has not been a national research project thoroughly examining the whole enterprise of having so many overseas-born priests working in parish ministry for over 20 years. The number and influence of these priests in church life and ministry is increasing in significance and there are many serious issues which need to be confronted, especially as there are no national policy settings for the time ahead.

We **recommend,** therefore, that the Plenary Council:

i)   make public the current policies and migration agreement(s) with the Commonwealth Government in relation to the recruitment of priests and seminarians from churches outside Australia;

ii)   review the current situation of overseas-born priests working in parish ministry in the territorial dioceses;

iii) recommend a full-scale research project looking at the origins, extent, arrangements, the welfare of the overseas-born priests, the quality and effectiveness of their ministry, present and future needs, and policy settings and implications; and

iv)   recommend that a major part of the research project include extensive consultation with the overseas-born priests themselves, with those parish communities who have experience of the ministry of these priests, with their Australian-born brother priests, with the Australian bishops, and with the bishops and superiors of the religious congregations in their own countries who have sent them to Australia.

4.13 Permanent deacons

The permanent diaconate, which had not been exercised in the Latin Church for more than one millennium, was restored by Pope Paul VI in 1967, who decreed that the order of deacon could be conferred for a life-long ministry upon married or celibate men. At December 2017 there were 46,894 permanent deacons throughout the world, with 97% in Europe and the Americas.[98]

After Vatican II the Australian bishops were slow to ordain permanent deacons. The first, Boniface Perdjert, an Aboriginal man, was ordained for the Darwin diocese in 1974. Four appeared in the *Official Catholic Directory* in 1981: 2 in Perth and 1 each in Townsville and Darwin. By 1997 there were 35 in 10 dioceses, by 2011, 102 in 17 dioceses, and at December 2017, 176 in 21 dioceses. The majority work in parish ministry and make up around 10% of all ordained clergy actively working in this ministry.

New norms and guidelines for the permanent diaconate were put in place by the ACBC in May 2017. In them the ACBC states:

> The presence of permanent deacons who live faithfully and happily the vocation of marriage is a powerful witness of the Gospel to Catholic and non-Catholic alike. The experience of these 'diaconal' families may be a valuable contribution to the ministry to families that the Church seeks to provide to all its married members. Though some are unmarried, most permanent deacons bring the wealth of the vocation of marriage and family life to the sacramental presence of Christ as a deacon in the Church. Their wives have explicitly consented to allow their husbands to follow this vocation of service outside the home and family. This is these women's

gift to our local Church. The deacons' love of their family will give a different and fresh flavour to their preaching and to their sacramental ministrations at such significant moments in family life as baptism, marriage and funerals. [99]

Following Vatican II, Pope Paul VI set down the ministerial functions of permanent deacons under the direction of the bishop:
- To assist the bishop and the priest during liturgical actions;
- To administer baptism solemnly;
- To reserve the Eucharist, distribute it, bring it as Viaticum to the dying, and impart it to the people in Benediction;
- In the absence of a priest, to assist at and bless marriages in the name of the Church by delegation from the bishop or pastor;
- To administer the sacramentals, and to officiate at funeral and burial services;
- To read the Scripture to the faithful and to instruct and exhort the people;
- To preside at the worship and prayers of the people when a priest is not present;
- To direct the liturgy of the Word, particularly in the absence of a priest;
- To carry out, in the name of the hierarchy, the duties of charity and of administration, as well as works of social assistance;
- To guide remote communities in the name of the parish priest and the bishop;
- To promote and sustain the apostolic activities of laity;
- To carry out all these function in communion with the bishop and his presbytery;
- To have a part in pastoral councils. [100]

Both the statement of the ACBC and ministerial functions of permanent deacons reinforce our view that suitable and mature single, married, and widowed women should be permitted to be ordained to the permanent diaconate.

4.14 Pastoral Associates

As an institution, the Catholic Church appears at odds with the trend in the wider community to accept the intrinsic human value of women, to oppose their subjugation, and to recognise their equality with men. It is almost as if the Church, as an institution, has sought to impede the contribution of women in the Church. In some areas, the opportunities for women to realise their potential as leaders in the Church are more retarded now than in previous decades. The 'rise and fall' of pastoral associates (PAs), most of whom are women, is a case in point.

... the Catholic Church appears at odds with the trend in the wider community to accept the intrinsic human value of women, to oppose their subjugation, and to recognise their equality with men ...

Following Vatican II, many Catholic men and women, married and unmarried, in several Australian dioceses, wanted to make a greater contribution to the mission and ministry of the Church. Having reflected on and discarded the self-doubt that ensued from being socialised into feeling no more than 'second class citizens' in their Church, and encouraged by many priests and bishops at that time to take up their baptismal calling and vocation to serve the church, and to minister to parish communities, they undertook special training in the 1970s and 1980s to become pastoral associates. Some dioceses recognised their need and accredited and appointed pastoral associates to work in parishes with parish priests and others in a leadership capacity. They saw them as offering a model of collaborative ministry for the whole community, and witnessing to the vision of Vatican II calling all women and men, equal in the eyes of God, to baptismal co-responsibility for the mission of the Church.[100b]

In 1975, the Archdiocese of Melbourne formalised the Pastoral Associate Ministry as a "formal, public, responsible leadership in a parish".[101] The Pastoral Associate would have "significant areas of involvement at parish planning level, and [be] a point of reference for others in ministry".[102] In 1990, there were some 160 pastoral associates ministering in Melbourne parishes[103] with many undertaking (and continuing to undertake) further theological, pastoral and post-graduate education, and committing themselves to ongoing professional development, supervision and spiritual direction. Many were lay women with families, and offered alternative leadership to which parishioners could connect and relate, consult with or confide in. Their unique experience, knowledge and skills offered a rare resource for the parish to enhance the overall life of the community.

Pastoral associates share in the leadership of the parish community, and in doing so bear witness to all that lay people, including women, have an important and necessary place in the decision-making of and for the community. Working in a collaborative relationship with the priest, they demonstrate that ecclesial leadership is not confined to the ordained or exercised in a solitary way, and that there is much benefit in listening, learning, giving and taking, and sharing decision-making. Their role is to invite and encourage all the faithful to exercise their baptismal rights and responsibilities by taking up their share in the ministry of the parish – that together they may advance God's reign of justice, peace, forgiveness, love and healing. Working with the community and as part of a parish team, they develop, shape and refine their mission in the light of Scripture and Tradition.

To carry out their role effectively, pastoral associates must be trained theologically, formed spiritually, and have practical experience and pastoral abilities. Their personal formation should be focused on the ability to have wholesome relationships as they witness to God's compassion and love thorough their words and actions.

Today, in many dioceses the number of pastoral associates has significantly diminished due to a variety of factors: a claim that there is insufficient funding;[104] the refusal of some priests (mostly conservative and often from overseas)[105] to embrace a sense of partnership required for the pastoral associate to succeed; and the evil of clericalism. Many priests feel threatened by competent, intelligent and professionally-trained women, and believe that all they need is loyal parishioners who will do whatever they direct them to do.

We **recommend** that the Plenary Council formally recognise and support the ministry of pastoral associates and their leadership role in parish communities.

We **recommend** that their employment conditions include just remuneration, a reasonable workload and work-life balance, the opportunity for advancement in responsibility and remuneration, support for professional development, supervision and spiritual direction, security of employment, and encouragement to belong to professional associations.

> ... Many priests feel threatened by competent, intelligent and professionally-trained women, and believe that all they need is loyal parishioners who will do whatever they direct them to do ...

We **recommend** that all dioceses put in place dedicated support services for pastoral associates and lay ecclesial ministers, with a special ministry to them – similar to the Ministry to Priests office – with full-time staff, an adequate budget, and space.

We **recommend** that seminary formation prioritise education and training in collaborative team ministry, especially with women; that all ministers – lay and clerical – in all dioceses receive the same education and training; and that special education and training, with women, be given to priests from overseas churches, to assist them in understanding collaborative team ministry, particularly at the early stage of their ministry in Australia.

We **recommend** that all parishes in all dioceses, regardless of size or wealth, be given the opportunity to employ pastoral associates or other qualified lay leaders; and that these persons be given the resources and support needed to gain the necessary skills to minister effectively to their parish communities.

4.15 Pastoral Strategies for parish ministry

In the 2015 report *Building Stronger Parishes*, 223 parishioners of 21 parishes across Australia gave 5 main reasons why they thought a parish is successful:

- it has a strong sense of belonging and community;
- the parishioners are committed to their parish;
- it is welcoming;
- it has active parish groups;
- it is inclusive.

We **recommend** that the Plenary Council re-evaluate the recent practice of amalgamating, merging, and clustering parishes, and consider the establishment of smaller parishes with qualified religious and lay leaders, supported by structures which bolster co-responsible pastoral ministry and good governance between the lay faithful and the ordained clergy.

We **recommend** that all diocesan bishops make more frequent parish pastoral visitations, and during these, give the highest priority to listening to all Christ's faithful in the community in a setting that allows meaningful dialogue.[106]

We **recommend** that all diocesan bishops recognise and support the various leadership roles within parishes, commission their ministry, and provide appropriate structures.

We **recommend** that all diocesan bishops instruct all the parishes in their diocese to develop, in a synodal and co-responsible manner, a parish pastoral plan which articulates the parish vision, mission and goals, in harmony with the diocesan pastoral plan. The plan should be reviewed and updated on a periodic (e.g. 5-yearly) basis.

We **recommend** that the Plenary Council legislate for the establishment of a consultative process for parishes when a new parish priest is to be appointed; and that it should respect parish traditions and the giftedness of the incoming pastor.

We **recommend** that diocesan bishops actively promote and support co-responsible and consensus decision-making in diocesan and parish pastoral councils, and discourage autocratic decision-making.

We **recommend** that parish communities more actively identify and reach out to those parishioners who have drifted away from active participation in parish life, visit them, and assure them of a welcome should they return.

Parishioners overwhelmingly believe that a sense of belonging and community is the most important reason for a parish being successful.[107] This is true not only for parishes, but also for dioceses. We are concerned that the Archdiocese of Melbourne has become more like a big corporation run by a CEO than a community of Christ's faithful led by a chief pastor with the smell of the sheep. With its 208 parishes, 328 Catholic schools, 124 health and aged care services, 480 priests (230 active), spread over an extensive geographical area and divided into 3 regions with auxiliary bishops, it is beyond the capacity of a single diocesan bishop to LISTEN adequately to the *sensus fidei* of all the people who have been committed to his care, even if all the listening and dialogue structures were in place – which they are not.[108]

... Parishioners overwhelmingly believe that a sense of belonging and community is the most important reason for a parish being successful...

We **recommend** that the Council consider the possibility of the Archdiocese of Melbourne being broken up into 2 or 3 smaller dioceses to afford Christ's faithful in the archdiocese a greater sense of ecclesial community, and to enjoy a closer pastoral relationship with their diocesan bishop. We are sure it has already been considered, but the Plenary Council 2020/21 – as was the case with previous plenary councils - would be the appropriate time and event for a decision to be taken.

The *Building Better Parishes* report found that the Eucharist was the central liturgical experience at the heart of the parish, that parishes must accommodate a wide range of spiritual needs, that parishes are the primary agents of evangelisation in the local community, especially through outreach services to people with special needs, and that parish vitality is greatly influenced by the quality of its leadership.

The 2011 National Church Life Survey found that adult Mass attenders across Australia most valued the Eucharist and Holy Communion, praying together, traditional worship or music, and homilies. But they wanted to see a stronger parish community, more people at Mass, increased ministry to children and youth, and spiritual growth.[109]

Earlier research into why once active Catholics had stopped going to Mass found that there was usually no single reason, but two sets of factors at play: some Church-related and others personal. The Church-related factors were:
- a perception that the Church was irrelevant to life today
- the misuse of power and authority in the Church
- problems of leadership or moral behaviour by priests and bishops
- loss of a sense of belonging in the parish
- a sense of being excluded by Church rules.

The personal factors were:
- family or household related issues
- a crisis of faith
- going to Mass was simply not a priority.

It found that as the various factors gradually accumulated in significance, people began to 'drift away' from Church life rather than suddenly cease participation, and that most still identify as Catholics and are open to returning to active participation "if they can see that the issues for them are being addressed". The research concluded that the Church could deal with almost all the factors if it really wanted to.[110]

4.16 Recommendations

Recommendation 4.1:

that the Plenary Council review the role of the ministers of the sacraments to ensure that the priorities of their ministry reflect a sound understanding of the relationship between Word, sacrament and ministry.

Recommendation 4.2:

that the Plenary Council thoroughly examine the empirical evidence of the reception of the sacraments to:
i) identify the failures in the life of the community to which it attests; and
ii) address the causes of and remedies to those failures.

Recommendation 4.3:

that the Plenary Council re-examine the Pastoral Strategies recommended by the Pastoral Projects Office in 2007 and legislate for appropriate action at diocesan and parish level.

Recommendation 4.4:

that all adult catechumens, before being baptised, be given a copy of the proposed Charter of Rights and Duties for Christ's Faithful in Australia and have it explained to them.

Recommendation 4.5:

that bishops who confer the sacrament of Confirmation be more mindful of the gifts of the Spirit received in the sacrament, particularly wisdom, knowledge and understanding, and understand that they have a duty to respect those gifts in the confirmed and to listen to what Christ's faithful have to say.

Recommendation 4.6:

that the Plenary Council legislate to restore the use of the Third Rite of Reconciliation in the Church in Australia to at least twice each year, during Lent and Advent, and that this Rite be properly explained to Christ's faithful.

Recommendation 4.7:

that, as there is a critical need to ensure that child sexual abusers are not left unidentified and at large in the community, the Plenary Council should carefully examine the seal of confession as it currently operates in the First Rite,[111] with a view to:

i)   maintaining its essential purpose while conforming to civil laws requiring reporting knowledge of child sexual abusers at large obtained in a sacramental confession; and

ii) mandating that absolution be deferred, conditional on the abuser penitent self-reporting the crime(s) committed to the civil authorities of the jurisdiction where the crime(s) was committed and providing proof of the self-reporting.

Recommendation 4.8:

that the sexual abuse of a child or minor[112] be declared a 'reserved sin' with absolution reserved to a diocesan bishop; and that absolution be deferred, conditional on the abuser penitent self-reporting the crime(s) committed to the civil authorities of the jurisdiction where the crime(s) were committed and providing proof of the self-reporting.[113]

Recommendation 4.9:

that the Plenary Council legislate to ensure that all priests, permanent deacons, religious and lay members of Christ's faithful in a diocese are given the opportunity to have a co-responsible and participatory role in the selection of their own bishop(s).[114]

Recommendation 4.10:

that the Plenary Council legislate to ensure that the Apostolic Nuncio, as part of his responsibility, must seek out and welcome any nominations, recommendations or expressions of concern from Christ's faithful in particular dioceses in regard to the selection or appointment of a new bishop for that diocese.

Recommendation 4.11:

that the Plenary Council legislate to make it obligatory for the Apostolic Nuncio to advise Christ's faithful in a particular diocese when the selection process for a bishop of their diocese is to begin and end, and to invite their participation.

Recommendation 4.12:

that all metropolitan archbishops and diocesan bishops are to encourage and facilitate the participation of Christ's faithful in every selection process where the appointment of a new auxiliary bishop in needed.

Recommendation 4.13:

that bishops be persons of prayer, humility, faith and courage, live close to the people committed to their care, and be true pastors, leaders, and agents of renewal for the sake of the Kingdom of God.[115]

Recommendation 4.14:

that all bishops develop and adopt a mindset of pastoral ministry which LISTENS carefully and constantly to the *sensus fidei* of Christ's faithful in their diocese, learn to govern with synodality, co-responsibility, accountability, transparency, inclusion, and subsidiarity, and embrace women as equals.

Recommendation 4.15:

that all bishops engage:

i)   a professional supervisor to 'look over' or 'oversight' how they personally approach and conduct their ministry; and
ii) a regular spiritual director.

Recommendation 4.16:

that the program of priestly formation present the priesthood as a gift of service to the community of Christ's faithful, not as something that elevates the priest above the lay faithful or separates the priest from them.

Recommendation 4.17:

that the program of priestly formation must instil a mindset that:
i)   welcomes collaborative and co-responsible lay and ordained ministries;
ii) respects the inherent value of lay ministry; and
iii) does not view ordained persons as superior to laypersons.

Recommendation 4.18:

that priests and bishops retain close ties with their own family members, and with colleagues and parishioners who will support them outside their professional and ministerial roles, and tell them what they need to hear, not what they want to hear.

Recommendation 4.19:

that priests and bishops allow some trusted persons into their personal lives as close friends – including but not limited to brother priests - who know them well, who will be honest with them and keep them grounded, and who will always be there for them.

Recommendation 4.20:

that the review of the *National Program of Priestly Formation,* as recommended by the Royal Commission, be immediate, independent, and comprehensive, with particular focus on the systemic factors related to:

i) initial selection and ongoing assessment of candidates for the priesthood;

ii) adequate personal and psychosexual development and integration; and

iii) initial and on-going professional education and formation for pastoral ministry.

Recommendation 4.21:

that candidates seeking admission to the program of formation for the priesthood should:

i) be at least 24 years of age;

ii) have gained a university degree or trade qualification;

iii) have worked for three years in their chosen field or trade;

iv) have demonstrated financial independence; and

v) have demonstrated a capacity for independent living.

Recommendation 4.22:

that a National Protocol for the Assessment of Candidates for the Priesthood be immediately developed and adopted. It should include:

i) having access to a highly skilled, multi-disciplinary team of professional persons, external to seminary staff, with extensive expertise in clinical psychiatry and psychology and a comprehensive understanding of the sub-cultures of religious life and diocesan priesthood;

ii) using this team for the initial and on-going assessment of candidates for the priesthood (and religious life);

iii) establishing a training and mentoring program for selected clinicians to become members of this team; and

iv) a clear statement of the pre-requisites for candidates for formation for the priesthood.

Recommendation 4.23:

that during their formation for the diocesan priesthood, seminarians remain living, for the most part, in the general community, and preferably in non-institutional settings with a model to be developed.

Recommendation 4.24:

that all staff involved in the formation of candidates for the priesthood must have an adequate and accurate self-knowledge, a high level of professional training and substantial pastoral experience.

Recommendation 4.25:

that the personal, professional and pastoral formation of priests be holistic, ongoing and reviewable, covering their relational, psychological, emotional, and spiritual development. They must be trained to understand that they will be accountable to predetermined standards of ethical behaviour set out in an official code of conduct.

Recommendation 4.26:

that priests and bishops always approach and conduct their ministry with humility and in the spirit of service, according to Gospel values and for the building up of the Kingdom of God.

Recommendation 4.27:

that those candidates who voluntarily embrace celibacy for the sake of the Kingdom of God, be fully informed of the loss of generativity it involves, guided in how to embrace and grieve for this loss, and how to live celibacy creatively and lovingly.

Recommendation 4.28:

that the Plenary Council take particular note of the outcomes of the Pan-Amazonian Synod, especially as it relates to the ordination of *viri probati*.

Recommendation 4.29:

that Plenary Council reflect seriously on the grave shortage of priests in certain dioceses and the impediments hindering faithful from frequent access to the Eucharist and the other sacraments, and legislate to permit the ordinaries of such dioceses, in consultation and collaboration with the Australian Catholic Bishops Conference, to put forward to the Holy See concrete proposals for the ordination to the priesthood of suitable and mature married men of deep faith and proven virtue, who are natural leaders and have the support and respect of their communities.[116]

Recommendation 4.30:

that, if after a period of trial, the ministry of married priests proves successful and acceptable to the clergy and other faithful in the dioceses where it exists, a later plenary council should review the situation and, if opportune, recommend that the presence and ministry of married priests be accepted as a normal and permanent part of priestly ministry throughout Australia.

Recommendation 4.31:

that discussion and study of women's ordination to the priesthood not be shut down, but allowed to continue, as it is an issue which calls for new efforts of analysis and synthesis within the context of a more dynamic and evolutionary concept of reality.[117]

Recommendation 4.32:

that the Plenary Council, although it cannot legislate on this issue, respectfully listens to the *sensus fidei* of Christ's faithful in Australia on the matter of the ordination of women, and reports in full what it hears to the Holy See.

Recommendation 4.33:

that the Plenary Council or the ACBC legislate or make provision, with the approval of the Holy See, for the ordination of suitable and mature singe, married, and widowed women to the permanent diaconate and appointment for this ministry.

Recommendation 4.34:

that each diocesan bishop, after consulting his council of priests and diocesan pastoral council, should convene a diocesan synod to hear the *sensus fidei* of the faithful of the diocese on women deacons in ministry, and make his decision in the Spirit based on the needs of the diocese and what he has heard.

Recommendation 4.35:

that the Plenary Council or the ACBC develop suitable criteria for the selection and screening of suitable female candidates for the diaconate, and a suitable program with active mentorship for their initial and on-going formation.

Recommendation 4.36:

that the Plenary Council or the ACBC develop and implement a suitable program for the preparation and education of the faithful of the dioceses where women deacons are introduced, so that their ministry will be welcomed and appreciated.

Recommendation 4.37:

that the approved ministries of women deacons include:
i)   the solemn conferral of Baptism;
ii)   keeping and dispensing the Eucharist;
iii) assisting at and blessing marriage in the name of the Church;
iv)   bring Viaticum to the sick and dying;
v)   reading and explaining the Sacred Scriptures to the faithful;
vi)   instructing and exhorting the faithful;
vii) presiding at the worship and prayer of the faithful;
viii) administering the sacramentals; and
ix)   officiating at funeral and burial services.[118]

Recommendation 4.38:

that the ACBC support lay Catholic civil celebrants and encourage them to include prayers and blessings in the marriage services of Catholics if and when the Catholic spouse(s) request(s) them.

Recommendation 4.39:

> that more ministers be available to young people when they are preparing for marriage, and to accompany them at their time of great happiness as they set out on their marriage journey.

Recommendation 4.40:

> that the Plenary Council legislate to allow diocesan bishops to give lay Catholic male and female civil marriage celebrants the authority to witness marriages in the name of the Church.[119]

Recommendation 4.41:

> that the Plenary Council legislate to allow people to be married in parks and gardens, in the bush, on beaches, or wherever they feel the presence of God is more powerfully present; and that it simplify the system for granting permission (e.g. delegating authority to Parish Priests and Administrators).[120]

Recommendation 4.42:

> that the Plenary Council make an unequivocal national commitment to widespread liturgical education in the spirit and principles of *Sacrosanctum Concilium*.

Recommendation 4.43:

> that the Plenary Council make a similar commitment to immediately establish a professional training program for liturgists in the spirit of Vatican II throughout Australia, with the aim of having them develop, promote and implement meaningful liturgical reform in all dioceses.

Recommendation 4.44:

> that the Plenary Council reawaken in parishes and dioceses throughout Australia a passion for the Rite of Christian Initiation of Adults (RCIA) which is true to the Vatican II spirit.

Recommendation 4.45:

that the Plenary Council seek to ensure that parish communities have meaningful liturgies, supported by quality resources, especially for baptism, liturgical presiding, and homiletics.

Recommendation 4.46:

that the Plenary Council strongly encourage the creation and renewal of sacred spaces in the spirit of Vatican II.

Recommendation 4.47:

that all formation programs for candidates for the priesthood and diaconate include professional training in Vatican II liturgical teaching and the best of contemporary liturgical insights.

Recommendation 4.48:

that all diocesan bishops and superiors of religious institutes provide adequate and ongoing training in Vatican II liturgical celebration and homiletics for all their priests and deacons – especially those sourced from overseas – who are engaged in parish ministry and experience difficulty in communicating. The training must include pastoral eloquence, speech therapy, accent modification, voice production, and homiletics.

Recommendation 4.49:

that diocesan bishops and superiors of religious institutes take steps to identify those of their priests and deacons who are experiencing difficulty in providing the faithful with balanced and dignified liturgical celebrations and easily understood and scripture-related homilies.

Recommendation 4.50:

that on an annual basis, a professionally prepared qualitative and quantitative survey be conducted anonymously in every parish and church throughout the nation, with an adequate sample of respondents, to assess the pastoral effectiveness of priests and deacons. Those surveyed are to be shown the results and offered the opportunity for further professional development.

Recommendation 4.51:

that there be an urgent retraining of all clerics – including overseas-trained priests - whose liturgical understanding and practices, especially in homiletics, are not in tune with Vatican II, or suited to the needs of the local worshipping community. This is necessary for the sake of the clerics themselves, but above all in justice to the people of God.

Recommendation 4.52:

that the Plenary Council legislate for the conduct of a regular and thorough review of liturgical music to ensure that it is suited to our times and Australian culture.

Recommendation 4.53:

that the Plenary Council legislate for the urgent and ongoing review the liturgical texts, including a reconsideration of previous texts which were prepared using a synodal process.

Recommendation 4.54:

that the Plenary Council carefully examine how the spirituality, sacred rituals, dance, music and customs of Australia's First Peoples might be more effectively incorporated into Australian liturgical celebrations and worship.

Recommendation 4.55:

that the Plenary Council:
i)   make public the current policies and migration agreement(s) with the Commonwealth Government in relation to the recruitment of priests and seminarians from dioceses outside Australia;
ii) review the current situation of overseas-born priests working in parish ministry in the territorial dioceses;

iii) recommend a full-scale research project looking at the current policies' origins, extent, arrangements, the welfare of the priests, the quality and effectiveness of their ministry, present and future needs, and policy settings and implications; and

iv) recommend that a major part of the research project include extensive consultation with the overseas priests themselves, with those parish communities who have experience of the ministry of these priests, with their Australian-born brother priests, with the Australian bishops, and with the bishops and superiors of the religious congregations in their own countries who have sent them to Australia.

Recommendation 4.56:

that the Plenary Council formally recognise and support the ministry of pastoral associates and their leadership role in parish communities: and that their employment conditions include just remuneration, a reasonable workload and work-life balance, the opportunity for advancement in responsibility and remuneration, support for professional development, supervision and spiritual direction, security of employment, and encouragement to belong to professional associations.

Recommendation 4.57:

that all dioceses put in place dedicated support services for pastoral associates and lay ecclesial ministers, including a special ministry to them – similar to the Ministry to Priests office – with full-time staff, an adequate budget, and space.

Recommendation 4.58:

that seminary formation prioritise education and training in collaborative team ministry, especially with women; that all ministers – lay and clerical – in all dioceses receive the same education and training; and that special education and training, with women, be given to priests from overseas churches, to assist them in understanding collaborative team ministry, particularly at the early stage of their ministry in Australia.

Recommendation 4.59:

that all parishes in all dioceses, regardless of size or wealth, be given the opportunity to employ pastoral associates or other qualified lay leaders; and that these persons be given the resources and support needed to gain the necessary skills to minister effectively to their parish communities.

Recommendation 4.60:

that the Plenary Council re-evaluate the recent practice of amalgamating, merging, and clustering parishes, and consider the establishment of smaller parishes with qualified religious and lay leaders, supported by structures which bolster co-responsible pastoral ministry and good governance between the lay faithful and the ordained clergy.

Recommendation 4.61:

that all diocesan bishops make more frequent parish pastoral visitations, and during these, give the highest priority to listening to all Christ's faithful in the community in a setting that allows meaningful dialogue.[121]

Recommendation 4.62:

that all diocesan bishops recognise and support the various leadership roles within parishes, commission their ministry, and provide appropriate structures.

Recommendation 4.63:

that all diocesan bishops instruct all the parishes in their diocese to develop, in a synodal and co-responsible manner, a parish pastoral plan which articulates the parish vision, mission and goals, in harmony with the diocesan pastoral plan. The plan should be reviewed and updated on a periodic (e.g. 5-yearly) basis.

Recommendation 4.64:

> that the Plenary Council legislate for the establishment of a consultative process for parishes when a new parish priest is to be appointed; and that it should respect parish traditions and the giftedness of the incoming pastor.

Recommendation 4.65:

> that diocesan bishops actively promote and support co-responsible and consensus decision-making in diocesan and parish pastoral councils, and discourage autocratic decision-making.

Recommendation 4.66:

> that parish communities more actively identify and reach out to those parishioners who have drifted away from active participation in parish life, visit them, and assure them of a welcome should they return.

Recommendation 4.67:

> that the Plenary Council consider the possibility of the Archdiocese of Melbourne being broken up into two or more smaller dioceses to afford Christ's faithful in the archdiocese a greater sense of ecclesial community and to enjoy a closer pastoral relationship with their diocesan bishop.

Some discussion questions:

- Do you agree with the proposition that if sacraments like the Eucharist fail to attract or retain participants, this is a sign that the quality of our community life of faith, hope and love is failing to radiate the love of God? Why? (4.2)
- If during confession, a person admits to having sexually abused a child, should absolution be withheld until the perpetrator reports themselves to police? If they do not report themselves, should the priest report them to police? Why? (4.3)
- There are a number of recommendations regarding the Office of Bishop. Share one that you would most like implemented. (4.5)
- According to Canon Law, only a baptised male can validly receive sacred ordination as a priest. Do you think this law should be changed to allow women to be priests? Why? (4.4; 4.6.5).
- The 2015 Report *Building Stronger Parishes* lists 5 qualities of a successful parish. How would you assess your parish according to these criteria? (4.15)

Notes

1 *Ibid.* n. 5
2 Vatican II, *Gaudium et Spes*, n. 4
3 *2 Cor* 6:18
4 Sterland, S., Powell, R., Hancock, N., Pepper, M. (2018) *A Snapshot of Effective and Sustainable Leadership Issues: Catholic Church in Australia 2016,* NCLS Local Church Leaders Report, Sydney. Retrieved from https://pro.catholic.org.au/wp-content/uploads/2018/09/NCLS2016ChurchLeadersEffectiveness-TA000000res.pdf
5 For the leaders of all other churches, this role was important for 60%. Cf. Table 2.
6 Molari, C, 2, 'La convivenza. E la Chiesa?', *Matrimonio in ascolto delle relazioni d'amore*, vol. Anno XXXVII, no. 2, pp. 13-20. [English translation by Dr. Michael Leahy]
7 The National Count is conducted once every 5 years over 4 consecutive weeks in all parishes and wherever Mass is celebrated publicly. It takes place in the same year as the Commonwealth Census.
8 ACBC Pastoral Projects Office, *Catholics who have stopped attending Mass*, Final Report, February 2007, Melbourne. Cf. pp. 50-51. Cf. also ACBC Pastoral Projects Office, *Pastoral Strategies*, October 2007
9 *Ibid.* Cf. accompanying document, *Pastoral Strategies*, October 2007
10 *Gen* 1:1-2. The Hebrew words '*tohu*' and '*bohu*' mean 'trackless waste' and 'emptiness' and are images which attempt to address the idea of creation from nothing.
11 *Rom* 8:19-23
12 Vatican II, *Sacrosanctum Concilium*, n. 72
13 Retrieved from https://www.liturgybrisbane.net.au/Learn/Liturgy-Lines/sacrament-of-penance-rites-of-reconciliation/
14 *Statement of Conclusions,* Rome, 14 December 1998. Retrieved from http://www.vatican.va/roman_curia/congregations/ccdds/documents/rc_con_ccdds_doc_20000630_dichiarazione-vescovi-australiani%20_lt.html
15 McGillion, C. & O'Carroll, J., *Our Fathers: what Australian Catholic Priests really think about their lives and their church*, John Garrett, Mulgrave, 2011. Cf. pp. 85-100
16 Royal Commission, *Criminal Justice Report*, August 2017, Chapter 16. Recommendation 7.4.; *Final Report*, Chapter 17
17 Royal Commission, *Final Report, Preface and Summary*, 2017, p. 73
18 Recommendations 33-35 of the Royal Commission into Institutional Responses to Child Sexual Abuse, *Criminal Justice Report*, Sydney, Aug. 2017, pp 123-4. Retrieved from https://www.childabuseroyalcommission.gov.au/sites/default/files/file-list/final_report_-_criminal_justice_report_-_executive_summary_and_parts_i_to_ii.pdf
19 Cf. Part 4, Section 4.3
20 Canon 97 defines a minor as a person under the age of 18 years. A minor over the age of 8 years is presumed to have the use of reason. In Australia, a minor is a person under the age of 18 years.
21 Cf. Pope Francis, Christmas Eve address to Curia, 2018. C. 982 could provide a template for conditional absolution. See also Kieran Tapsell's submission to the 21-24 February 2019 Summit of Presidents of Episcopal conferences in Rome to discuss child sexual abuse.

22   Vatican II, *Lumen Gentium* n. 10

23   We recommend a reading of the most recent document of the Australian Lutheran-Roman Catholic Dialogue, *THE MINISTRY OF OVERSIGHT: THE OFFICE OF BISHOP AND PRESIDENT IN THE CHURCH,* 2000 – 2007. Retrieved from https://www.cam.org.au/Portals/66/Resources/Documents/LutheranChurch/Ministry_of_Oversight2007.pdf

24   Matt 19:12

25   Cf. McGillion, *op. cit.* p. 85–100

26   Pope Benedict XVI, Synod of Rome Diocese, 2009

27   Boston College Seminar, 2016-2018. "To Serve the People of God: Renewing the Conversation on Priesthood and Ministry, in *Origins,* 2018

28   Royal Commission, *Final Report, Preface and Executive Summary,* p. 68-69

29   We do not believe this is an accurate figure.

30   Cf. Gerardine Taylor Robinson, "A church in crisis needing attention" in *The Swag,* Vol. 26, No. 4 (Summer 2018), pp. 5-9

31   Cf. Gerardine Taylor Robinson, *op. cit.,* p. 7

32   Pope Francis, Interview on plane from Panama to Rome 28 January 2019.

33   Vatican II, *Gaudium et Spes,* n. 5

34   Royal Commission into Institutional Responses to Child Sexual Abuse, *Final Report: Preface and Executive Summary,* 2017, p. 71

35   Pope Francis, interview on 28 January 2109

36   At the 1895 2nd Australian Plenary Council, significant attention was given to those priests with alcohol problems. Alcoholism and excessive drinking was a major problem for many priests, especially those living in the outback with isolation and loneliness. The Council recommended the promotion of temperance societies in all seminaries (mainly Irish) sending priests to Australia, that a religious congregation be asked to establish a permanent rehabilitation house for alcoholic priests, and that each diocese establish a special fund to help treat these priests (Decrees 71-72).

37   Cf. https://www.americamagazine.org/faith/2018/06/08/vatican-releases-preparatory-document-pan-amazonian-synod

38   Cf. Vatican II, *Lumen Gentium,* n. 29 as a potential model for the restoration of a married priesthood in the Latin Church.

39   Paul VI, Response to the Letter of His Grace the Most Reverend Dr. F.D. Coggan, Archbishop of Canterbury, concerning the Ordination of Women to the Priesthood (November 30, 1975); AAS 68 (1976), 599.

40   Cf. Congregation for the Doctrine of the Faith, Declaration Inter Insigniores on the question of the Admission of Women to the Ministerial Priesthood (October 15, 1976): AAS 69 (1977), 98-116.

41   Pontifical Biblical Commission, Can Women be Priests? 1976. Retrieved from http://www.womenpriests.org/articles-books/biblical-commission-report-can-women-be-priests-appendix/

42   Two texts forbid women to speak and teach in assemblies. 1 *Cor* 14: 33-35; *1 Tim* 2:11-15. Questions have been raised about their Pauline authenticity.

43   Matt 28:19; Mark 16:15 ff

44   For the story of the licit ordination of Ludmilla Javorova, the first woman priest in Europe during the Communist era in Czechoslovakia, and three others, cf. Winter, M T, *Out of the Depths,* Crossroad, New York, 2001, pp. 144-148

45   Pope John Paul II, Apostolic Letter *Ordinatio Sacerdotalis,* 22 May 1994, n. 4

46 Retrieved from https://www.reuters.com/article/us-pope/pope-reaffirms-ban-on-women-priests-assails-disobedience-idUSBRE83500U20120406

47 Retrieved from https://theconversation.com/pope-francis-wont-support-women-in-the-priesthood-but-heres-what-he-could-do-91555

48 Joan Chittister OSB, *Discipleship for a Priestly People in a Priestless Period*, Dublin, 2001.

49 Boston College Seminar, 2016-2018. "To Serve the People of God: Renewing the Conversation on Priesthood and Ministry, in *Origins*, 2018

50 Coherence does not mean closure within a system, but rather dynamic fidelity to a received light. Cf. Address to Cultural Centre of Belém, Lisbon, 12 May 2010; cited by Molari, ('Tradizione e innovazione nella chiesa', Rocca, vol. 12, no. 15 giugno 2010, p. 1). Doctrinal coherence does not consist in verbal consistency between formulas down through the centuries but in a continuity of fidelity to the light of the Holy Spirit manifested in the events of those times. The latter is 'living tradition' as opposed to verbal tradition.

51 Vatican II, *Gaudium et Spes*, n. 5

52 Pope Benedict XVI, Apostolic Letter 'Motu Proprio' *Omnium in Mentem*, 26 October 2009,

53 *1 Cor* 12:4; *1 Tim* 3:11

54 *1 Cor* 11:4

55 *Acts* 16:14-15, 12:12; *Rom* 16:5; *Phil* 4:2

56 *Rom* 16:1-2

57 Syriac *Didascalia Apostolorum* (*The Teaching of the Twelve Apostles*), 3rd Century CE, II, 26.

58 The *Constitutiones Apostolorum*, 8, 28, 6. This document appeared in Syria towards 380, used and interpolated the Didascalia, the *Didache* and the *Traditio Apostolica*. However, they were never considered to be an official canonical collection.

59 International Theological Commission (2002) *From the Diakonia of Christ to the Diakonia of the Apostles*. Cf. Retrieved from http://www.vatican. va/roman_curia/congregations/cfaith/cti_documents/rc_con_cfaith_ pro_05072004_diaconate_en.html

60 In *Constitutiones Apostolorum*

61 Cf. Retrieved from https://www.americamagazine.org/faith/2019/01/15/ vatican-commission-members-women-served-deacons-millennium

62 Pope Francis, *Evangelii Gaudium*, n. 103

63 *Ibid*. n. 104

64 McElwee, J. (2016). Francis institutes commission to study female deacons, appointing gender-balanced membership. National Catholic Reporter.

65 On 7 May 2019, Pope Francis, with a cautionary statement, revealed that the 12 members of the Study Commission he established had been unable to find consensus on the role of female deacons in the early Church and on whether the ordination they received was 'sacramental' or not – that is, whether it was the same as the ordination of male deacons. While the Commission has formally concluded its work, the various members are continuing their research individually. Retrieved from https://www.americamagazine.org/ faith/2019/01/15/vatican-commission-members-women-served-deacons-millennium

66 Vatican II, *Lumen Gentium*, n. 29

67 Cf. CARA Survey. Retrieved from https://www.ncronline.org/news/people/

survey-assesses-views-bishops-diaconate-directors-women-deacons?utm_so
urce=NCR+weekend+edition+Jan+26-27%2C+2019&utm_
campaign=cc&utm_medium=email

68   Cf. Retrieved from https://www.ncronline.org/news/opinion/just-catholic/
its-not-about-women-priests?utm_source=NCR+weekend+edition+J
an+26-27%2C+2019&utm_campaign=cc&utm_medium=email

69   Cf. Retrieved from https://cruxnow.com/global-church/2019/01/16/papal-
advisers-say-francis-will-know-right-moment-to-act-on-women-deacons/

70   *Lumen Gentium*, n. 29

71   Pope Francis, Post-Synodal Exhortation, *Amoris Laetitia*, 2015, n. 1

72   Charles Curran, "Encyclical left Church credibility stillborn", NCR, 16 July
1993.

73   McGillion & O'Carroll, *op. cit.,* p. 164

74   See our recommendation 2.10

75   ACBC, 2013

76   Dixon, R, "Proposals regarding the celebration of marriage and the exercise of
parish leadership", an extract from "The Science of Listening", *ACR*, Vol. 91,
No 3 (September 2014), pp. 264-80

77   Cf. Canon 1112 §1. Where there are no priests and deacons, the diocesan
Bishop can delegate lay persons to assist at marriages, if the Episcopal
Conference has given its prior approval and the permission of the Holy
See has been obtained; §2. A suitable lay person is to be selected, capable of
giving instruction to those who are getting married and fitted to conduct the
marriage liturgy properly.

78   Current law should permit this: Canon 1118 §1. A marriage between
Catholics, or between a Catholic party and a baptised non-Catholic, is to be
celebrated in the parish church. By permission of the local Ordinary or of
the parish priest, it may be celebrated in another church or oratory; §2. The
local Ordinary can allow a marriage to be celebrated in another suitable place;
§3. A marriage between a Catholic party and an unbaptised party may be
celebrated in a church or in another suitable place.

79   Vatican II, *Sacrosanctum Concilium*, n. 1

80   *Ibid*. n. 2

81   In one formerly thriving rural parish, a barely intelligible priest exchanged
the homily for a meditation on a sin-ridden mystic and fulfilled every
liturgical role himself, except the collection.

82   Vatican II, *Sacrosanctum Concilium*, Constitution on the Sacred Liturgy, 1963

83   Massimo Faggioli, speaking at a seminar in Newcastle, 2017

84   Vatican II, *Sacrosanctum Concilium*, Constitution on the Sacred Liturgy, 1963

85   Wilkinson, Peter J., *Catholic Parish Ministry in Australia: Facing Disaster?*
Catholics for Ministry & Women and the Australian Church, 2011,
pp. 22, 31 Retrieved from http://www.catholica.com.au/editorial/
CatholicParishMinistry.pdf

86   *The Official Directory of the Catholic Church in Australia, July 2010-July 2011.*

87   The Mass attendance census of 2011 found a regular attendance rate of 12.2%.

88   This number is not accurate, as only 1269 were actually functioning.

89   The word 'autochthonous' (from Greek αὐτόχθων, meaning 'sprung from the
land itself') is used throughout this paper to denote persons whose primordial
culture, acquired in childhood through the process of enculturation, is
Australian. It is not intended to be interchangeable with 'indigenous', may

include persons born outside Australia, but does not include persons whose primordial culture is other than Australian.

90 This number represents all priests residing in Australia, including those belonging to the Eastern Churches and to the Military and Anglican Ordinariates. The total number of diocesan and religious priests residing in the 28 territorial dioceses at end-2018 was 2718.

91 Parish priests (pastors) are required to tender their resignation to their diocesan bishop when they reach age 75 years (C. 538 § 3).

92 Another 162 priests and bishops residing in the parishes were making a casual or part-time contribution to the parishes, including 93 who are retired.

93 National Church Life Survey, Ruth Poweell et al., *A demographic profile of senior clergy in local churches: Catholic Church in Australia, 2016 NCLS Local Church Leaders Report,* March 2018. This report, outlining the demographic characteristics of a small same of 120 senior clergy in the Catholic Church in Australia, found the average age of Catholic priests in ministry was 58 years, with 24% aged 60-69 years, 21% aged 70-79 years, and 6% aged 80 years and over. It also found that 3.8% of Catholic priests were in their 'first marriage', and that 64 % of the 120 senior Catholic clergy who participated in the survey were Australian-born, with 2% born overseas in an English-speaking country, and 34% born overseas in a non-English-speaking country (pp. 5-7). However, the sample is too small to be reliable.

94 Vatican II, *Christus Dominus*, n. 23,3

95 McGillion, C. & O'Carroll, J., *Our Fathers: what Australian Catholic Priests really think about their lives and their church,* John Garrett, Mulgrave, 2011. Cf. p. 162

96 Vatican II, *Christus Dominus*, n. 6. These priests are often referred to as *'fidei donum'* (gift of faith) priests.

97 Some of these, especially those born in Vietnam, arrived at a young age; some have arrived for seminary formation; the majority have been recruited after they were ordained in their own country. The margin of error for this figure is around 3%.

98 *Annuarium Pontificium Ecclesiae,* Vatican, 2019. The data is for 2017

99 Retrieved from https://clergy.org.au/images/pdf/Norms_&_Guidelines.pdf

100 Pope Paul VI, *Sacrum diaconatus ordinem*, n. 21.

100b McGrath, Aoife, Hughes, Philip, Reid, Stephen, *Exploring Lay Pastoral Ministry in the Catholic Church*, Christian Research Association, Nunawading, January 2016

101 Introductory Statement, *Policy for the Accreditation of Pastoral Associates* in the Archdiocese of Melbourne, 30 June, 1995, reissued August 2002), p.1

102 *Ibid,* p. 1

103 Dixon, R (1991), *The Work of Pastoral Associates*, Catholic Research Office for Pastoral Planning, p. 2.

104 This reason is sometimes given as an excuse to terminate their employment.

105 Some priests from other countries still harbour social constructions of women as somehow 'less than men'.

106 It is insufficient for the bishop to meet only the parish pastoral council or address only the faithful attending the parish Mass.

107 ACBC, Pastoral Research Office, *Building Stronger Parishes*, Project Report, May 2015, p. vii

108 The last diocesan synod was held in Melbourne in 1916 and a diocesan pastoral council has never been established.

109 National Church Life Survey Research, 2013

110 ACBC Pastoral Projects Office, *Pastoral Strategies: Catholics Who have Stopped Attending Mass*, Fitzroy, 2007, p. 3

111–112 CIC, Canon 97 defines a minor as a person aged under 18 years, while a minor at the age of 8 years is presumed to have the use of reason. In Australia, a minor is a person under the age of 18 years.

113 Cf. Pope Francis, Christmas Eve address to Curia, 2018. C. 982 could provide a template for conditional absolution. See also Kieran Tapsell's submission to the 21-24 February 2019 Summit of Presidents of Episcopal conferences in Rome to discuss child sexual abuse.

114 Cf. Recommendations 2.7 and 3.12

115 Matt 19:12

116 Cf. Vatican II, *Lumen Gentium*, n. 29 as a potential model for the restoration of a married priesthood in the Latin Church.

117 Vatican II, *Gaudium et Spes*, n. 5

118 Vatican II, *Lumen Gentium*, n. 29

119 Cf. Canon 1112 §1. Where there are no priests and deacons, the diocesan Bishop can delegate lay persons to assist at marriages, if the Episcopal Conference has given its prior approval and the permission of the Holy See has been obtained; §2. A suitable lay person is to be selected, capable of giving instruction to those who are getting married and fitted to conduct the marriage liturgy properly.

120 Current law should permit this: Canon 1118 §1. A marriage between Catholics, or between a Catholic party and a baptised non-Catholic, is to be celebrated in the parish church. By permission of the local Ordinary or of the parish priest, it may be celebrated in another church or oratory; §2. The local Ordinary can allow a marriage to be celebrated in another suitable place; §3. A marriage between a Catholic party and an unbaptised party may be celebrated in a church or in another suitable place.

121 It is insufficient for the bishop to meet only the parish pastoral council or address only the faithful attending the parish Mass.

*Photo of the assembled bishops of Australia at the
1895 2nd Australian Plenary Council. Photo taken in the
Aula Maxima of St Patrick's College, Manly, NSW*

PART 5

PLENARY COUNCIL: PROCESS AND PROCEDURES

For centuries the sole participants in Catholic Church councils and synods were bishops and ordained clerics. When the 2nd Vatican Council called for the "venerable institution of synods and councils to flourish with new vigor" (Christus Dominus, n. 36), it also stated that "the body of the faithful, as a whole, cannot err in matters of belief" for it has a "supernatural sense of faith" which manifests this unerring quality (Lumen Gentium, n. 12). In 1983 the revised Code of Canon Law gave to the lay faithful an official voice and vote at plenary and provincial councils and diocesan synods, and at the 2020/21 Plenary Council a number of religious and non-religious lay Catholics will be called to participate with a 'consultative' vote. However, Catholics for Renewal *believes that there are far too many restrictions on the lay presence at this Council and is calling for substantial changes.*

- Peter Wilkinson, President of *Catholics for Renewal*, author of articles on the role of synods in the Church.

5.1 Synods and councils in Australia

Eighty-two years ago, at the Pontifical Mass in St Mary's Cathedral, Sydney, to open the Fourth Australasian Plenary Council, the homilist, Archbishop Giovanni Panico, Apostolic Delegate to Australia, told the bishops and clerics assembled that the purpose of the Council was "to give yourselves an opportunity to decide on the policy which will most favour the preservation and propagation of the faith in these lands."

For that Council, the decision makers were the local bishops only, and their advisors were local clerics only.

The homilist at the opening Mass of the Fifth Australian Plenary Council at St Francis Xavier's Cathedral in Adelaide on 11 October 2020, might repeat some of what the Delegate said in 1937, but there will be much that is new.

The decision-makers on policy and legislation in 2020/21 will still be the bishops, including some who have retired, for they alone have a 'deliberative' vote; and many of their advisors will still be priests in senior diocesan positions, major superiors of some male religious congregations, and some other diocesan priests, all with a 'consultative' vote. Entirely new, however, will be the presence of non-religious lay men and women – their numbers still to be decided – who will also have a 'consultative' vote. Also new will be the presence of invited 'guests', who can be clerics and laypersons, men and women, experts in various fields, Catholic bishops and clerics from outside Australia, local representatives of other Christian churches, and even representatives of non-Christian faiths. All these may be invited to speak at the Council, but will not have a vote.

As in 1937, the Plenary Council 2020/21 will have authority to decide policy for the Church in Australia and to translate it into legislation. The policy aim of the 1937 Council was to safeguard and propagate the faith in Australia and New Zealand; the policy aim of the Plenary Council 2020/21 will be to "make provision for the pastoral needs of the people of God", and more specifically to decide what "seems opportune for the increase of the faith, the organisation of common pastoral action, and the regulation of morals and of the common ecclesiastical discipline which is to be observed, promoted and protected" (C. 445). It will be policy and legislation for Australia only, suited to Australian circumstances, but it cannot prejudice the universal law of the Church.

… For the first time ever in Australia, all Christ's faithful have been asked to engage in a program of listening, dialogue, and consultation, and invited to contribute their voices to the Plenary Council …

Also new is the process for drawing up the agenda. For the first time ever in Australia, all Christ's faithful have been asked to engage in a program of listening, dialogue, and consultation, and invited to contribute their voices to the Plenary Council. Australian Catholics are not used to being asked for their views on church matters, and the Australian bishops are not known for synodality, even though Vatican II called for synods "to flourish with vigour" and encouraged every layperson to "openly reveal to their pastors their needs and desires with the freedom and confidence that befits a son of God and a brother in Christ", and even at times to feel "obliged to express their opinion on things which concern the good of the Church"[1].

These statements of Vatican II were never taken seriously in Australia. Most bishops never even bothered to establish a diocesan pastoral council, much less a synod, an indication of their aloof disposition of paying little attention to the "needs and desires" of their people.

Even in 2019, very few diocesan bishops have committed to meeting with their people in synod or assembly prior to the Plenary Council to learn of their concerns. It is a continuation of the 'business as usual' autocratic mindset that has been a major cause of the Church's failings and, if unchanged, could certainly prejudice the workings of the Council.

Pope Francis has now re-established the principle of synodality and synods: the ancient and most traditional means of discerning the movement of the Spirit and legislating accordingly. From 1842, when the Australian hierarchy was established, until January 2019, the bishops of Australia had convened just 138 diocesan synods, and seven particular councils (provincial and plenary). All but six were convened as exclusively clerical gatherings, for it was only in 1965 that Vatican II, for the first time in centuries, provided for lay men or women to participate in these gatherings.

> ...A plenary council, on the other hand, gives witness to the Church as a hierarchically ordered community of believers, with legislative authority, witnessing the highest form of communion between all the particular churches of a nation ...

Traditionally, and at present, there are two types of synod or council that can be convened locally: a diocesan synod called by a diocesan bishop, and a particular council called by the bishops of an ecclesiastical province (provincial council) or by an Episcopal conference (plenary council). Since Vatican II, only five Australian diocesan bishops have convened a diocesan synod,[2] while the bishop of a province or the Bishops Conference (ACBC) has not convened a single particular council, either 'provincial' or 'plenary' for over 80 years.[3] (Table 5.1).[4]

Australia's bishops have generally shied away from synods and councils, preferring to exercise their collegial pastoral and governance ministry via the national bishops' conference which meets in plenary session *in camera* twice a year. However, a bishops' conference – an assembly of bishops expressing 'collegiality' – was never intended to replace a plenary council – a gathering of churches expressing '*communio*' –where a more comprehensive discussion of issues takes place, not just among bishops, but among a much wider group of Christ's faithful from all the particular churches (dioceses, eparchies, ordinariates).

Eminent canonist, James Provost, states that for a long time bishops have been ruling by 'emergency decree', finding this form of governance more efficient, smoother and less messy than governing through a plenary council. However, this may be causing a loss of the 'sense of law' in the Church, protecting the prerogatives of administrators, and denying access to traditional instruments of justice in the Church.[5] A plenary council, on the other hand, gives witness to the Church as a hierarchically ordered community of believers, with legislative authority, witnessing the highest form of communion between all the particular churches of a nation.

5.2 Plenary Council 2020/21

Canon law permits an episcopal conference to celebrate a plenary council whenever it deems it necessary or useful, and the Apostolic See approves (C. 439). Its purpose is to "ensure that the pastoral needs of the people of God in its territory are provided for [and it can] determine whatever seems opportune for the increase of faith, for the ordering of common pastoral action, for the direction of morality and for the preservation, introduction and defence of a common ecclesiastical discipline" (C. 445). A plenary council has the power of governance for these purposes, especially the power to make local laws binding on all the particular churches.

> … purpose is to "ensure that the pastoral needs of the people of God in its territory are provided for [and it can] determine whatever seems opportune for the increase of faith, for the ordering of common pastoral action, for the direction of morality and for the preservation, introduction and defence of a common ecclesiastical discipline" …

Proposals for a fifth Australian plenary council arose in 2007, but no decision was taken until 2015 when the ACBC voted unanimously to move towards a 'national ecclesial event'.[6] In 2016, with a majority of the bishops in favour (30 to 5), the ACBC decided to seek approval from the Apostolic See for a plenary council in 2020.

No specific reasons were given for the decision, but Archbishop Coleridge said that it was a "recognition that we can no longer put up a sign saying 'Business as usual', for the Royal Commission has made it abundantly clear that the culture has to change, and that bishops and others will have to make bold decisions about the future."[7] The bishops, he added, must "listen to all the voices and try to bring them into harmony", and for this "synods are necessary, even if they might reveal differences and unresolved issues, be exhausting, and struggle to find the way ahead. For all their messiness, synods are a serious process of discernment, can be exhilarating and refreshing in deeper ways, and should produce real fruit".[8]

In March 2018, the Apostolic See approved the Plenary Council, as well as the ACBC's selection of Archbishop Timothy Costelloe of Perth as the Council's president.

5.3 Three stages of a plenary council

A plenary council has three stages: preparation, celebration, and implementation. The preparatory stage for the Plenary Council 2020/21, which was officially launched at Pentecost 2018, will run until 11 October 2020 when the first of two council sessions will commence.[9]

... The most important and immediate of these are determining who and how many are to be called and invited to attend the Council, and setting the agenda ...

Preparations made by the ACBC to date[10] include: the establishment of a 5-member Plenary Council Bishops Commission[11], the appointment of a 3-member Facilitation Team and 14-member Executive Committee[12], the decision to hold the Council over two sessions (in Adelaide on 11-17 October 2020, and in Sydney in May 2021), a 3-year planning schedule[13], and a dedicated website with significant helpful resources (www.plenarycouncil.catholic.org.au).

At the Pentecost launch of the Plenary Council, the entire Catholic community was urged to pray for the Council, to gather for local 'listening sessions' to discern under the guidance of the Spirit what God is asking of the Church in Australia at this present time, and to make written submissions.

Steps still to be taken by the ACBC, on the advice of the Plenary Council Bishops Commission, include:

i)   Issuance of a call to attend the council to those who must be called and to those who can be called; and to invite others as guests;[14]

ii) Determine the number of major superiors (male and female) of religious institutes and societies of apostolic life in Australia who must to be called (to be selected by their peers);[15]

iii) Determine the number of rectors of major seminaries in Australia who must to be called (to be selected by their peers);

iv) Determine:
   a) the number of retired bishops to be called;
   b) the number of priests who may to be called; and
   c) the number of other members of the Catholic faithful who may be called and how they are to be selected;

v) Determine who and how many to invite to the Council as 'guests', and what role they will have;

vi) Determine the agenda for the council and the questions to be treated; and (if necessary)

vii) Transfer, extend or dissolve the council.

The most important and immediate of these are determining who and how many are to be called and invited to attend the Council, and setting the agenda.

5.4 Who are called to attend the Council?

Canon 443 of the 1983 *Code of Canon Law* specifies two groups to be 'called': Group A - those who 'must' be called; and Group B - those who 'can' be called (cf. Table 5.2).

Until Vatican II only clerics could be called to attend a plenary council. Those called to the Plenary Council 2020/21 will be bishops, priests, religious men and women, and non-religious lay men and women. No mention is made of deacons, even though they are part of the Church's hierarchical structure, and should be called.

> ... the special formula in Canon 443 § 4: "the number of presbyters and other members of the Christian faithful who can be called cannot exceed one half of the combined number of all the other participants who are mentioned in §§ 1-3 ...

At this stage it is not possible to determine the exact number of all who will be called, as the ACBC has yet to announce the numbers for three sub-groups:

i)   the major superiors of (male and female) religious institutes and societies of apostolic life;
ii) the rectors of major seminaries; and
iii) retired bishops.[16]

With all 3 sub-groups, the ACBC has latitude.

A further complication is the special formula in Canon 443 § 4: "the number of presbyters and other members of the Christian faithful who can be called cannot exceed one half of the combined

238

number of all the other participants who are mentioned in §§ 1–3", namely, all those who must be called, plus the retired bishops resident in Australia who can be called. In effect, just one third of the total to be called will be ordinary priests, deacons, religious who are not superiors, and non-religious laypersons. This formula was probably designed to limit the number attending with a vote, and to prevent pressure groups from attempting to take over a council.

Relying exclusively on C. 443 to decide the total number to be called to the council will be both complex and difficult, and will almost certainly result in an unbalanced and unsatisfactory outcome. The reason is contained in the data for the various groups and sub-groups specified in C. 443 §§ 1–3 (Table 5.3).

Group A: those who must be called from all the particular churches

This group will include (at 31.12.2017): diocesan bishops (35), coadjutor bishops (0), auxiliary bishops (8), titular bishops with a special function (0)[17], vicars general (37), episcopal vicars (35), major superiors of religious institutes and societies of apostolic life (number to be determined by ACBC), rectors of Catholic and ecclesiastical universities (4), deans of faculties of theology and canon law (6), and rectors of major seminaries (number to be determined by ACBC). If the ACBC were to decide to call 20–30 religious superiors (male and female balanced) and 10–14 seminary rectors, the total number to be called in this group might vary from 153 to 167. At most, this number would include 10–16 women.

Group B: those who can be called from all the particular churches

This group may include (at 31.12.2017) retired titular bishops living in Australia (31), some priests (number not specified), and some other members of Christ's faithful (number not specified). While the retired bishops 'can' be called, there is no obligation on the ACBC to call any of them.[18] However, we assume some will be called. Using the formula in C. 443 §4 (cf. below), the total number of priests and others called might vary from 87 (if 20 retired bishops attend) to 97 (if 31 retired bishops attend). If half these are priests and half lay persons, an average 1.2-1.4 priests and 1.2-1.4 lay persons would be called from each particular church. If the lay persons called were gender balanced, the number of women might total 21 to 24, less than 1 per particular church.

All who are called to a plenary council must attend, unless they are impeded for a just reason, and they must inform the president of the Council (C. 444).

The formula for calling priests and other members of Christ's faithful is:

$$\text{Group A} + \text{Retired Bishops} = \text{Sub-Total} \div 2 =$$
$$\text{Other members of Christ's faithful.}$$

Because of the variables, it is impossible at this stage to arrive at a final number for those who will be called to attend the Council. However, it is possible to present some scenarios based on the rules and formula in C. 443, the data in Table 5.3, and making certain assumptions (Table 5.4).

The outcomes of each scenario (1-4) are concerning. In scenario 1, only 58 non-religious lay persons might be called to the Council, including 10 from tertiary institutions. They would constitute just 20% of all those called to attend, while total clerics might constitute up to 76%, and lay religious 5%. This outcome would, we believe, be totally unacceptable to Australian Catholics. Scenario 2 could also result in only 20% non-religious laity being called, equally unacceptable. Scenarios 1-4 all include a large number (20-30) of retired bishops, more than seems appropriate, but necessary (because of the formula) to maximize the number of priests and laity that can be called.

A fifth scenario, which would require an exemption from some aspects of C. 443, might provide a call to 5 retired bishops (selected by their peers), to 35 ordinary priests (1 per particular church and elected by their peers), to 5 permanent deacons (elected by their peers), and to some 150 non-religious lay men and women selected in a manner best determined at diocesan synods or assemblies held prior to the Council.

In this scenario, clerics might make up around 53% of all those called and lay persons (including lay religious 3%) 47%, with some 23-24% being women. We believe that something like this allocation of calls would likely satisfy the broad Catholic community.

In September 2018 *Catholics for Renewal* asked the ACBC President to lodge a request with the Holy See to grant a dispensation from the restrictive formula contained in C. 443. If the request has not yet been made, we again **recommend** that the ACBC immediately seek from the Holy See an exemption from certain aspects of C. 443 to ensure that at least one third of all those called to the Council are non-religious lay men and women, and gender balanced.

If a dispensation is granted, we **recommend** that every particular church (diocese, eparchy, ordinariate) have a minimum representation at the Council of 1 ordinary (not *ex officio*) priest (elected by his peers), and a minimum of 1 male and 1 female non-religious layperson, to be selected/ elected in a manner determined at a diocesan synod or assembly convened prior to the Council.

> ... The presence of a large body of non-religious lay men and women at the Plenary Council is essential if the Council is to understand the sensus fidei fidelium of Christ's entire faithful in Australia ...

The presence of a large body of non-religious lay men and women at the Plenary Council is essential if the Council is to understand the *sensus fidei fidelium* of Christ's entire faithful in Australia, for

> the body of the faithful as a whole, anointed as they are by the Holy One, cannot err in matters of belief. Thanks to a supernatural sense of the faith which characterizes the People as a whole, it manifests this unerring quality when, 'from the bishops down to the last member of the laity', it shows universal agreement in matters of faith and morals.[19]

As the number of non-religious laypersons must be sufficient to represent the diversity of experience in all the particular churches and ensure the full expression of the *sensus fidei fidelium* across Australia, we also **recommend** that for the 22 particular churches with more than 50,000 faithful, there be a scaled-up non-religious lay representation – always gender balanced – increasing to a maximum of 10 non-religious laypersons for the 3 dioceses with more than 500,000 faithful. This is not intended to be proportional representation, but simply to ensure that the Plenary Council hears adequately from the full diversity of voices within the particular churches.[20]

Among that diversity of voices we **recommend** that among the non-religious lay faithful to be selected/elected to represent the particular churches, special consideration be given to members of the indigenous, ethnic, LGBTIQ, and youth communities.

5.5 Who and how many can be invited as guests to the Council?

A third group (Group C) can also be invited to attend the Council if the ACBC considers it expedient. C. 443 § 6 refers to them as 'guests'. Whereas all others are to be "called', guests are to be 'invited'. Johnson (2000) comments that guests cannot be regarded as 'participants' and have no right to speak; but may be invited to speak and, if they do, should be listened to with attention.[21]

However, on 15 September 2018, just weeks before the Ordinary Assembly of the Synod of Bishops met to discuss Young People, Faith and Vocational Discernment, a new Apostolic Constitution, *Episcopalis communio*, was published by Pope Francis, listing those who may be invited to the Synod without voting rights. They included experts, auditors, fraternal delegates and special guests.[22] At the October 2018 Ordinary Assembly, 339 participants gathered, including 267 'Fathers', 23 'experts' and 49 'auditors'. The auditors included 34 young men and women (aged 18-29) selected to represent youth across the world, and they were permitted to deliver a 4-minute 'intervention' at the general assembly meetings, and to participate in the small working groups (14 by language), but not to vote. Only the 267 'Fathers'[23] had a vote, which was consultative,[24] and no female was included among them.

At a diocesan synod, a diocesan bishop can also, if he judges it opportune, invite 'observers', who can be other ministers or members of churches or ecclesial communities which are not in full communion with the Catholic Church; but they have no voting rights (C. 463).

As C. 443 places no limit on the number of guests that can be invited to a particular council, the ACBC has significant latitude in inviting guests to the Plenary Council 2020/21. Relying on precedents from other councils and synods, and *Episcopalis communio*, it may invite a wide variety of guests, including Catholic clerics and laypersons, ministers and members of other Christian churches, and also representatives of non-Christian faith communities. While guests have no right to speak or vote at the Council, the Council President can invite them to address the general assembly and participate in the working committee meetings. It should be expected that the ACBC will invite as experts a number of clerical and lay persons with professional competence in theology, canon law, and liturgy, as well as others who represent the various charisms and ministries of the People of God.

... The Plenary Council 2020/21 will be a significant event not only for the Church in Australia, but also for other churches outside Australia, particularly those in the Asia-Pacific region and those which share similar cultural values and historical ties. Representatives from these churches should certainly be invited as guests ...

The Plenary Council 2020/21 will be a significant event not only for the Church in Australia, but also for other churches outside Australia, particularly those in the Asia-Pacific region and those which share similar cultural values and historical ties. Representatives from these churches should certainly be invited as guests.[25] Moreover, in order to foster greater unity with other Christian churches in Australia, and more openness to dialogue and cooperation with non-Christian faith communities, some of their representatives should also be invited.

We **recommend** that the ACBC invite to the Plenary Council as guests a suitable number of experts, auditors, observers and special guests who may include:

i)   selected Catholic clerics, religious and laypersons with particular expertise;

ii) selected representatives of Catholic Episcopal conferences from the Asia–Pacific region;

iii) selected ministers and members of other Christian churches; and

iv) selected leaders of non–Christian faith communities.

All these guests may be invited to speak at a general assembly and in the working groups, but they cannot vote.

We **recommend** that the ACBC makes a decision as soon as possible on who and how many are to be called to the Council, and who and how many are to be invited as guests, and how they are to be selected or appointed.

5.6 Who can vote at the Plenary Council?

Canon 443 specifies two voting groups: those who have a 'deliberative' vote, and those who have a 'consultative' vote.

Those with a deliberative vote are all, and only, those bishops who have been called to the Council. Bishops who are called, but cannot attend for a just reason, can send a proxy, but the proxy will not have a deliberative vote (C. 444).

While all the retired titular bishops who currently live in Australia can be called, the ACBC is not obliged to call them, and it may call as many as it wishes. At 1 January 2019, there were 33 retired bishops resident in Australia. At 11 October 2020, there could be as many as 40. If all were called, they must attend.[26]

… Canon 443 specifies two voting groups: those who have a 'deliberative' vote, and those who have a 'consultative' vote …

We have two factors to consider regarding the calling of retired bishops. On the one hand, under the formula in C. 443, their number directly affects the number of priests and laity who can be called (C. 443 § 4): the more retired bishops who are called, the more priests and laypersons can be called. On the other hand, retired bishops were not generally known for their synodal approach to governance while in office and are unlikely to embrace the new synodality. If all 40 are still alive at October 2020, 24 will be aged 80 years or over, and 5 aged 90 years or over. None of them now have pastoral responsibilities and many are probably out of touch with the *sensus fidei* of the faithful. With their deliberative vote, they could have an undue influence on the Council's outcome.

We **recommend** that the ACBC, if it gains a dispensation from certain aspects of C. 443, limit to a maximum of 5 the number of retired titular bishops living in Australia who are called to the Council, but invite them all, as a group, to vote for those of their number whom they wish to be called. The 5 with the greatest number of votes can be called.

Those with a consultative vote include the others specifically listed in C. 443 §§ 3-4 who must be called or can be called, and can include priests, permanent deacons, male and female lay religious and male and female non-religious lay persons.

What does a consultative vote mean? Johnson (2000) states that all those mentioned in C. 443 §§ 3-4 "can speak but cannot vote" and that "the only participants who can vote on questions the council seeks to answer are the bishops and those equivalent to them", since voting is "so bound up with the bishop's leadership role".[27] This would suggest that it is the bishops alone who are the legislators, not the Council itself. At a diocesan synod, the sole legislator is the diocesan bishop (C. 466), since the general principle is that a diocesan bishop cannot delegate his legislative power (unlike his executive and judicial power) and must exercise it personally.[28]

Cusack (2000), however, argues that at a diocesan synod[29] the role played by those with a consultative vote is significant, and that "the entire decision-making process is a consultative one involving all the members of the faithful". While the bishop may seek the opinions of the synod members by means of a 'consultative vote' on the questions before them, since the synod is "not a college with decisional capacity, such votes are not intended as a binding majority decision, their purpose being to indicate the degree of concurrence among the synod members with regard to a given proposal".[30] While the diocesan bishop remains free in his ultimate decision, he may wish to accept the view expressed by the synod members; but he can reject it if, in his prudential judgment, there exists some grave obstacle.[31]

Waters (2018) believes that Canon 127 is "the fundamental canon for what should happen at the plenary council".[32] Canon 127 states that when a juridical decision is being made and the advice of some group of persons is to be given, the persons giving the advice must be convened and heard, and that there has to be an overriding reason for the superior (in this case, the bishops) to act against the vote of the advisors, especially if it is a unanimous one (C. 127 §§ 1-3).

At the two most recent Ordinary Assemblies of the Synod of Bishops, Pope Francis, the sole legislator, asked all the Fathers (with a consultative vote), to vote on each paragraph/proposition in the final document drafted by the Synod, and required a two-thirds majority vote in favour of each paragraph/proposition for 'moral unanimity', before it could be sent to him for his deliberative vote.[33] He also instructed that the votes be counted and the tally published. Bishops at the Council should also be mindful of Pope Francis' instruction on voting set out in his recent Apostolic Constitution *Episcopalis communio.*[34]

5.7 Plenary Council agenda

When the ACBC decided to convene the Plenary Council it stated that it "intends that the scope of consultation and discernment processes towards the Plenary Council will be inclusive of the whole Catholic community in its breadth and diversity".[35] Subsequently, it has said that the draft agenda will be developed from the input of local listening sessions, submissions made by Christ's faithful, consultations, a survey/questionnaire, more listening sessions, discernment, face-to-face encounters, immersion and spiritual retreats (see 3-year Schedule on Plenary Council website).

...Catholics for Renewal **is advocating strongly that diocesan synods or assemblies are integral to the preparation of the Plenary Council agenda ...**

Canon law specifically provides that the Christian faithful "are at liberty to make known their needs, especially their spiritual needs, and their wishes to the Pastors of the Church" and "they also have the right to make their views known to others of Christ's faithful" (C. 212 §§2-3). Until recently, the church structures – pastoral councils and synods – designed to promote and facilitate the expression of the faithful's desires and opinions have been largely denied them. *Catholics for Renewal* is advocating strongly that diocesan synods or assemblies are integral to the preparation of the Plenary Council agenda.

We **recommend** that each diocesan bishop, prior to the 2020 (First) session of the Council, convene a diocesan synod or assembly to ascertain the *sensus fidei* of the faithful in his care, and that this be an integral part of preparing the Plenary Council agenda. At this diocesan synod/assembly, the diocesan bishop should seek guidance on how to select the non-religious lay faithful who will best represent the diocese at the Plenary Council.

It might be expected that the clergy of the particular churches, particularly those engaged in parish and pastoral ministry, will be invited separately to formulate proposals for the agenda, based on the pastoral challenges they confront daily. Similarly, religious congregations, educational institutions such as universities, seminaries, theological faculties, diocesan education offices and boards, health and welfare organisations, and missionary institutes, should be invited to make specific contributions.

The matters and questions to be included on the agenda should be those that arise from and are shaped by the experiences of the particular churches in Australia. They should also be shaped by a careful reading of the signs of the times, and a thorough analysis of the submissions and results contained in the responses to a questionnaire or survey instrument prepared by experts.

...Archbishop Coleridge has pointed to some issues or 'signs of the times' which will need to be addressed if the Church in Australia is to stop drifting, revive hope and set a vision: ...

Archbishop Coleridge has pointed to some issues or 'signs of the times' which will need to be addressed if the Church in Australia is to stop drifting, revive hope and set a vision:

- better understanding of the culture in which the Church must proclaim the Gospel;
- how to deal with the fact that mass civic Christianity is 'over';
- facing the fact that the Catholic Church is not the power in Australia that it once was;
- planning the future of the Church in Australia at a very complex time;
- developing and revitalizing parish life and mission;
- confronting the critical issues of our times, such as same-sex marriage:
- the Church's response to the findings of the Royal Commission into child sexual abuse;

- contemporary issues of justice, peace, development and the environment;
- becoming a more missionary church, not one retiring behind defensive walls;
- reviewing ordained ministry and the diminishment of apostolic orders;
- examining the relationship between newer and older Catholic communities/parishes.[36]

The ACBC has indicated that some of the recommendations contained in the May 2017 *Open Letter to the Bishops3*7 signed by 3770 Australian Catholics, including the need for greater transparency, accountability and inclusion, and greater participation of the faithful in the selection of bishops, could be included in the council agenda.[38]

Overcaution in setting the Council agenda will almost certainly cause much angst, and suspicion that the bishops do not want to go forward, but are desirous to return to 'business as usual'.

5.8 Liturgy at the Plenary Council

Synods and councils are first and foremost "sacred gatherings where the participants open their hearts and minds to the guidance of the Holy Spirit".[39]

Each general assembly of the Plenary Council is an important opportunity for collective listening to what the Holy Spirit "is saying to the churches".[40] During the synodal deliberations, significant importance should be attached to liturgical celebrations and other forms of common prayer, to invoke the gifts of discernment and harmony on the members of the assembly. Following an ancient synodal tradition, at the start of each day, the Book of the Gospels is be solemnly enthroned, symbolically reminding all those in attendance of the need for docility to the Word, which is the 'Word of truth'.[41]

... Synods and councils are first and foremost 'sacred gatherings where the participants open their hearts and minds to the guidance of the Holy Spirit ...

We **recommend** that the liturgical celebrations at the Council incorporate in a symbolic and meaningful manner, wherever possible, the language, rituals, spirituality and culture of Australia's First Peoples.

5.9 How will voting at the Plenary Council take place?

The general rules of order and rules of procedure should be drawn up well before the first session of the Plenary Council in October 2020, so that discussion, interaction and voting can proceed with harmony and efficiency. The ACBC must ensure that they are transparent and provide accountability.

The President of the Council must ensure that these rules are put into practice and applied fairly. The usual procedural arrangement for voting at synods and councils is "*placet*" (in favour), "*non placet*" (not in favour), "*placet iuxta modum*" (in favour with reservation). It is assumed that this arrangement will be adopted.

In previous plenary councils all those attending were divided into several working groups or committees dealing with several broad areas, such as Faith, Discipline, Sacraments, Life and Ministry of Priests, and Catholic Education. Within these the detailed questions were addressed. It is assumed that a similar arrangement will be adopted.

The current legislation for the Church in Australia is essentially what is in the 1983 *Code of Canon Law.* With few exceptions, all the local Australian church legislation (371 decrees) that had been formulated at the 1844, 1869, 1885, 1895 and 1905 particular councils to deal with the peculiar needs, circumstances and conditions of Australia was abrogated at the 1937 4th Australasian Plenary Council.[42] Since 1985 only a handful of complementary legislation for Australia has been enacted by the ACBC.[43] If the Plenary Council 2020/21 is to compile a new body of legislation that meets the particular needs and circumstances of the People of God in Australia and responds to the current signs of the times, it will need to be bold and courageous and sublimely attentive and obedient to the Spirit.

We **recommend** that prior to the 2020 (first) session of the Council, the ACBC draw up and make public the agenda for the Council, which should contain a *Lineamenta* or 'preparatory document' which includes the questions to be addressed, a 'schemata' of the draft legislation or propositions to be presented at the Plenary Council, and well-researched background papers on the questions.

> ...While the Council is in progress, ordinary Catholics in Australia must feel satisfied that their voices and sensus fidei have been heard and are being taken into consideration. They must feel assured that that all decisions on legislation and pastoral issues will be arrived at through prayer, openness to the Spirit, discussion, dialogue, discernment, and consensus ...

While the Council is in progress, ordinary Catholics in Australia must feel satisfied that their voices and *sensus fidei* have been heard and are being taken into consideration. They must feel assured that all decisions on legislation and pastoral issues will be arrived at through prayer, openness to the Spirit, discussion, dialogue, discernment, and consensus.

Canon 127 provides some assurance, for it requires that when a juridical decision is being made, and the advice of some group of persons is to be given, the persons giving the advice must be convened and heard. Those whose advice is required must also give their opinions sincerely (C. 127 §3) for the sake of the pastoral needs of the People of God. It is not a trivial matter.[44]

Also, before any Council discussion takes place, all who have been called must make the profession of faith (C. 833), the purpose of this being to foster the *sensus fidei* amongst the members of the Council and to inspire them with love for the doctrinal and spiritual patrimony of the Church.[45]

Initial discussion of the questions to be treated will take place in the working committees and then in the general assemblies. If the guidelines set out in *Episcopalis communio* are followed, voting on draft texts and propositions developed in the working committees will take place at the general assemblies. The voting will gauge the degree of consensus and 'moral unanimity'. Drafts with a high level of consensus support will likely proceed directly to deliberative voting by the bishops.

At each session of the Plenary Council the opinions of the members with a consultative vote may be solicited by means of a vote, which is not intended as a binding majority decision, but rather to indicate the degree of concurrence amongst the synodal members with regard to a given proposal.

We **recommend** that the 'rules of procedure' for voting at the Council be drawn up well in advance of the first session, be put out for comment and feedback, and generally follow the guidelines set out in *Episcopalis communio* and the procedures used at the two recent ordinary assemblies of the Synod of Bishops.

The interval between the first and second sessions will be an important (6 months) period for further reflection and discernment.

We **recommend** that following the 2020 (first) session of the Plenary Council, the President of the Council commission a detailed report of the session, make it public, and invite comment and feedback from Christ's faithful. If necessary, he might seek further clarification of the *sensus fidei fidelium* on certain issues.

From this follow-up input, an *Instrumentum laboris* or 'working document' for the second session should be prepared, containing all the detailed draft legislation to be put before the Council members for their final consultative and deliberative voting at the 2021 (second) session.

We **recommend** that after the working committees have discussed the detailed draft legislation on specific issues with advice from experts (*periti*), the drafts be voted on by those with a consultative vote, and if they have majority support, they are to go forward to the general assembly of the 2021 (second) session of the Council.

We **recommend** that all draft laws and propositions which have received majority support from the working committees, should be voted on in the general assembly, paragraph by paragraph, by all those with a consultative vote. If the draft paragraph or proposition receives the support of two-thirds or more of those with a consultative vote, it should immediately go forward to the bishops for their deliberative vote. Draft paragraphs which gain the support of less than two-thirds but more than half, may be redrafted and put to another vote. Draft paragraphs which gain the support of half or less of those with a consultative vote should be set aside completely.

We **recommend** that all draft legislation which receives the support of two-thirds or more of those with a consultative vote, must go forward to the bishops for their deliberative vote; and that the bishops, unless they perceive some grave doctrinal or other reason to be an obstacle, should vote in favour of the draft legislation. The tally of consultative and deliberative votes should be made public.

We expect that approval of the proposed legislation or propositions by the bishops with a deliberative vote would require at least a two-thirds majority of votes in favour, as is the case with Episcopal conference legislation.[46] Even then, it would still require the approval (*recognitio*) of the Holy See, before it could become law for the whole Church in Australia.

We **recommend** that if a draft law or proposition fails to gain the support of a two-thirds majority of the bishops, the reasons why it failed, in their prudential judgment, and the vote tally, must be made public and recorded in the minutes of the Council to be sent to the Holy See.

5.10 Writing the legislation

We **recommend** that the text of the Council's legislation be written in a tone that is welcoming, and pastoral; in a style that is clear, open and inviting, not moralising, judgmental or controlling; that it be framed in the context of the Council's understanding of contemporary Australian society and the place of the Church in that society; and that it set out clearly its vision of how the Church might better progress God's mission in Australia.

5.11 Recommendations

Recommendation 5.1:

> that the ACBC immediately seek from the Holy See an exemption
> from certain aspects of C. 443 to ensure that at least one third of
> all those to be called to the Council are non-religious lay men
> and women and gender balanced; and that every particular church
> will have a basic representation at the Plenary Council of 1 priest
> (elected by his peers), and minimal 1 male and 1 female non-
> religious layperson, to be selected in a manner determined at a
> diocesan synod or assembly convened prior to the Plenary Council.

Recommendation 5.2:

> that the ACBC allocate to the 22 particular churches with
> more than 50,000 faithful a scaled-up gender-balanced lay
> representation, increasing to a maximum of 10 non-religious lay
> representatives for dioceses with more than 500,000 faithful, to
> ensure that the Plenary Council hears adequately from the full
> diversity of voices within the particular churches.[47]

Recommendation 5.3:

> that among the non-religious lay faithful to be selected/elected
> to represent the particular churches, special consideration be
> given to members of the indigenous, ethnic, LGBTIQ, and
> youth communities.

Recommendation 5.4:

> that the ACBC limit to 5 the number of retired titular bishops

living in Australia who may be called to the Plenary Council; and that it invite all these bishops, as a group, to vote for those of their number whom they wish to be called. The 5 with the greatest number of votes are to be called.

Recommendation 5.5:

that among those called to attend the Plenary Council, there be up to 5 permanent deacons.

Recommendation 5.6:

that the ACBC invite to the Plenary Council as guests a suitable number of experts, auditors, observers and special guests who may include:

i) selected Catholic clerics, religious and laypersons with particular expertise;

ii) selected representative of Catholic Episcopal conferences from the Asia-Pacific region;

iii) selected ministers and members of other Christian churches; and

iv) selected leaders of non-Christian faith communities.

All these guests should be invited to speak at the general assemblies and in the working groups, but they cannot vote.

Recommendation 5.7:

that the ACBC make a decision as soon as possible on who and how many are to be called to the Council, and who and how many are to be invited as guests to attend the Council, and how they are to be selected or appointed.

Recommendation 5.8:

that each diocesan bishop, prior to the first session of the Council, convene a diocesan synod or assembly to ascertain the *sensus fidei* of the faithful in his care, and that this be an integral part of preparing the Plenary Council agenda. At this diocesan synod/assembly, the diocesan bishop should seek guidance on how on how to select the lay faithful who will best represent the diocese at the Plenary Council 2020/21.

Recommendation 5.9:

that prior to the first session of the Council, the ACBC draw up and make public the agenda for the Council, which should contain a *Lineamenta* or 'preparatory document' including the questions to be addressed, a 'schemata' of the draft legislation or propositions to be presented at the Plenary Council, and well-researched background papers on the questions.

Recommendation 5.10:

that the 'rules of procedure' for voting at the Council be drawn up well in advance of the first session, be put out for comment and feedback, and generally follow the guidelines set out in *Episcopalis communio* and the procedures used at the two recent ordinary assemblies of the Synod of Bishops.

Recommendation 5.11:

that, after the 2020 (first) session of the Plenary Council, the President of the Council should commission a detailed report on the session, make it public, and invite comment and feedback from Christ's faithful. If necessary, he might seek further clarification of the *sensus fidei fidelium* on certain issues.

Recommendation 5.12:

that, after the working committees have discussed the detailed draft legislation on specific issues with advice from experts (*periti*), the drafts be voted on by those with a consultative vote, and if they have majority support, they are to go forward to the general assembly of the 2021 (second) session of the Council.

Recommendation 5.13:

that all draft laws and propositions which have received majority support from the working committees, should be voted on in the general assembly, paragraph by paragraph, by all those with a consultative vote. If the draft paragraph or proposition receives the support of two-thirds or more of those with a consultative vote, it should immediately go forward to the bishops for their deliberative vote. Draft paragraphs which gain the support of less than two-thirds but of more than half, may be redrafted and put to another vote. Draft paragraphs which gain the support of half or less of those with a consultative vote should be set aside completely.

Recommendation 5.14:

that all draft legislation which receives support from two-thirds or more of those with a consultative vote, must go forward to the bishops for their deliberative vote; and that the bishops, unless they perceive some grave doctrinal or other reason to be an obstacle, should vote in favour of the draft legislation. The tally of the consultative and deliberative votes should be made public.

Recommendation 5.15:

that if a draft law or proposition fails to gain the support of a two-thirds majority vote of the bishops, the reasons why it failed, in their prudential judgment, and the vote tally, must be made public and recorded in the minutes of the Council to be sent to the Holy See.

Recommendation 5.16:

that the text of the Council's legislation be written in a tone that is welcoming and pastoral; in a style that is clear, open and inviting, not moralising, judgmental or controlling; that it be framed in the context of the Council's understanding of contemporary Australian society and the place of the Church in that society; and that it set out clearly its vision of how the Church might better progress God's mission in Australia.

Recommendation 5.17:

that the liturgical celebrations at the Council incorporate in a symbolic and meaningful manner, wherever possible, the language, rituals, spirituality and culture of Australia's First Peoples.

Some discussion questions:

- In reflecting upon the preparatory period for the 2020/21 National Plenary Council what are your views about the processes for listening, contributing, receiving feedback and engaging in ongoing dialogue? (5.3)
- These sections indicate potential participants for the Plenary Council and the extent of their representation. Is this an appropriate mix? Are there other people/groups who should be involved, even if they are not entitled to vote? (5.1-5.6)
- How do you understand the difference between consultative and deliberative voting as it will operate at the Council? (5.6)
- Archbishop Coleridge has pointed to *signs of the times* to be addressed at the Council. Are there others you believe could be added? (5.7)
- Is your bishop convening a Diocesan Assembly or Synod prior to the Plenary Council in 2020? What would be the value of such an event? (Rec. 5.8)

Notes

1   Vatican II, *Lumen Gentium*, n. 37.
2   These were held in Canberra & Goulburn (1989 and 2004), Maitland-Newcastle (1992-93), Brisbane (2003), Cairns (2008-11), and Broken Bay (2011-12).
3   The last provincial council was convened in the Melbourne Province in 1907, and the last plenary council in 1937.
4   Worldwide, since Vatican II, only one plenary council has been convened (Philippines in 1991).
5   Provost, J., "Canon Law: The Next 25 Years" in CLSANZ, *Proceedings: Twenty-Fifth Annual Conference*, 1991, 192-3
6   Three of the earlier plenary councils (1869, 1885 and 1937) were convoked at the direction of the Holy See. The Councils of 1844, 1895 and 1905 were convoked on the initiative of the Australian bishops.
7   *The Catholic Leader*, 1 December 2016
8   Knox Lecture, May 2016
9   Plenary Council 3-year timeline. The 2nd session will be held in Sydney in May 2021. Retrieved from http://plenarycouncil.catholic.org.au/wp-content/uploads/2018/05/ThreeYearTimeline.pdf
10 Date of writing was 15 January 2019
11 Members include Archbishops Costelloe (President) and Comensoli, and Bishops Randazzo, Tarabay, and Kennedy.
12 Members include 8 women and 6 men.
13 Published on the Plenary Council website: www.plenarycouncil.catholic.org.au
14 Canon 443 §6
15 All figures cited in ii), iii) and iv) are those provided in *The Official Catholic Directory of the Catholic Church in Australia, 2018-2019*. The major superiors represent 5879 male and female religious. There are 300 diocesan and religious seminarians. The number of permanent deacons (not mentioned in C. 443) is 176.
16 At 31 December 2018 there were 33 retired bishops resident in Australia, another 4 who had tendered their resignation due to age but not retired, and another 3 who will have to tender their resignation due to age, before 11 October 2020. Of these 40 bishops, if all are still alive on 11 October 2020, 24 will be aged 80 years or more, and 6 will be aged 90 years or more.
17 Canon 443 § 1 3° does not explicitly include the Apostolic Nuncio, as his role is ambassador between the Holy See and the ACBC, not a bishop with pastoral responsibilities in Australia. He could however, be invited to the Council as a guest, without a vote.
18 While retired bishops are not members of an Episcopal conference, they have the right to attend ACBC plenary meetings, and are invited to make available to the Conference their special wisdom and experience. They have a consultative vote (Letter of Congregation for Bishops, 13 May 1999).
19 Vatican II, *Lumen Gentium*, n. 12
20 At 31 December 2017 there were 13 particular churches with a Catholic population of less than 50,000, 9 with 51,000-100,000, 6 with 100,000-200,000, 4 with 200,000-500,000 and 3 with more than 500,000. Cf. *Official Catholic Directory*, 2018-2019, *op. cit.*

21 Beal J et al., *New Commentary on the Code of Canon Law*, Paulist Press, NY, 2000. Johnson comments that C. 443 distinguishes between 'participants' (§§ 1-5) and 'guests' (§6), and between participants who can both speak and vote (§§ 1-2), participants who can speak but cannot vote (§§ 3-5), and guests, who are not to be regarded as participants in conciliar discussions. However, in footnote 69 he quotes Provost who states: "This does not mean that they [guests] might not be invited to speak to the assembly if they would wish to do so; on the contrary, at least courtesy would require that they ought to be so invited, and if they accept, that their expressions of opinion or advice be given careful attention" (p. 585).

22 Cf. Pope Francis, *Episcopalis communio*, Apostolic Constitution on the Synod of Bishops, 15 September 2018, n. 10, Art. 12. Cf. n. 8: "Besides the members, certain invited guests without voting rights may attend the Synod Assembly. These include Experts (*Periti*), who help with the redaction of documents; Auditors (*Auditores*), who have particular competence regarding the issues under discussion; Fraternal Delegates from Churches and Ecclesial Communities not yet in full communion with the Catholic Church. To these may be added further special guests (*Invitati Speciales*), chosen because of their acknowledged authority." Retrieved from: http://w2.vatican.va/content/francesco/en/apost_constitutions/documents/papa-francesco_costituzione-ap_20180915_episcopalis-communio.html

23 The 267 Fathers included 55 cardinals and patriarchs, 46 archbishops, 102 diocesan bishops, 37 auxiliary bishops, 6 vicars apostolic, 1 bishop prelate, 8 religious priests, 2 religious lay brothers (i.e. non-clerics), and 10 diocesan and religious priests nominated by the Pope. No women were included in this group.

24 The Synod of Bishops is an advisory body to the Pope (C. 342), but unless specifically granted by the Pope, it does not have deliberative power (C. 343).

25 The bishops of New Zealand were full participants in the 1st and 4th Australasian Plenary Councils in 1885 and 1937. Archbishop Coleridge has already spoken informally to them about some form of presence. The ACBC is one of 4 members (ACBC, CE PAC, NZCBC, PNG-SI) of the Federation of Catholic Bishops Conferences of Oceania. It would be expected that the other members will be invited as guests to the Council.

26 In addition to the already 33 retired titular bishops resident in Australia, there are another 4 who have already tendered their resignation due to age, and another 3 due to tender their resignation due to age before 11 October 2020. If they are all still alive on 11 October 2020, their number could total 40, with 24 aged 80 years or over, and 6 aged 90 years or over.

27 Beal, J et al. *op. cit.*, p. 584

28 Beal et al., *op. cit.,* p. 621

29 Cusack, B.A. in Beal et al., *op. cit*, p. 621. Cusack quotes Kennedy, R, "Shared responsibility in Ecclesial decision-making" in *Stud. Can.* 14 (1980) 5-23.

30 *Origins* 27 (October 23, 1997) 328, quoted by Cusack in Beal. Et al. op. cit., p. 621

31 *Ibid.* p. 621

32 Waters, Ian, "The Plenary Council and Canon Law", in *The Australasian Catholic Record*, 95 (2018), 399-411cf. p. 405

33 Cf. Pope Francis. (2018) *Episcopalis communio*, Apostolic Constitution on the Synod of Bishops. Retrieved from http://w2.vatican.va/content/

francesco/en/apost_constitutions/documents/papa-francesco_costituzione-
ap_20180915_episcopalis-communio.html Pentin, E. *Concerns Generated by
Lack of Clarity on Synod Voting Procedures in NCR*, Retrieved from http://
www.ncregister.com/blog/edward-pentin/concerns-generated-by-lack-of-
clarity-on-synod-voting-procedures

34 *Ibid.*
35 ACBC. Summary of Plenary Meeting 4-11 May 2017
36 *The Catholic Leader*, 17 August 2016
37 *The Swag*, Vol. 25, No. 2, Winter 2017, p. 15
38 ACBC, Summary Minutes of ACBC Plenary Meeting, May 2017
39 *Acts* 15:28
40 *Rev* 2:7
41 *Col* 1:5
42 Waters, I. (2006). *The Fourth Plenary Council of Australia and New Zealand* in
    Annuarium Historiae Conciliorum, Vol. 38, No. 6 pp. 451-466 Cf. Retrieved
    from https://repository.divinity.edu.au/3000/1/2008JA_Waters%252CIB_
    The_Fourth_Plenary_Council.pdf
43 Cf. Lucas, B., Slack, P. & d'Apice, W, *Church Administration Handbook*, St Pauls
    Publications, Sydney, 2011, Appendix D – "Complementary Legislation for
    Australia enacted by the Australian Catholic Bishops Conference".
44 Waters, Ian, "The Plenary Council and Canon Law" in *The Australasian
    Catholic Record*, 95 (2018), 399-411
45 Congregation for Bishops and Congregation for Evangelization of Peoples,
    Instruction on Diocesan Synods, 1997, IV, n. 3
46 Pope John Paul II, Motu Proprio, *Apostolos Suos*, 21 May 1998, cf. IV, Art.
    1: "In order that the doctrinal declarations of the Conference of Bishops
    referred to in No. 22 of the present Letter may constitute authentic
    magisterium and be published in the name of the Conference itself, they must
    be unanimously approved by the Bishops who are members, or receive the
    recognitio of the Apostolic See if approved in plenary assembly by at least two
    thirds of the Bishops belonging to the Conference and having a deliberative
    vote."
47 At 31 December 2017 there were 13 particular churches with a Catholic
    population of less than 50,000, 9 with 51,000-100,000, 6 with 100,000-
    200,000, 4 with 200,000-500,000 and 3 with more than 500,000. Cf. *Official
    Catholic Directory*, 2018-2019, *op. cit*. Cf. Table 5.5 for possible formulae for
    allocation of numbers.

Conclusion

In 2011 *Catholics for Renewal* sponsored an *Open Letter* to Pope Benedict XVI and the Australian Bishops (Appendix 1) signed by 8635 Australian Catholics. They lamented that the Church has been tainted by injustice and blemished by bad decisions, and they referred particularly to the sexual abuse scandal where the Church's initial response was manifestly inadequate and where some Church authorities, in their attempts to protect the institution, had exposed innocent young children to grave harm.

Those Australian Catholics prayed for:

a renewed Church that follows Christ more closely in every way ... a Church committed to authentic collegiality and subsidiarity ... open, transparent and accountable ... which respects due process, rejects every form of discrimination, listens to its people, promotes co-responsibility in every facet of its mission and ministry, and is compassionate to its core ... an outward-facing Church totally committed to justice, peace, ecumenism and dialogue with other faiths ... which advocates unequivocally for the rights of the oppressed and disadvantaged while tending practically to their needs ... a Church where all are 'one in Christ, with no more distinctions between male and female', and a Church whose leaders read well the signs of the times and interpret them in the light of the Gospel.

... respects due process, rejects every form of discrimination, listens to its people, promotes co-responsibility in every facet of its mission and ministry, and is compassionate to its core ...

In 2012, the Commonwealth Government established the Royal Commission into Institutional Responses to Child Sexual Abuse, which over 5 years of inquiry uncovered conclusive evidence of dysfunctional governance in the Catholic Church. The implications of this went far beyond the crimes of the clerical abusers and the cover-up by bishops; they went to the fundamental efficacy of the Church in pursuing its God-given mission.

The 2017 *Open Letter to the Australian Bishops* (Appendix 2) also sponsored by *Catholics for Renewal* and calling on the bishops to 'Please Listen and Act Now', identified the most urgent imperatives for what had to be done, for the Church in Australia had gone 'off mission'.

Vatican II made it very clear: "the Church, inspired by no earthly ambition, seeks but a solitary goal: to carry forward the work of Christ himself under the lead of the befriending Spirit".[1] The work of Christ is the proclamation and inauguration of the Kingdom of God on earth, but in Australia the Church had become a counter-sign of the Kingdom. That has to change and our Church must be renewed.

We rejoice that the present bishops of the Church in Australia have decided to convene a Plenary Council in 2020/21, for we see it as a graced opportunity to get our Church back 'on mission': proclaiming and building up God's Kingdom of Justice, Peace, Love, Unity, Equality, Compassion, and Freedom. Australia needs a healthy Catholic Church, a church at the service of all its people.

Catholics for Renewal has prepared this submission to the Plenary Council in faith, hope and prayer. We have trust in the Spirit and pray that the Council will find the best way to bring our Church back 'on mission' – God's mission, for which Jesus founded it.

Catholics for Renewal Inc.
PO Box 178
Doncaster Heights VIC 3109
www.catholicsforrenewal.org.au

Note

1   Vatican II, *Gaudium et Spes*, n. 3

APPENDICES

Appendix 1

Open Letter to Pope Benedict XVI and the Catholic Bishops of Australia (August 2011)

Dear Pope Benedict and Bishops of Australia,

We, the undersigned Catholics of Australia, write to you regarding our concerns for the Church. We ask that you consider these matters during the 2011 *Ad Limina* visit.

As Christ's faithful, we must speak out. Under Canon Law we have a right and a duty in keeping with our knowledge, competence and position, to manifest to our pastors our views on matters which concern the good of the Church (C. 212, §§ 2-3).

The Church no longer adequately inspires many of our communities. It has alienated too many adults who were born of Catholic parents, attended Catholic schools, and lived a sacramental life. It has become disconnected from, and irrelevant to the lives of too many of our children. With fewer priests, its ability to provide regular Eucharist in our parishes, especially in rural areas, has become increasingly limited. As an institution it does not yet embody the vision of Vatican II for a truly collegial Church in which decisions respect local cultures, communities and circumstances. Rather, it appears as an institution focussed on centralism, legalism and control, with few effective structures for listening and dialogue, and often more concerned with its institutional image and interests than the spirit of Christ.

Our Church has been tainted by injustice and blemished by bad decisions. We still reel from the sexual abuse scandal where the Church's initial response was manifestly inadequate and where some authorities, in their attempts to protect the institution, exposed innocent young people to grave harm. We were shocked at the lack of due process in the way Bishop Morris, a dedicated pastor, was removed from his diocese. We were dismayed by the failure to consult properly on the new English translations of our liturgy. We can no longer accept the patriarchal attitude towards women within our Church, and we fear that an extended claim to infallibility is stifling discussion on many important issues. These issues include some teachings on human sexuality, as well as new forms of ministry for women and married men; the latter an anomaly for a Church committed to equality, and which welcomes married ministers from other Christian traditions. These concerns undermine confidence and trust in you our leaders.

We want and pray for a renewed Church that follows Christ more closely in every way. We need a Church committed to authentic collegiality and subsidiarity. We seek an open, transparent and accountable Church, which respects due process, rejects every form of discrimination, listens to its people, promotes co-responsibility in every facet of its mission and ministry, and is compassionate to its core. We call for an outward-facing Church totally committed to justice, peace, ecumenism and dialogue with other faiths, and which advocates unequivocally for the rights of the oppressed and disadvantaged while tending practically to their needs. We need and want a Church where we are 'all one in Christ, with no more distinctions ... between male and female' (Galatians, 3:28) and whose leaders read well the signs of the times and interpret them in the light of the Gospel.

As a first step towards collegiality and subsidiarity, we call on each diocesan bishop to convene at an early date a synod in his diocese, under the provisions of Canon Law (CC. 460-468), to discuss how the local Church might be a more authentic witness in the 21st century. We also ask that Pope Benedict allow a return to a more accountable and consultative process for the appointment of bishops, giving both priests and people a real voice as was earlier Church practice. This could commence with the appointment of the next bishop of Toowoomba.

For all of us Jesus is the way, the truth and the life. As the People of God and your sisters and brothers in Christ, who together seek the Kingdom of God, we pray that the Spirit will guide us all ever closer to Jesus in the critical task of renewal.

Sincerely,

Note: The above letter was launched on 8 July 2011 and signed by 8635 Australian Catholics by 30 September 2011. The Open Letter was personally delivered to the Holy See by Archbishop Philip Wilson, President of the Australian Catholic Bishops Conference, during the bishops' Ad Limina visit in 2011. Despite follow-ups, there has been no response nor even acknowledgement.

Appendix 2

Open Letter to the Bishops of Australia:
'Please Listen and Act Now' (May 2017)

Dear Bishops,

The Royal Commission into Institutional Responses to Child Sexual Abuse has exposed grave governance failures in our Church, failures that undermine its very mission. We, the undersigned Catholics of Australia, write to you as Pilgrim People of God, accepting shared responsibility for our Church, expressing our sense of faith which Vatican II recognised as critical to the life of the Church, and asking you our bishops to listen and to act decisively, executing necessary reforms now.

Over several decades we have seen our Church declining steadily to its now shameful state. Countless Catholics have been alienated, particularly younger generations who are our Church's future. The Royal Commission has now exposed dysfunctional governance, an entrenched culture of clericalism, and a leadership not listening to the people. Too many bishops have denied the extent of clerical child sexual abuse and its systemic cover-up, and even protected paedophiles ahead of children.

The Victorian Parliamentary Inquiry also found that the Church's governance contributed to cover-ups and further abuse. Yet the failings go beyond the scandal of child sexual abuse. Archbishops have admitted to "a catastrophic failure of leadership", and some have spoken of "criminal negligence". Church credibility has been squandered. To rebuild trust, there must be reform of governance based on Gospel values, reflecting servant leadership and engagement with the faithful. There has to be accountability, transparency, and inclusion particularly of women.

Changing processes is not enough. We ask each and every bishop to **act now** on these reforms:

1. Eradicate **the corrosive culture of clericalism** – "an evil . . . in the Church" (Pope Francis).

2. Become truly **accountable with full involvement of the faithful**, including diocesan pastoral councils, and diocesan assemblies or synods; with pastoral plans and annual diocesan reports.

3. Appoint **women to more senior diocesan positions**, such as chancellor and delegate of bishops.

4. Hold **diocesan synods/assemblies** in 2018, with deanery and parish listening sessions, to develop the agenda for the national 2020/21 Plenary Council; and as part of normal diocesan governance.

5. Further remodel **priestly formation**, including ongoing development, assessment and registration.

6. **Reconcile publicly and fully** with all the persons abused, their families and communities, and commit to just redress.

7. Send **an urgent delegation, including lay persons, to Pope Francis**:

    i) urging him to **purge child sexual abuse** from the Church: legislating civil reporting of abuse, and ensuring effective discipline, major canon law reform, and review of priestly celibacy;

    ii) advising him of the Royal Commission's **exposure of the Church's global dysfunctional governance**; particularly its clericalist culture and lack of accountability, transparency, and inclusion, especially the exclusion of women from top decision-making positions; and

    iii) requesting immediate **reform of bishop selection** processes, fully including the faithful in identifying the needs of dioceses and local selection criteria.

None of the above proposals requires deferral to the Holy See or awaiting the Royal Commission's report before acting. All these actions are within your own competence. We ask you to lead the reform of our Church now, acting promptly and decisively – anything less would be a betrayal of the Gospel.

We pray that the Spirit guide us all at this critical time.
Catholics of Australia

Note: The above Open Letter was launched in February 2017 and signed by 3770 Australian Catholics by 15 June 2017

Appendix 3

A model Catholic Charter of Rights and Responsibilities of Christ's Faithful

- **Primacy of Conscience.** Every Catholic has the right and responsibility to develop an informed conscience and to act in accord with it.
- **Community.** Every Catholic has the right and responsibility to participate in a Eucharistic community and the right to responsible pastoral care.
- **Universal Ministry.** Every Catholic has the right and responsibility to proclaim the Gospel and to respond to the community's call to serve in appropriate ministries.
- **Freedom of Expression.** Every Catholic has the right to freedom of expression and the freedom to dissent, but always within the context of the Christian obligation to protect the rights and human dignity of others.
- **Sacraments.** All Catholics, according to their age and disposition, have the right and responsibility to participate in the liturgical and sacramental life of the Church.
- **Reputation.** All Catholics have the right to a good name and to due process.
- **Governance.** All Catholics, and their communities, have the right to a genuine participation in decision making, including the selection of leaders.
- **Participation.** All Catholics have the right and responsibility to share in the discernment of the Gospel message and Church tradition.

- All Catholics have the right and responsibility to enjoy and participate in regular Faith education, particularly in the Scriptures and the various theological disciplines.
- **Councils.** Catholics have the right to convene and speak in assemblies where diverse voices can be heard.
- **Social Justice.** Every Catholic has the right and the responsibility to promote social justice in the world at large as well as within the structures of the Church.

Note: This model charter was prepared in 2018 by the Yarra Deanery of the Archdiocese of Melbourne in collaboration with *Catholics for Renewal*.

Appendix 4

Tables and figures

FIGURE 1.1: RELIGIOUS IDENTITY OF AUSTRALIAN POPULATION, 1966 AND 2016

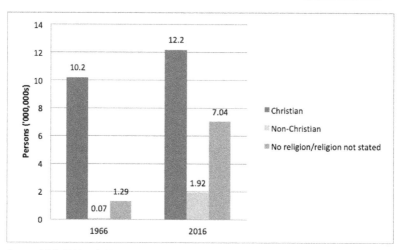

Source: ABS, 1966 and 2016 Commonwealth Census.

Figure designed by *Catholics for Renewal*.

Notes: 1. The 1966 Census contained no specific data on the Muslim population. In the 1971 Census, Muslims numbered 22,311. 2. 'No religion' includes secular and other spiritual beliefs. 3. In the 2016 Census, since the question on religious identity is 'optional', the total of respondents (21.2 million) does not equal the total population of 23.4 million.

FIGURE 1.2: RELIGIOUS AFFILIATIONS OF AUSTRALIAN POPULATION, 2016

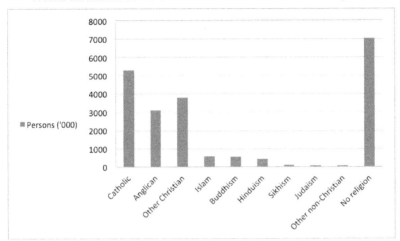

Source: ABS, Cat. 2071.0: Census of Population and Housing, 2016. Religion in Australia.
Figure designed by *Catholics for Renewal*.

FIGURE 1.3: TOTAL AUSTRALIAN AND CATHOLIC POPULATION, 1835-2017

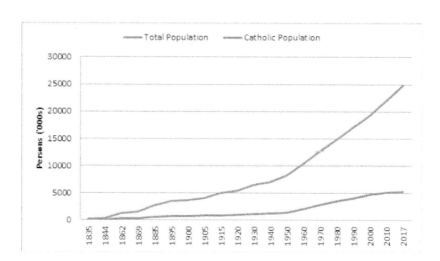

Source: Colonial and Commonweath Censuses, various years; ABS. Cat. no. 3105.0.65.001, *Australian Historical Population Statistics.* Official Catholic directories, various titles and various years.

Figure designed by *Catholics for Renewal.*

TABLE 1.1: BIRTHPLACE OF AUSTRALIAN CATHOLICS, 1961, 2011 AND 2016

Birthplace	1961	%	2011	%	2016	%
Australia	2,029,969	77.5	4,065,104	74.0	3,895,007	73.6
Italy	209,995	8.0	168,801	3.1	149,899	2.8
UK/Ireland	86,106	3.3	193,518	3.6	186,020	3.5
NZ	7243	0.3	73,145	1.3	68,837	1.3
Netherlands	41,241	1.6	24,861	0.5	21,037	0.4
Poland	38,257	1.5	36,117	0.7	31,974	0.6
Malta	36,514	1.4	37,816	0.7	33,473	0.6
Germany	35,763	1.4	30,478	0.6	27,015	0.5
Yugoslavia	32,451	1.2	49,197	0.9	43,490	0.8
India	3,108	0.1	48,209	0.9	59,699	1.1
Vietnam	n/a	n/a	39,892	0.7	44,227	0.8
Philippines	261	0.01	134,655	2.5	174,621	3.3
China/HK	2,039	0.08	22,423	0.4	23,677	0.4
Sri Lanka	n/a	n/a	20,216	0.4	22,778	0.4
Indonesia	1,437	0.05	16,821	0.3	17,602	0.3
South Korea	n/a	n/a	16,705	0.3	17,363	0.3
Other Asia	7,624	0.3	39,098	0.7	41,413	0.8
Central &South America	464	0.02	61,625	1.1	77,168	1.5
Middle East	5,395	0.2	55,787	1.0	65,811	1.3
Africa	11,577	0.4	27,961	0.5	34,410	0.7
Total Catholics	2,619,984		5,439,268		5,291,817	

Source: ABS, Commonwealth Census, 1961, 2011, 2016.

Table designed and calculations made by *Catholics for Renewal*.

TABLE 4.1: ADMINISTRATION OF SACRAMENTS OF INITIATION,
AUSTRALIA, 2001-2017

Year	Total Catholics	Baptisms 0-7 yrs	Baptisms Over 7 yrs	Total Baptisms	Confirmations	First Communions
2001	5,001,600	60,878	4,935	65,813	54,938	58,499
2006	5,126,884	61,844	6,428	68,272	54,466	49,000
2011	5,439,200	59,446	5,061	64,407	50,183	44,263
2017	5,291,817*	50,480	4,735	55,215	48,481	48,625
Change 2001-17	+ 5.8%	-17.1%	-4.1%	-16.1%	-11.8%	-16.9%

Source: *Annuarium Statisticum Ecclesiae,*Various years.

Notes: 1.* Figure is for the 2016 Census. 2.Vatican statistics do not show the number of adults (aged 18 and over) who specifically come through the RCIA process. Figures for many adults who are baptised in parishes at Easter are not collected consistently across dioceses. Also some who are baptised as infants complete their initiation much later by receiving the sacraments of Holy Communion and Confirmation as adults. Data on these groups are not currently available at a national level and better data collection methods are needed to have a complete picture of all who are received into the Catholic Church in Australia every year.

Table designed and calculations made by *Catholics for Renewal.*

**FIGURE 4.1: AUSTRALIAN CATHOLIC POPULATION AND
REGULAR MASS ATTENDERS: 1947-2016**

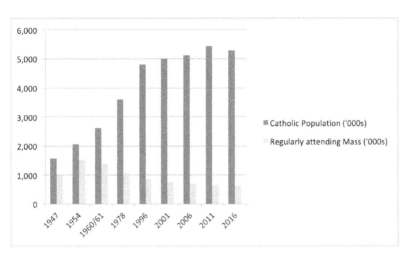

Sources: ABS Census Data, 1647, 1954, 1961, 1976, 1996, 2001, 2006, 2011, 2016; *Catholic Church Life Survey* 1996 and 2001; *National Church Life Survey* 2001 and 2006; *National Count of Attendance 2006;* CROPP, 1978; Mol, Hans, *The faith of Australians,* Allen & Unwin, North Sydney, 1985; O'Farrell, Patrick, *The Catholic Church and Community in Australia: A History,* Nelson, West Melbourne, 1977, p. 428, Gallup Polls, 1947, 1960, 1976 (Note: Gallup Poll rates have tended to be higher than actual attendance rates); Robert Dixon, Stephen Reid and Marilyn Chee, *Mass Attendance in Australia: A Critical Moment,* ACBC, 2013, cf. Table 3, page 7. Retrieved from https://ncpr.catholic.org.au/national-count-of-attendance/; and ACBC, NCPR, *2016 National Count of Attendance – National Summary. Retrieved from* https:// ncpr.catholic.org.au/wp-content/uploads/2019/04/Pastoral-Research-Online-Edition-44-April-2019.pdf
Figure designed by *Catholics for Renewal.*

TABLE 4.2: AVERAGE WEEKLY MASS ATTENDANCE IN 28 TERRITORIAL DIOCESES AND OTHER PARTICULAR CHURCHES, 2006 AND 2016

Diocese	2006 Catholic population	2006 Av. week attend	2006 Attend rate	2016 Catholic population	2016 Av. week attend	2016 Attend rate	Change 2006-2016 Change in Catholic Population	Change in attendance: number & (%)
Adelaide	278,017	34,085	12.3	274,135	28,340	10.3	-3,882	-5,745 (-16.9%)
Armidale	44,284	5,184	11.7	42,490	3,875	9.1	-1,794	-1,309 (-25.3%)
Ballarat	98,985	14,499	14.6	95,696	10,024	10.5	-3,289	-4,475 (-30.9%)
Bathurst	66,394	8,131	12.2	65,677	5,562	8.5	-717	-2,569 (-31.6%)
Brisbane	645,765	70,923	11.0	708,701	57,539	8.1	+62,936	-13,384 (-18.9%)
Broken Bay	213,285	29,502	13.8	215,449	22,586	10.5	+2,164	-6,916 (-23.4%)
Broome	8,308	830	10.0	8,480	694	8.2	+172	-136 (-16.4%)
Bunbury	53,640	4,805	9.0	64,296	5,573	8.7	+10,656	+768 (+16.0%)
Cairns	57,157	5,005	8.8	60,977	4,266	7.0	+3,820	-739 (-14.8%)
Canberra & Goulburn	159,670	20,814	13.0	155,088	16,156	10.4	-4,582	-4,658 (-22.4%)
Darwin	40,423	4,140	10.2	45,151	5,994	13.3	+4,728	+1854 (+44.8%)
Geraldton	23,004	2,150	9.3	27,596	1,962	7.1	+4,592	-188 (-8.7%)
Hobart	87,782	7,175	8.2	79,454	5,352	6.7	-8,328	-1,823 (-24.4%)
Lismore	108,168	12,072	11.2	104,580	8,699	8.3	-3,588	-3,373 (-27.9%)
Maitland-Newcastle	153,857	15,642	10.2	154,475	10,465	6.8	+618	-5,177 (-33.1%)
Melbourne	1,062,789	155,513	14.6	1,067,030	138,724	13.0	+4241	-16,789 (-10.8%)
Parramatta	319,228	51,684	16.2	322,677	47,005	14.6	+3,449	-4,679 (-9.1%)

Perth	379,012	54,449	14.4	429,715	58,119	13.1	+50,703	+3,670 (+6.7%)
Port Pirie	27,176	3,760	13.8	27,069	2,857	10.6	-107	-903 (-24.0%)
Rockhampton	97,847	10,382	10.6	108,566	8,119	7.5	+10,719	-2,263 (-21.8%)
Sale	103,645	11,838	11.4	123,594	11,960	9.7	+19,949	+122 (+1.0%)
Sandhurst	90,135	11,438	12.7	90,189	8,572	9.5	+54	-2,866 (-25.1%)
Sydney	594,730	103,310	17.4	594,145	93,365	15.7	-555	-9,945 (-9.6%)
Toowoomba	62,822	8,615	13.7	62,212	5,510	8.4	-610	-3,105 (-36.0%)
Townsville	72,956	6,177	8.5	79,008	5,544	7.0	+6,042	-633 (-10.2%)
Wagga Wagga	62,933	9,395	14.9	60,674	7,274	12.0	-2,309	-2,121 (-22.6%)
Wilcannia-Forbes	33,439	3,519	10.5	29,264	2,275	7.8	-4,175	-1,244 (-35.4%)
Wollongong	179,447	22,306	12.4	189,834	18,108	9.5	+10,387	-4,198 (-18.8%)
Other[1]	1,924[2]	21,279[3]		2,193[2]	30,777[1]		+259	+9,498 (+44.6%)
TOTAL	5,126,834	708,618	13.8	5,291,817	623,376	11.8	+164,933	- 85,242 (- 12.0%)

Source: Robert Dixon, Stephen Reid and Marilyn Chee, *Mass Attendance in Australia: A Critical Moment*, ACBC, 2013, cf. Table 3, page 7. Retrieved from https://ncpr.catholic.org.au/national-count-of-attendance/; ACBC, NCPR, *2016 National Count of Attendance – National Summary. Retrieved from* https://ncpr.catholic.org.au/wp-content/uploads/2019/04/Pastoral-Research-Online-Edition-44-April-2019.pdf

The National Count is conducted once every 5 years over 4 consecutive weeks in all parishes and wherever Mass is celebrated publicly. It takes place in the same year as the Commonwealth Census. Notes: 1. 'Other' includes the Chaldean, Maronite, Melkite, Syro-Malabar and Ukrainian Churches, and the Military and Anglican Ordinariates. 2. This figure includes only Catholics of the Military Ordinariate who live on military bases. Numbers for all the 'other' particular churches (Note 1) are included in the totals for the 28 territorial dioceses. 3. 'Average weekly total attendance' is the average for the 4 weeks of the Count. It does not take into account special circumstances.

Table designed and calculations made by *Catholics for Renewal*.

FIGURE 4.2: ALL SEMINARIANS (DIOCESAN AND RELIGIOUS), AUSTRALIA, 1835-2017

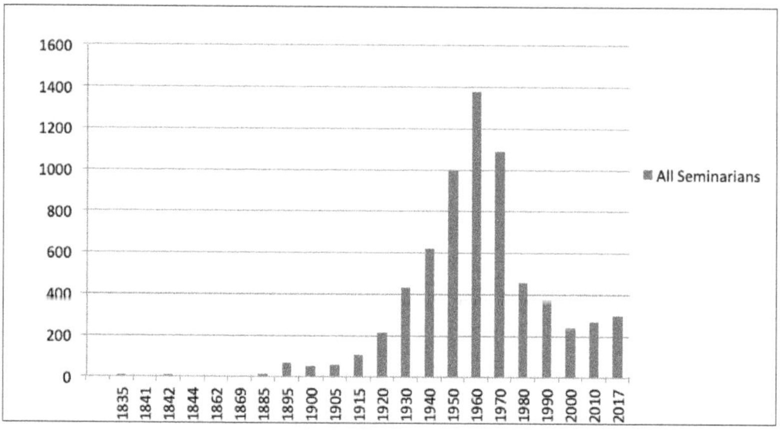

Source: Official Catholic Directories, various titles and various years.

Figure designed by *Catholics for Renewal*.

**TABLE 4.3: CATHOLIC CHURCH–REGISTERED MARRIAGES OF
CATHOLICS IN AUSTRALIA, 2001-2017**

Year	Catholic Population	Church marriages between Catholics	Mixed Marriages	Total church Marriages
2001	5,001,600	8,180	7,835	16,015
2006	5,126,884	8,043	6.942	14,985
2011	5,439,200	6,557	5,823	12,380
2017	5,291,817★	4,458	3,437	7,895
Change 2001–2017	+ 5.8%	-45.5%	-56.1%	-50.7%

Source:Vatican, *Annuarium Statisticum Ecclesiae*, various years.

Table designed and calculations made by *Catholics for Renewal*.

Notes: 1. The marriages in the table are those celebrated according to the rites of the Catholic Church and registered by a registered Catholic celebrant.

2. A 'mixed' marriage is one between a baptised Catholic and a baptised non-Catholic.

**TABLE 4.4: REGISTERED MARITAL STATUS OF CATHOLICS IN AUSTRALIA
AGED 15 YEARS AND OVER, BY GENDER, 2016**

Marital status by Age	Males	Males %	Females	Females %	Total	Total %
Never Married	727,287	36.7	684,790	30.3	1,412,077	33.3
Married	1,007,990	50.9	1,100,345	48.6	2,108,335	49.7
Separated/ Divorced	197,677	10.0	278,648	12.3	476,325	11.2
Widowed	47,189	2.4	199,548	8.8	246,737	5.8
All aged 15 yrs and over	1,980,143	100.0	2,263,331	100.0	4,243,474	100.0
Aged under 15 yrs	534,976		513,383		1,048,359	
Total Catholics	2,515,119		2,776,714		5,291,833	

Source: *ABS Census of Population and Housing, 2016 – National Centre for Pastoral Research, Social Profile of the Catholic Community in Australia based on the 2016 Australian Census, Canberra, March 2019, p. 13, Table 12.*

TABLE 4.5: PARISHES IN TERRITORIAL DIOCESES OF AUSTRALIA: 1986-2017

Diocese	Parishes in 1986	Parishes in 1996	Parishes in 2006	Parishes in 2016	Parishes in 2017	Change in Parish numbers +/- since 1986	Total Priests 2017	Priests F/T in Parish Ministry, 2017	Overseas-born priests, 2017 estimate	OS-born priests as % of priests F/T in parish ministry, 2017
Adelaide	75	78	67	56	57	-18	130	64	27	42
Armidale	26	25	25	25	25	-1	42	22	13	59
Ballarat	54	53	52	51	50	-4	55	27	4	15
Bathurst	25	25	21	17	17	-8	35	14	6	43
Brisbane	116	111	109	100	98	-18	265	120	68	57
Broken Bay	39	39	40	26	26	-13	98	56	39	70
Broome	11	10	9	9	9	-2	13	13	9	69
Bunbury	26	26	27	28	28	+2	43	29	24	83
Cairns	25	24	25	23	23	-2	29	16	5	31
Canberra & Goulburn	63	59	55	55	55	-8	73	44	18	41
Darwin	11	16	17	15	15	+4	23	20	14	70
Geraldton	21	21	12	16	16	-5	19	12	7	58
Hobart	41	40	27	27	27	-14	49	28	14	50
Lismore	32	30	28	22	22	-10	49	27	9	33
Maitland-Newcastle	53	53	45	39	38	-15	50	32	12	38

Melbourne	231	233	228	216	208	-23	479	230	115	50
Parramatta	45	45	48	47	47	+2	128	70	41	59
Perth	105	104	104	108	109	+4	276	133	92	69
Port Pirie	28	24	26	16	16	-12	27	17	6	35
Rockhampton	41	36	34	31	31	-10	39	18	11	61
Sale	30	29	26	26	27	-2	36	25	13	52
Sandhurst	41	41	41	40	40	-1	55	30	11	37
Sydney	141	137	141	136	136	-5	475	159	84	53
Toowoomba	36	35	35	35	37	+1	41	17	6	35
Townsville	29	30	27	27	27	-2	27	16	10	63
Wagga Wagga	30	29	31	34	32	+2	55	34	7	21
Wilcannia–Forbes	21	20	20	20	20	-1	26	15	7	47
Wollongong	31	32	31	32	32	+1	82	33	4	12
TOTAL PARISHES	1427	1405	1350	1277	1268	-159	2718	1321	676	51%

Source: *The Official Directory of the Catholic Church in Australia*, various years. Note: 1. No Official Directory was published for 1986/87, 1987/88 or 1989/90. 2. The last two territorial dioceses to be established were Broken Bay and Parramatta in 1986. 3. There is a 3% margin of error for data on overseas-born priests.

Table design, estimates and calculations made by *Catholics for Renewal*.

FIGURE 4.3: TOTAL PRIESTS IN AUSTRALIA AND CATHOLICS PER PRIEST, 1820-2017

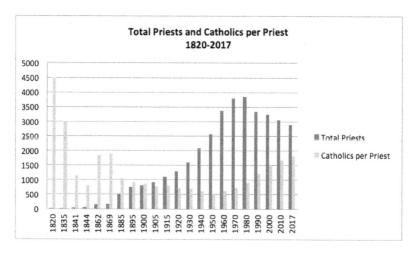

Source: Official Catholic directories, various titles and years.

Note: 1. Catholics per priest is based on total priests, both active and retired. If the ratio in territorial dioceses in 2017 was based on active full-time priests in parish ministry, there would be one priest for every 4070 Catholics.

**TABLE 4.6: BIRTH REGIONS OF ACTIVE FULL-TIME PRIESTS IN
1268 TERRITORIAL PARISHES, AUSTRALIA, AT 31 DECEMBER 2017**

Priest Type	Aust-ralia	Africa	Asia[1]	Eur-ope	Amer-icas	Mid-East	Oce-ania	Other OS[2]	Total Overseas	Grand Total
Diocesan	517	69	193	39	14	5	8	18	346	863
Religious	128	16	209	74	2	0	4	25	330	458
Total	645	85	402	113	16	5	12	43	676	1321

Source: *The Official Directory of the Catholic Church in Australia, 2018-2019* (for Grand Totals only). The table design, estimates and calculations were made by Catholics for Renewal relying on a multiplicity of Catholic diocesan and other website sources. In identifying the birth regions, Catholics for Renewal acknowledges a possible margin of error of around 3%-5%. Notes: 1. A significant number of the overseas-born priests, especially the Vietnamese, arrived in Australia with their parents as children and grew up in Australia. 2. It was not possible to identify particular birth regions for these priests.

TABLE 5.1: PARTICULAR COUNCILS HELD IN AUSTRALIA: 1844–1937

Particular Synod/Council	Year	Place Held	Bishops (or equivalent) attending	Clerics attending	Decrees enacted
1ˢᵗ Australian Provincial Council, (Follow-up meeting)[1]	1844, (1862)	Sydney, (Melbourne)	3 (Australian only) (4) (Australian only)	33	48 (Supplement)
2ⁿᵈ Australian Provincial Council	1869	Melbourne	8 (Australian only)	30	38
1ˢᵗ Australasian Plenary Council	1885	Sydney	18 (Australian & NZ)	52	272
2ⁿᵈ Australian Plenary Council	1895	Sydney	23 (Australian only)	49	344
3ʳᵈ Australian Plenary Council	1905	Sydney	21 (Australian only)	49	371
1ˢᵗ Melbourne Provincial Synod	1907	Melbourne	4 (Victorian only)	18	112
4ᵗʰ Australasian Plenary Council	1937	Sydney	33 (Australian & NZ)	59	685

Note: 1. The Provincial Councils in 1844 and 1869 were 'plenary' in character, as there was only one ecclesiastical province (Sydney) covering the whole country. 2. A 2ⁿᵈ Provincial Council was planned for 1862, but only 4 of the 6 bishops met and it was not convened or celebrated in the canonical manner. The Holy See did not recognise it as a canonical provincial council or approve its legislation. The document it prepared on the discipline for priests was published only as a Supplement to the decrees of the 1844 1ˢᵗ Provincial Council. 3. In 1922 the Australian bishops agreed to hold a plenary council in 1925, but no action was taken. In 1932 Archbishop Kelly of Sydney proposed a provincial council, but was advised by his suffragans that a plenary council would be more appropriate. A proposal for a plenary council was also put forward in 1962, but deferred until after the 2ⁿᵈ Vatican Council and the publication of the Revised *Code of Canon Law* in 1983.

Table designed by *Catholics for Renewal*.

TABLE 5.2: PARTICIPANTS IN THE 2020/21 PLENARY COUNCIL (BASED ON CANON 443)

Those who **must** be called	Voting Rights	Those who **can** be called	Voting Rights
Diocesan bishops	Deliberative	Titular bishops retired or living in Australia	Deliberative
Coadjutor & auxiliary bishops	Deliberative	Priests of Christ's faithful	Consultative
Titular bishops with special function	Deliberative	Other members of Christ's faithful[4]	Consultative
Vicars general of all particular churches	Consultative		
Episcopal vicars of all particular churches	Consultative		
Major superiors of religious institutes[1]	Consultative		
Rectors of Catholic universities[2]	Consultative	Those who **can** be invited as guests	
Deans of theology & canon law faculties	Consultative		
Rectors of major seminaries[3]	Consultative	Others (as guests, but not participants)	Nil

Notes: 1. Includes societies of apostolic life for both men and women. The number of those to be called will be determined by the ACBC and they are to be elected by all the major superiors with a presence in Australia. 2. Includes ecclesiastical universities in Australia. 3. The number will be determined by the ACBC and they will be elected by all the rectors. 4. These can include deacons, non-ordained male and female religious and other lay men and women. Their numbers will be determined using a special calculation (see text).

Table designed by *Catholics for Renewal*.

TABLE 5.3: SUB-GROUPS OF THOSE WHO MUST OR CAN BE CALLED TO THE PLENARY COUNCIL 2020/21 (DATA CORRECT AT 31 DECEMBER 2017)

Particular Churches/Religious Institutes	Dioc. Bish.	Auxil. Bish.	Ret. Bish.	Vicars Gen.	Episc. Vicar	Relig. Instit.	Cath. Unis.	Major Sems.	Th/CL Facul.	Sub-Totals	Total Catholics
Sydney	1	3	2	1	3		3	2	4	19	594,145
Armidale	1		1	1						3	42,490
Bathurst	1			1	1					3	65,677
Broken Bay	1		1	1	1					4	215,449
Lismore	1		1	1	1					4	104,580
Maitland-Newcastle	1		1	1						3	154,475
Parramatta	1	2	2	2	7			1		13	322,677
Wagga	1		1	1				1		4	60,674
Wilc/Forbes	1		1	1	2					5	29,264
Wollongong	1		1	2						4	189,834
Canb/Goulb	1		2	1	1					5	155,088
Melbourne	1	3	2	1	5		2	2	3	19	1,067,432
Ballarat	1		1	1	1					3	95,696
Sale	1			1	1					3	123,594
Sandhurst	1			1	1					3	90,189
Hobart	1		1	1						3	79,454
Adelaide	1			2				0		3	274,135
Darwin	1		1	1						3	45,151
Port Pirie	1			1						2	27,069

Particular Churches/Religious Institutes	Dioc. Bish.	Auxil. Bish.	Ret. Bish.	Vicars Gen.	Episc. Vicar	Relig. Instit.	Cath. Unis.	Major Sems.	Th/CL Facul.	Sub-Totals	Total Catholics
Perth	1	1	1	1	3			2		9	429,715
Broome	1			1						2	8,480
Bunbury	1			1						2	64,296
Geraldton	1		1	1						3	27,596
Brisbane	1	1	3	1				1		7	708,701
Cairns	1			1	2					4	60,977
Rockhampton	1		1	1						3	108,566
Toowoomba	1		1	1						3	65,212
Townsville	1			1						2	79,008
Melkite Greek	1			1						2	2,579
Ukrainian	1			1	1					3	2,906
Maronite	1		2	1	4					8	36,434
Chaldean	1		1	1						3	10,029
Syro-Malabar	1			1				1		3	8,353
Military	1			1	2					4	2,193
Anglican	1									1	
Elsewhere			3								
Religious Instities								13			
Clerical Religious						41					

Particular Churches/Religious Institutes	Dioc. Bish.	Auxil. Bish.	Ret. Bish.	Vicars Gen.	Episc. Vicar	Relig. Instit.	Cath. Unis.	Major Sems.	Th/CL Facul.	Sub-Totals	Total Catholics
Relig. Brothers						5					
Relig. Women						93					
Soc. of i Ap. Life						7					
Totals	35	8	31	37	35	146	5	23	6	165	5,291,817

Source: *The Official Directory of Catholic Church in Australia, 2018-2019.*

This data was accurate at 31 December 2017. Notes: 1. The dioceses of Adelaide and Wagga Wagga at 15 January 2019 had Apostolic Administrators. In law, these are equivalent to diocesan bishops. 2. The Ordinary of the Anglican Ordinariate is not a bishop, but is the equivalent of a diocesan bishop. 3. Retired bishops include those who served outside Australia but now reside in Australia. They include Cardinal Cassidy and Bishops O'Grady OP and Crapp OFM. At 15 January 2019 the number of retired bishops eligible to attend the Council is 33. 4. Several Vicars General are also Episcopal Vicars. They have not been double-counted in the table. 5. Lay vicars, usually Vicars for Religious (5 in Australia) are only the 'delegates' of the bishop and are not equivalent to Episcopal Vicars. 6. The total number of major seminaries (23) listed in the Official Directory is dubious. 7. The Catholic ecclesiastical universities and (faculties) are: ACU (Theology), Catholic Institute of Sydney (Theology), Notre Dame University (Theology), Broken Bay Institute (Theology & Canon Law), and possibly the University of Divinity (Melbourne) with CTC (Theology) and YTU (Theology). 8. There are 146 major superiors of religious orders: 46 for male clerics, 93 for religious sisters, 5 for religious brothers, and 7 for Societies of Apostolic Life. The ACBC will decide the number for each group, and the relevant group will elect their own representatives. The major superiors represent 1039 clerics, 4161 sisters and 679 brothers, many of whom are quite old and retired from ministry.

(Table designed and calculations made by *Catholics for Renewal*.)

**TABLE 5.4: VARIOUS SCENARIOS FOR WHO IS CALLED TO
ATTEND THE PLENARY COUNCIL**

	Status	Scenario 1	Scenario 2	Scenario 3	Scenario 4	Scenario 5★★
GROUP A						
-Ordinaries	Bishop	35	35	35	35	35
-Aux. Bishops	Bishop	8	8	8	8	8
-Vicars General	Cleric	37	37	37	37	37
-Episc.l Vicars	Cleric	35	35	35	35	35
-Uni. Rectors	Lay	4	4	4	4	4
-Facult. Deans	Cleric/Lay	6	6	6	6	6
-Sem. Rectors★	Cleric	10	10	10	10	10
-Rel. Superiors★	Cleric/Lay	30	25	20	20	20
TOTAL GROUP A		165	160	155	155	155
GROUP B						
-Ret. Bishops★	Bishop	30	25	20	25	5
-Other priests★	Cleric	48	46	44	45	40
-Other Faithful★	Lay	48	46	44	45	140
TOTAL GROUP B		126	117	108	115	185
GROUPS A + B		291	277	263	270	340
Clerics		218 (75%)	211 (76%)	201 (76%)	207 (77%)	180 (53%)
Lay Religious		15 (5%)	12 (4%)	10 (4%)	10 (3%)	10 (3%)
Laity		58 (20%)	54 (20%)	52 (20%)	53 (20%)	150 (44%)

Table design and calculations made by *Catholics for Renewal*.

Notes: '★' signifies that the number of members from these groups are variable, and will be determined by the ACBC. 2. No provision is made for permanent deacons in C. 443 and they should be allocated some places among the 'Other members of Christ's Faithful' (Scenario 5 allocates 5 places among the priests in Group B. 3. '★★' This scenario would require dispensation from C. 443. It could allow an increase in the lay membership of up to 47%, including at least 150 non-religious lay men and women and gender balanced.

TABLE 5.5: POSSIBLE FORMULAS FOR ALLOCATION OF SUPPLEMENTARY LAY FAITHFUL NUMBERS TO THE PARTICULAR CHURCHES

Catholic population of the 35 particular churches in Australia	Number of particular churches	Number of lay faithful who may be called (Formula 1)	Number of lay faithful who may be called (Formula 2)
Less than 50,000	13	2	2
50,000– 100,000	9	4	4
101,000–200,000	6	6	6
201,000–500,000	4	8	6
More than 500,000	3	10	8
Total	35	160	146

Source: *The Official Directory of the Catholic Church in Australia*, 2018-2019, p. 795.

Table design and calculations made by *Catholics for Renewal.*

SUPPLEMENTS

Supplement 1

1. Contact details for Apostolic nuncio, diocesan bishops, eparchs, other ordinaries, auxiliary bishops, and Australian Catholic Bishops Conference

Apostolic Nunciature in Australia
Most Rev Adolfo Tito Yilana
Apostolic Nuncio in Australia
PO Box 3633
MANUKA ACT 2603
Email: nuntius@nunciature.com.au
Tel: (02) 6295 3876

Province of Sydney (NSW & ACT)
Most Rev Anthony Fisher OP
Archbishop of Sydney
Catholic Church Offices
Polding Centre,
133 Liverpool Street
SYDNEY NSW 2000
Email: archbishop@sydneycatholic.org
Tel: (02) 9390 5188

Most Rev Terence Brady
Auxiliary Bishop for the Northern Region (Sydney)
15 Quirk Street
ROZELLE NSW 2039
Email: terry.brady@sydneycatholic.org
Tel: (02) 9390 5992

Most Rev Anthony Randazzo
Auxiliary Bishop for the Western Region (Sydney)
Polding Centre
133 Liverpool Street
SYDNEY NSW 2000
Email: bishop.tony@sydneycatholic.org
Tel: (02) 9390 5100

Most Rev Richard Umbers
Auxiliary Bishop for the South-Eastern Region (Sydney)
Polding Centre
133 Liverpool Street
SYDNEY NSW 2000
Email: richard.umbers@sydneycatholic.org
Tel: (02) 9390 5100

Most Rev Michael Kennedy
Bishop of Armidale
PO Box 93
ARMIDALE NSW 2350
Email: chancery@armidale.catholic.org.au
Tel: (02) 6771 8700

Most Rev Michael McKenna
Bishop of Bathurst
PO Box 246
BATHURST NSW 2795
Email: bishop@bathurst.catholic.org.au
Tel: (02) 6334 6400

Very Rev David Ranson
Administrator of Broken Bay Diocese
PO Box 340
PENNANT HILLS NSW 1715
Email: bishop@bbcatholic.org.au
Tel: (02) 8379 1614

Most Rev Gregory Paul Homeming OCD
Bishop of Lismore
PO Box 1
LISMORE NSW 2480
Email: chancery@lismore.catholic.org.au
Tel: (02) 6622 0407

Most Rev William Wright
Bishop of Maitland-Newcastle
PO Box 780
NEWCASTLE NSW 2300
Email: bishopsoffice@mn.catholic.org.au
Tel: (02) 4979 1109

Most Rev Vincent Long Van Nguyen OFM Conv
Bishop of Parramatta
PO Box 3066
NORTH PARRAMATTA NSW 1750
Email: bishop@parramattacatholic.org
Tel: (02) 8838 3400

Most Rev Christopher Prowse
Administrator of Wagga Wagga Diocese
PO Box 473
WAGGA WAGGA NSW 2650
Email: kwilliams@wagga.catholic.org.au
Tel: (02) 6937 0003

Most Rev Columba Macbeth-Green OSPPE
Bishop of Wilcannia-Forbes
PO Box 775
FORBES NSW 2871
Email: chancery@wf.catholic.org.au
Tel: (02) 6853 9340
Mob: 0427 003 612

Most Rev Brian Mascord
Bishop of Wollongong
PO Box 1239
WOLLONGONG NSW 2500
Email: bishop@dow.org.au
Tel: (02) 4222 2400

Most Rev Christopher Prowse
Archbishop of Canberra & Goulburn
PO Box 89
CANBERRA ACT 2601
Email: archbishop@cg.org.au
Tel: (02) 6939 9811

Province of Melbourne (VIC & TAS)

Most Rev Peter A Comensoli
Archbishop of Melbourne
PO Box 146
EAST MELBOURNE VIC 8002
Email: archbishop@cam.org.au
Tel: (03) 9926 5612

Most Rev Terence Curtin
Auxiliary Bishop for the Northern Region (Melbourne)
Bishop's House
22A Robinson Street
MOONEE PONDS VIC 3039
Email: terry.curtin@cam.org.au
Tel: (03) 9375 7161

Most Rev Mark Edwards OMI
Auxiliary Bishop for the Western Region
386 Geelong Road
KINGSVILLE VIC 3012
Email: mark.edwards@cam.org.au
Tel: (03) 9412 8404 (Office)

Most Rev Paul Bird CSsR
Bishop of Ballarat
PO Box 121
BALLARAT VIC 3353
Email: paul.bird@ballarat.catholic.org.au
Tel: (03) 5337 7121

Most Rev Patrick O'Regan
Bishop of Sale
PO Box 1410
WARRAGUL VIC 3820
Email: bishop@sale.catholic.org.au
Tel: (03) 5622 6690

Most Rev Leslie Tomlinson
Bishop of Sandhurst
PO Box 201
BENDIGO VIC 3552
Email: chancery@sandhurst.catholic.org.au
Tel: (03) 5441 2544

Most Rev Julian Porteous
Archbishop of Hobart
GPO Box 62
HOBART TAS 7001
Email: archbishop@aohtas.org.au
Tel: (03) 6208 6222

Province of Adelaide (SA & NT)

Most Rev Gregory O'Kelly SJ
Administrator of Adelaide Archdiocese
GPO Box 1364
ADELAIDE SA 5001
Email: cco-reception@adelaide.catholic.org.au
Tel: (08) 8210 8210

Most Rev Gregory O'Kelly SJ
Bishop of Port Pirie
PO Box 1206
PORT PIRIE SA 5540
Email: diocoffice@pp.catholic.org.au
Tel: (08) 8632 0550

Most Rev Charles Gauchi
Bishop of Darwin
GPO Box 476
DARWIN NT 0801
Email: diocadmin@darwin.catholic.org.au
Tel: (08) 8942 6008

Province of Perth (WA)
Most Rev Timothy Costelloe SDB
Archbishop of Perth
PO Box 3311
EAST PERTH WA 6892
Email: archexec@perthcatholic.org.au
Tel: (08) 6104 3650

Most Rev Donal Sproxton
Auxiliary Bishop of Perth
PO Box 3311
EAST PERTH WA 6892
Email: don.sproxton@perthcatholic.org.au
Tel: (08) 6104 3650

Most Rev Christopher Saunders
Bishop of Broome
PO Box 76
BROOME WA 6725
Email: bishop@broomediocese.org
Tel: (08) 9192 1060

Most Rev Gerard Holohan
Bishop of Bunbury
PO Box 2005
BUNBURY WA 6231
Email: dio@bunburycathholic.org.au
Tel: (08) 9721 0515

Most Rev Michael Morrissey
Bishop of Geraldton
PO Box 46
GERALDTON WA 6531
Email: bishop@diocese-geraldton.org
Tel: (08) 9921 3221

Province of Brisbane (QLD)

Most Rev Mark Coleridge
Archbishop of Brisbane
GPO Box 282
BRISBANE QLD 4001
Email: archbishop@bne.catholic.net.au
Tel: (07) 3324 3415

Most Rev Kenneth Howell
Auxiliary Bishop of Brisbane
GPO Box 282
BRISBANE QLD 4001
Email: archbishop@bne.catholic.net.au
Tel: (07) 3324 3415

Most Rev James Foley
Bishop of Cairns
PO Box 625
CAIRNS QLD 4870
Email: bishop@cairns.catholic.org.au
Tel: (07) 4051 2071

Most Rev Michael McCarthy
Bishop of Rockhampton
PO Box 611
ROCKHAMPTON QLD 4700
Email: bishop@rok.catholic.net.au
Tel: (07) 4887 3070

Most Rev Robert McGuckin
Bishop of Toowoomba
PO Box 756
TOOWOOMBA QLD 4350
Email: bishop@twb.catholic.org.au
Tel: (07) 4632 4277

Most Rev Timothy Harris
Bishop of Townsville
PO Box 6149
TOWNSVILLE QLD 4810
Email: bishop@tsv.catholic.org.au
Tel: (07) 4726 3202

Eastern Rite Churches

Most Rev Robert Rabbat
Eparch of Melkite Eparchy of Australia and New Zealand
PO Box 620
GREENACRE NSW 2190
Email: bishoprobert@melkite.org.au
Tel: (02) 9786 3444

Most Rev Peter Stasiuk CSsR
Eparch of the Ukrainian Eparchy of Australia and New Zealand
Bishops Chancery
35 Canning Street
NORTH MELBOURNE VIC 3051
Email: eparchy@catholicukes.org.au
Tel: (03) 9320 2566

Most Rev Antoine-Charbel Tarabay OLM
Bishop of the Maronite Diocese of St Maroun
PO Box 385
STRATHFIELD NSW 2135
Email: bpoffice@maronite.org.au
Tel: (02) 8831 0000

Most Rev Amel Nona
Eparch of Chaldean Eparchy of St Thomas
PO Box 3120
WETHERILL PARK NSW 2164
Email: st.thomasdiocesensw@gmail.com
Tel: (02) 9823 1856

Most Rev Bosco Puthur
Eparch of Syro-Malabar Eparchy of St Thomas
6 Greenock Court
GREENVALE VIC 3059
Email: bishop.melbourne@syromalabar.org.au
office.melbourne@syromalabar.org.au
Tel: (03) 9480 5379 (Office); (03) 9745 2299 (Home)

Military Ordinariate
Most Rev Max Davis
Military Ordinary
PO Box 63
CAMPBELL ACT 2612
Email: bishop@cmoa.org.au
Tel: (02) 6248 0511

Personal Ordinariate of Our Lady of the Southern Cross (Anglican)

Very Rev Carl Reid

Ordinary Designate

The Personal Ordinariate of Our Lady of the Southern Cross

40A Mary Street

HIGHGATE WA 6003

Email: ordinary@ordinariate.org.au

office@ordinariate.org.au

Tel: (08) 9422 7988 (Office)

Australian Catholic Bishops Conference

Rev Dr Stephen Hackett MSC

General Secretary

ACBC General Secretariat

GPO Box 368

CANBERRA ACT 2601

Email: gensec@catholic.org.au

Tel: (02) 6201 9845

Supplement 2

Media Release of the Australian Catholic Bishops Conference and Catholic Religious Australia[1]

MEDIA RELEASE MAY 1, 2019

Respected leaders named to conduct
Church governance review

A panel of experts has been convened to conduct a national review of the governance and management structures of Catholic dioceses and parishes, including in relation to issues of transparency, accountability, consultation and lay participation.

The review was a recommendation of the Royal Commission into Institutional Responses to Child Sexual Abuse after the Commission concluded that the governance and management of some dioceses and parishes contributed to the child sexual abuse crisis.

Among other organisations, the review will consider the approaches to governance of Catholic health, community services and education agencies – as suggested by the Royal Commission.

Archbishop Mark Coleridge, president of the Australian Catholic Bishops Conference (ACBC), said the review of governance will examine how Church structures – some of which were devised centuries ago – can be improved.

"We cannot ignore the wisdom that the Church has handed down through the years, but we must also be mindful that some of our practices fail to acknowledge and draw upon the best practice of other large, contemporary organisations," he said.

Sr Monica Cavanagh rsj, president of Catholic Religious Australia (CRA), added: "The Royal Commission uncovered some practices that could have exacerbated the abuse of children and hampered the response to that tragic reality.

"The establishment of this panel is another step in our serious response to the Royal Commission and will help establish a way forward for the Church into the future."

The members of the panel are:

- Ms Pauline Connelly, chancellor of the Archdiocese of Adelaide, deputy director of Centacare Catholic Family Services, Adelaide;
- Rev Dr Brendan Daly, lecturer in canon law, Good Shepherd College, Auckland, New Zealand;
- Mr Jack de Groot, CEO of the St Vincent de Paul Society NSW and chair of the Church's Implementation Advisory Group;
- Sr Professor Isabell Naumann ISSM, president, Catholic Institute of Sydney;
- Justice Neville Owen, former Supreme Court justice in Western Australia, former chair of the Truth, Justice and Healing Council, which facilitated the Church's engagement with the Royal Commission, current member of the Pontifical Council for the Protection of Minors;
- Adjunct Professor Susan Pascoe AM, president and chair of the Australian Council for International Development, former Commissioner of the Australian Charities and Not-for- profits Commission and former executive director of the Catholic Education Commission of Victoria;
- Professor John Warhurst, Emeritus Professor of Political Science at the Australian National University and chair of Concerned Catholics Canberra Goulburn.

The panel produced a progress report for the presidents of ACBC and CRA today and will produce an interim report by the end of October. A final report should be provided to CRA and the ACBC in the first half of 2020.

The governance review project plan **can be found at** https://www.catholic.org.au/acbc-media/media-centre/media-releases-new/2188-governance-review-project-plan/file

Media enquiries:
Implementation Advisory Group – Anna Tydd (Executive Officer): 0437 745 325.

Supplement 3

KIERAN TAPSELL: Pope Francis and the Closed Door Syndrome
(Posted on **21 May 2019**)

For all his good points, Pope Francis has a credibility problem over child sexual abuse. Public statements are made, but once the door is closed, the paper that comes out contradicts what has been said. His latest Apostolic Letter, Vos Estis Lux Mundi, is no exception.

In March 2017 Marie Collins, an abuse survivor, resigned as a member of Pope Francis' Pontifical Commission for the Protection of Minors, because what was happening behind closed doors conflicted with what was said in public.

From 1996 onwards, four national Catholic bishops conferences requested the Holy See to allow mandatory reporting of all allegations of child sexual to the civil authorities.

They were rebuffed. In 2003, the Attorney General for Massachusetts (remember *Spotlight*?) found that Church officials in Boston believed that canon law prohibited them from reporting abuse to the civil authorities. In 2009, the Murphy Commission in Ireland came to the same conclusion about the cover up in Dublin.

On 16 January 2014, members of the United Nations Committee for the Rights of the Child asked Bishop Scicluna why Church policy did not provide for mandatory reporting of all cases to the civil authorities, and not just where there were civil reporting laws. His answer was the Church required domestic laws to be followed, but otherwise, it was up to the victims (children or those who 'habitually have **the imperfect use of reason**') to report the abuse.

On 6 May 2014, Archbishop Tomasi told the United Nations Committee against Torture that the Holy See's responsibility towards children under the Convention was limited to the 30 or so who lived inside the 44 hectares of the Vatican City, despite the fact that within those walls, the Holy See was deciding whether some 4,000 priest sex rs from all over the world should have access to children by remaining as priests.

On 26 September 2014, Pope Francis told the United Nations that any attempt by the Church to impose mandatory reporting under canon law could constitute a violation of the principle of non-interference in the internal affairs of States. The Church, like so many other international organisations, creates rules for its members living in different countries. This response was like the International Olympic Committee saying that it could not provide codes of conduct against sexual harassment, bribery or even rough play because that is a matter for the governments of the place where the athletes live.

On 15 February, 2016 Cardinal O'Malley, the President of the Pontifical Commission for the Protection of Minors, stated: '... our obligations under civil law must certainly be followed, but even beyond these civil requirements, we all have a moral and ethical responsibility to report suspected abuse to the civil authorities.' The doors closed, and on 16 December 2016, the Commission issued guidelines for national protocols on child sexual abuse. O'Malley's statement was not included.

On 17 February 2016, after seeing the movie, *Spotlight,* Archbishop Scicluna said that 'all bishops and cardinals must see this film, because they must understand that it is reporting that will save the church, not 'omertá', a reference to the Sicilian Mafia's code of silence.

On 17 December 2017, the Australian Royal Commission into Institutional Responses to Child Sexual Abuse in its Final Report found that the **pontifical secret** over allegations of child sexual abuse against clergy still applied where there are no applicable civil reporting laws. Its recommendation 16.10 was that canon law should be amended "so that the pontifical secret does not apply to any aspect of allegations or canonical disciplinary processes relating to child sexual abuse". One way of complying with this was to have mandatory reporting to the civil authorities under canon law.

On 12 September 2018, Pope Francis summoned the heads of Catholic bishops conferences to a **conference** in Rome in February 2019 to discuss the sexual abuse crisis. Two speakers, Linda Ghosina and Cardinal Marx called for the repeal of the pontifical secret over child sexual abuse. Archbishop Scicluna said it was "counterproductive". The doors closed.

On 29 March 2019, Pope Francis imposed mandatory reporting of child sexual abuse to the Vatican City's judicial authorities. That protection only applies to the 30 or so children who reside there. The millions of children under the Church's care throughout the world had to wait for a change in canon law to have the same protection.

On 7 May 2019, Pope Francis issued his Apostolic Letter, _Vos estis lux mundi_. It made no mention of the pontifical secret being abolished, and it did not expressly impose mandatory reporting. Article 1§1(b) created a canonical crime for bishops and religious superiors for 'actions or omissions intended to … avoid civil investigations …' It was at least arguable that if they failed to report, they breached this provision. In other words, it could be interpreted, by a roundabout method, that the new law imposed mandatory reporting.

However, when Archbishop Scicluna was asked about the failure of _Vos estis lux mundi_ to provide for mandatory reporting, he made no mention of Article 1§1(b), and said, "we cannot tell states what their citizens should be doing". This was essentially the same answer that Francis gave to the United Nations in 2014.

Another _excuse_ given was that different legal systems make a universal reporting law impossible, and that imposing one could endanger the church in places where Catholics are a persecuted minority.

In 1842 there was a universal law of the Church that penitents should denounce priests who solicited sex in the confessional. The Holy Office under Pope Gregory XVI issued a decree relieving the faithful of this obligation in the lands of "schismatics, heretics and

Mohammedans". Every legal system creates exceptions to general laws, and the *Code of Canon Law* creates such exceptions 1,300 times. Canon 87 of the Code also allows for dispensations.

It seems that the closed door syndrome mentioned by Marie Collins is still alive and well in the Vatican. The expectations raised at the Vatican child sex abuse conference about the pontifical secret and reporting to the civil authorities have not appeared in *Vos estis lux mundi*, the document arising from it.

(Reproduced with permission from John Menadue – Pearls and Irritations, 21 May 2019.)

• Kieran Tapsell is a retired civil lawyer and the author of *Potiphar's Wife: The Vatican's Secret and Child Sexual Abuse* and of a submission to the Royal Commission into Institutional Responses to Child Sexual Abuse: Canon Law, A Systemic Factor in Child Sexual Abuse in the Catholic Church. He was also a member of the canon law panel before the Royal Commission.

Supplement 4

The Australian Catholic Coalition for Church Reform (ACCCR) is a network of 13 Catholic renewal groups across Australia established in 2012. The Renewal Propositions below were developed in 2019 in the light of the common commitments of the Coalition.

Australian Catholic Coalition for Church Reform

RENEWAL PROPOSITIONS FOR THE CATHOLIC CHURCH

The Australian Catholic Coalition for Church Reform (ACCCR) recognises that all Christ's faithful have *"the right and even at times the duty to manifest to the sacred pastors their opinion on matters which pertain to the good of the Church and to make their opinion known to the rest of the Christian faithful"*. (Canon 212 §3)

The Church in Australia faces continuing decay unless its bishops recognise the essential role and responsibility that lay Catholic women and men share in the wellbeing of their Church. Bishops must learn to trust and value the wisdom and advice of their people, whom they have too long ignored and treated as irrelevant.

ACCCR now calls for a systemic reform of the Catholic Church so that it:

1. ensures that all doctrines and practices reflect the teachings and spirit of Jesus;
2. seeks to heal not to hurt, to include not to exclude, to nurture not control;

3. reflects the Christian values of love, justice, compassion, peace, equality and freedom;
4. is trusted by the wider Australian community;
5. is free of the pervasive culture of clericalism;
6. recognises the innate dignity of every human person and rejects all discrimination;
7. welcomes women and men equally into all its roles of leadership, ministry and service, so that everyone shares co-responsibly in the mission of the Church:
8. calls on all its members to accept their responsibility to live their lives by Gospel values;
9. is guided by the sense of faith of the faithful (*sensus fidei fidelium*);
10. works for a world that is more just, compassionate, egalitarian, and committed to peace;
11. is truly safe for children and vulnerable adults, and prioritises their welfare:
12. adopts the very best models and practice of governance and leadership;
13. uses authority wisely and justly, ever open to new knowledge and experience;
14. is genuinely transparent and accountable to the faithful and to the community at large;
15. maintains an ongoing and open dialogue with all Christ's faithful, and
16. selects and forms candidates for the priesthood in a spirit of service and rejection of clericalism.

ACCCR seeks a Church committed to:
1. **Synodality:** with regular plenary councils (at least every 15 years), diocesan synods or assemblies (at least every 5 years) – to identify key concerns of the time, and to discern and put in place the necessary plans to address them;
2. **Co-responsibility:** with participatory processes for the selection of bishops, and mandatory diocesan and parish pastoral councils which are truly representative of the diversity of people – including gender – within the diocese and parish.

The members of these councils should be selected through a consultative process, and their vote must have real value;

3. **Inclusion:** with the recruitment and appointment of suitably qualified and experienced women and men, attuned to the *sensus fidei fidelium*, to the most senior roles in dioceses, national bodies, and parishes;

4. **Accountability:** with every diocese and parish to provide an annual report to its people on its mission: its ministries, services, personnel, assets, finances, and pastoral plans;

5. **Subsidiarity:** with decisions being taken by competent authorities closest to those affected by the decisions, as directed by Pope Pius XI.

In preparing for the Plenary Council, ACCCR calls on **each and every diocesan bishop** to:

1. convene a diocesan synod or assembly in 2019 or early 2020, so that he can LISTEN to the sense of faith of the diocesan faithful, understand their priority concerns, and seek their advice on the selection of diocesan representatives to attend the Council;

2. establish immediately – if one does not already exist – a diocesan pastoral council, using a process that ensures a genuine voice for the diversity of the faithful within the diocese, including gender, ethnicity, age, social condition, work, apostolate, and the regions;

3. appoint, on merit, a balanced number of suitably qualified and experienced women and men to the most senior roles in his diocese;

4. prepare and publish – commencing in 2019 – an annual report to all the faithful of the diocese, which includes a full account of its ministries, services, personnel, assets, finances, and pastoral plans:

5. require every parish to prepare and publish a similar annual report commencing in 2019.

Since all the above matters also apply to the Universal Church, ACCCR calls on the 2020/21 Plenary Council to draw them to the attention of the Holy See.

Members of the Australian Catholic
Coalition for Church Reform
Catholics Speak Out
Catholics for Renewal
Women and the Australian Church
Australian Reforming Catholics
Inclusive Catholics
Aggiornamento
The Friendship Group WA
The Cyber Community
Concerned Catholics Canberra Goulburn
Rainbow Catholics InterAgency for Ministry
For the Innocents
Women's Wisdom in the Church
Voice of Catholic Australian Laity

Each ACCCR member group has its own focus and history; all are united in the call for renewal in the Church. The role of ACCCR, established in 2012, is to foster collaboration and support among its member groups and to disseminate messages of hope and opportunity. For further information, contact the Convener at: pjgovernance@gmail.com

INDEX

A

absolution 21–22, 159–60, 207, 220
abuse (see also *clerical child sexual abuse*) ix–x, xiii, 1–2, 12, 21, 59–60, 66, 102, 122, 135, 145, 153, 155, 159, 166, 267, 272, 275–276, 317–19
    child sexual vii–x, xii–xiii, 1, 4, 7–8, 18, 21, 38, 43, 66–67, 79, 94, 111–12, 116–117, 119, 122, 124, 128, 134–135, 142, 146–147, 155, 159–160, 106–107, 109–71, 207, 221, 222, 226, 250, 268, 275–76, 314, 317–20
accountability v–vii, xiii, 8, 12, 18–19, 23, 66–67, 83, 102, 110, 119–20, 122, 125, 129, 135–36, 141–42, 164, 208, 251, 253, 276, 314, 323
adult 2, 3, 16, 21, 29, 140, 155, 160, 188, 205–6, 214, 272, 284, 322
apostolic exhortation 11, 101, 136
Apostolic nuncio xii, xix, 20, 22, 143, 163, 208, 304
Apostolorum successors 101
Apostolos suos 265
assembly 14–16, 34–6, 87, 137, 139, 187, 231–32, 241–45, 249, 252, 255, 258–62, 323
assessment 20, 24, 25, 125, 126, 143, 169–70, 210, 276
Australasian Catholic Record 264–65
Australian Catholic Bishops Conference xii, xiii, 116, 125, 134, 159, 168–69, 171, 181, 314
Australian Catholic Coalition for Church Reform xiv, 321
Australian Research Council 78
authority xvi, 3, 28, 86, 90, 93–4, 96, 110, 113–17, 119, 121–22, 124–25, 128–29, 166, 175, 183, 185, 214, 231, 233, 264, 322
autocratic 33, 110–12, 124, 127, 204

B

baptism xvi, 27, 29, 88, 95–6, 114, 152–53, 161, 179, 181, 188, 199, 200, 201, 213, 215, 284
birth control 183, 184
bishop
    appointment 20, 22, 129, 143, 163–64, 208, 273
    auxiliary xii, xix, 22, 164, 204, 208, 239, 264, 295, 304, 305, 307, 309–10
    conference xii–xiii, xix, 26, 116, 121, 125, 134, 159, 168–69, 171, 174, 181, 212, 232, 264–65, 304, 313–14, 317, 319
    retired 34, 225, 230, 237–40, 246–47, 258, 263–64, 295, 298
    titular 20, 34, 143, 239, 246–47, 258, 264, 295
business as usual 232, 234, 251

C

canonical structures 9, 11, 101
Canon Law
    Canon 87 320
    Canon 97 38, 221, 226
    Canon 127 115, 247, 254
    Canon 129 18, 117, 141
    Canon 208 118
    Canons 210-223 11, 101
    Canon 212 321
    Canon 443 xviii, 238, 246, 263, 295
    Canon 511 115
    Canon 512 115
    Canon 1009 161, 178
    Canon 1024 161
    Canon 1112 39, 224, 226
    Canon 1118 39, 224, 226

Catechism of the Catholic Church 39, 99, 106
Catholic Church v–ix, xi–xiii, xv, xix, 2, 13, 39, 41, 43, 57, 60–1, 66–7, 70, 71, 73, 76, 83, 99, 103, 106, 110, 120, 127, 130–31, 135, 153, 159, 166, 182, 184, 200, 221, 224–25, 229, 243, 250, 263–64, 268, 284–85, 288, 291, 293, 298, 304, 320, 321

CPSIA information can be obtained
at www.ICGtesting.com
Printed in the USA
BVHW060212180220
572581BV00012B/1812